Your Pregnancy
Week-by-Week

Revised & Expanded Edition

Your Pregnancy
Week-by-Week

Revised & Expanded Edition

Glade B. Curtis, MD
FACOG

Illustrations
by Paul Gettler

Publishers: Bill Fisher
Helen Fisher
Howard Fisher

Editors: Judith Schuler
Bill Fisher

Book Design: Edgar H. Allard

Illustrations: Paul Gettler

Cover Design: B. Josh Young

Cover Photo: Joshua J. Young

Technical Readers: Elizabeth D. Warner,
MD, FACOG
Marcia Vavich,
RN, MA

Published by:
Fisher Books
4239 West Ina Road, Suite 101
Tucson AZ 85741
(520) 744-6110

**Library of Congress
Cataloging-in-Publications Data**

Curtis, Glade B.
    Your pregnancy week-by-week/
Glade B. Curtis; illustrations by Paul
Gettler.—[New rev. ed.]
        p. cm
    Includes bibliographical references
and index.
    ISBN 1-55561-068-4 : $12.95
    1. Pregnancy. 2. Fetus—Growth.
I. Title.
RG525.C92   1994
618.2—dc20   94-30005
                                            CIP

© 1989, 1994 Alta Publishing
Revised 1995, 1996
Printed in U.S.A.
Printing 20, 19, 18, 17, 16, 15, 14

Quotation on back cover reprinted with permission. *Women's Circle*, October 1990, House of White Birches, 306 East Parr Road, Berne, IN 46711.

Notice: The information in this book is true and complete to the best of our knowledge. This book is intended only as an informative guide for those wishing to know more about pregnancy. In no way is this book intended to replace, countermand or conflict with the advice given to you by your own physician. The ultimate decision concerning care should be made between you and your doctor. We strongly recommend you follow his/her advice. The information in this book is general and is offered with no guarantees on the part of the author or Fisher Books. The author and publisher disclaim all liability in connection with use of this book.

✧

Acknowledgments

This book contains many facts and figures, yet its spirit comes from the enthusiastic and questioning minds of many pregnant women and their partners. It is my special privilege to participate every day in the excitement of a positive pregnancy test, the anticipation of weekly changes and the miracle of birth. My sincere thanks to these women and their families.

Credit must also be given to my understanding and generous wife, Debbie, and our family, who support me in a profession that requires much of them. Beyond that commitment, they have supported and encouraged me to pursue the challenge of this project. And my parents have always offered their love and support.

Judi Schuler continues to be a fresh source of energy and enthusiasm. I appreciate her commitment to excellence and accuracy. Special thanks to Elizabeth Warner, M.D., and Marcia Vavich, R.N., for reviewing the text, and to Kathy Michael for her valuable help.

Contents

About the Revised & Expanded Edition

When we introduced this book several years ago, we were pretty sure that it would provide helpful, in-depth information that the pregnant woman could really use. Sales, ever increasing, have proved that our concept was correct.

Now Dr. Curtis has added new information throughout to keep the book totally up-to-date. Plus, there's an entire new chapter, Preparing for Pregnancy, for the woman who is planning to become pregnant. We know that you will read the book with great interest as your pregnancy progresses.

Your comments about this book are always appreciated.

About the Author

Glade B. Curtis, M.D., is a Fellow of the American College of Obstetricians and Gynecologists. He is in private practice in obstetrics, gynecology and infertility in Sandy, Utah.

One of Dr. Curtis' goals as a doctor is to provide patients with many types of information about gynecological and obstetrical conditions they may have, problems they may encounter and procedures they may undergo. In pursuit of that goal, he has written this book and an informative pregnancy guide entitled *Your Pregnancy Question & Answers,* and he has co-authored a book on female surgeries. His most recent book, published September, 1996 is a companion to this one. It is titled *Your Pregnancy After 30.*

Dr. Curtis is a graduate of the University of Utah and the University of Rochester School of Medicine and Dentistry, Rochester, New York. He was an intern, resident and chief resident in Obstetrics and Gynecology at the University of Rochester Strong Memorial Hospital. He now has a very active private practice in Sandy, where he lives with his wife Debbie, and their five children.

Preparing
for Pregnancy

Nothing can compare with the miracle and magic that occur while you are pregnant. It is your chance to be involved in the creative process. Planning ahead for this experience can improve your chances of doing well yourself and of having a healthy baby.

You can affect one of the most important factors in your baby's health—*your lifestyle.* By planning ahead, you can be certain you and your baby are not exposed to harmful things during your pregnancy.

Pregnancy is not an illness; a pregnant woman is not sick. However, major changes occur in you during the course of your pregnancy. Having good general health before pregnancy can help you deal with the physical and emotional stresses of pregnancy, labor and delivery. It can help you prepare to take care of a newborn baby.

You can harm your developing baby unintentionally and not know it. Getting in shape for pregnancy means physical *and* mental preparation. By the time most women realize they are pregnant, they are 1 to 2 months into their pregnancy. By the time they see their doctor, they are 2 or 3 months along. The first 12 weeks of pregnancy are extremely important. The baby is forming or may have already formed its major organ systems. Many important things happen before you realize you are pregnant or before you see your doctor.

Your General Health

There has been an explosion of technology, new medications, medical advances and medical treatments in recent years. Through these advances in technology, we have learned that your health at the beginning of your pregnancy and during your pregnancy can have a major effect on you and your developing baby.

In the past, the emphasis was on being healthy while being pregnant. Some doctors suggest a new way of looking at pregnancy that includes more than just the 9 months of pregnancy. It has been suggested *12 months* or more (to include a period of preparation) should be the "norm" for a pregnancy. Preparing your body with good general mental and physical health can certainly help. Questions to ask yourself as you prepare for pregnancy might include:

+ Am I the weight I want to be when I get pregnant?
+ Am I taking medications for other problems that could possibly be harmful to a developing fetus?
+ Do I exercise regularly?
+ Am I planning on undergoing tests, such as X-rays?
+ How does my pregnancy fit into my future plans (education, career, travel)?
+ Do I use drugs or alcohol?
+ Should I stop smoking before getting pregnant rather than waiting to try to stop while I am pregnant?

The answers to these questions become more complicated if they have to be decided *during* a pregnancy. Deal with these issues *before* pregnancy and know you are healthy. You won't have to worry about the risk of these problems while you're pregnant. It makes sense to continue birth control while you are seeking the answers to these questions.

Seeking Medical Advice

Seeing a doctor *before* you get pregnant is good preparation for pregnancy. It's also helpful to pick someone to take care of you during your pregnancy. Arrange a visit for a checkup and to discuss your plans for pregnancy with your doctor *before* you get pregnant. Then you will know that when you do get pregnant you are in the best health possible.

You may have a medical condition that requires attention before pregnancy. Taking care of these things before trying to conceive may affect your ability to get pregnant and may help ensure a healthy pregnancy. You may find you need to change medications you are taking. Or you may need to make changes in your lifestyle before trying to get pregnant.

Tests for You   A general physical exam before you get pregnant ensures you won't have to deal with new medical problems during a pregnancy. A Pap smear and a breast exam should be included in this physical. Lab tests to consider before pregnancy include tests for rubella, blood type and Rh factor. If you are 35 or over, a mammogram is also a good idea.

If you have been exposed to AIDS or hepatitis, have your doctor conduct tests for these problems. If you have a family history of other medical problems, such as diabetes, ask your doctor whether you should have any tests to rule out these problems. If you have other chronic medical problems, such as anemia or recurrent miscarriages, your doctor may suggest tests for these problems.

X-rays and Other Imaging Tests   When you are scheduled to have any test involving radiation, ask for a pregnancy test first. Use reliable contraception before these tests so you *know* you are not pregnant when you have the tests. These tests include X-rays, CT scans and MRIs. A good time to schedule these tests is right after the end of your period, so you know you're not pregnant. If you must receive a series of these tests, continue to use contraception. See pages 141-143.

I've had new patients come in who are pregnant and tell me they had a series of X-rays during the first or second month of pregnancy. They didn't know they were pregnant. It's very difficult to determine whether the tests will harm their pregnancy. It is much better to *know* you aren't pregnant before these tests are done.

Weight   Before trying to get pregnant, it's a good idea to pay attention to your weight; don't be too overweight or too underweight. Either of these conditions can make a pregnancy more difficult for you and more risky for your baby.

It's not a good idea to be on a weight-loss diet while you are trying to get pregnant or during pregnancy. Pregnancy is a time you are expected to gain weight, not lose weight. See pages 96-97.

Medical History

A visit with your doctor before you get pregnant is the best time to discuss your medical history and any problems you may have had in other pregnancies. Ask your doctor what you can do to eliminate or decrease the chances of the same problems occurring in your next pregnancy. This includes dealing with ectopic pregnancy, miscarriage, previous C-sections or other complications.

This is also a good time to talk about exposure to and problems with sexually transmitted diseases, such as AIDS or other infections. If you have had major surgery or any female surgery in the past, discuss it now. If you are being treated for other medical problems, discuss these with your doctor. Make plans to take medications that are safe during your pregnancy—*before* you try to get pregnant.

Discontinuing Contraception

It's important to continue using some form of contraception until you are *ready* to get pregnant. If you are in the middle of treatment for a medical problem or undergoing tests, finish the course of treatment or have the tests *before* trying to become pregnant. If you are not using some form of birth control, you *are* trying to get pregnant.

Oral contraceptives taken before pregnancy do not cause birth defects. When stopping birth-control pills, switch to another type of birth control such as a barrier method, condoms or the sponge.

Most doctors recommend you have two or three normal periods after you stop taking birth-control pills before you try to get pregnant. If you get pregnant immediately after stopping oral contraceptives, it may be difficult to know *when* you conceived. This can make it harder to determine your due date. This may not seem important now, but it will be very important to you during the pregnancy and at the end of the pregnancy.

If you have an IUD (intrauterine device), you will have to have it removed before you try to conceive. If you have any sign of infection with the IUD, this should be resolved before trying to get pregnant. The best time to remove an IUD is during a menstrual period. When you discontinue birth-control pills or have an IUD removed, use one of the barrier methods for birth control while you are waiting to conceive.

If you use Norplant®, a newer type of birth control, it should be removed and you should experience at least two or three normal menstrual cycles before trying to get pregnant. It may take a few months for your periods to return to normal after Norplant is removed. If you get pregnant immediately after removing Norplant, it may be difficult to determine when you got pregnant and what your due date is.

Depo-provera®, an injection of hormone used for birth control, should be discontinued for at least 3 to 6 months before trying to get pregnant. Wait until you have had at least two or three normal periods before trying to conceive.

After stopping Depo-provera or having a Norplant removed, use a barrier-type contraception until your periods become normal. With *any* type of birth control you use, it is important to consult with your physician about discontinuing its use and when to attempt pregnancy.

Current Medical Problems

Your health before you become pregnant includes your general lifestyle, your diet, your physical activity and any chronic medical problems, such as high blood pressure or diabetes. You may require extra care before and during your pregnancy. Tell your doctor about any medications you are currently taking, including amounts. Discuss with him or her any tests you may be planning to have, such as X-rays. Be sure to cover all of the medical problems you are being treated for.

It's much easier to answer questions about these problems and not worry about their complications *before* you get pregnant rather than after you are already pregnant.

Diabetes   Diabetes is a medical problem that can have serious effects during pregnancy. It is the third-leading cause of death in the United States. If you have diabetes, it may make it harder for you to become pregnant; it can also increase the chance of miscarriage, stillbirth and birth defects. These risks can be decreased by good control of blood sugar or control of your diabetes during pregnancy.

If your diabetes is not controlled, the combination of pregnancy and diabetes can be dangerous for you *and* your baby. Most problems or damage caused by diabetes occur during the first trimester (the first 13 weeks of pregnancy).

Pregnancy may affect diabetes by increasing your body's need for insulin. This can easily be determined by blood-sugar tests. Most doctors recommend you have your diabetes under good control for at least 2 to 3 months before pregnancy begins. This will help you lower your risks of miscarriage or other problems.

It is a good idea to have kidney problems and blood-pressure problems under control before pregnancy. This

✧

may require checking your blood sugar several times a day to get good control. Historically, women with diabetes have had serious problems with pregnancy. With good control, a woman with diabetes is often able to have a good outcome with her pregnancy.

If you have a strong family history of diabetes or any suspicion you might have diabetes, have it checked before trying to get pregnant. Also read pages 221-223.

Asthma   Asthma affects about 1% of all pregnant women. There is no way to predict ahead of time how pregnancy will affect your asthma. Half of those affected see no change in their asthma. About 25% actually have improvement in their asthma during pregnancy and about 25% see a worsening of their problems during pregnancy.

Most asthma medications are safe during pregnancy, but it is best to talk to your doctor about taking any medication. Most people with asthma *know* what triggers their asthma attacks. While you are trying to get pregnant and during pregnancy, avoid whatever triggers your attacks. Try to get your asthma under good control before trying to become pregnant.

Hypertension   Hypertension or high blood pressure can cause problems for the pregnant woman and her unborn baby. For the woman, these problems may include kidney damage, stroke or headaches. For the baby, high blood pressure in a mother-to-be can cause decreased blood flow to the placenta, resulting in a smaller baby or intrauterine-growth retardation (IUGR).

If you have high blood pressure before pregnancy, you *must* closely monitor your blood pressure during pregnancy. Your doctor may ask you to see an internist or family doctor to help in the control of your blood pressure.

Some high-blood-pressure medications are safe to take during pregnancy; others are not. Do *not* stop or decrease any medication on your own! This can be dangerous. If you

✧

are planning a pregnancy, ask your doctor about any medication you take for high blood pressure and the safety of this medication.

Heart Disease   During pregnancy, the workload on your heart increases about 50%. If you have any kind of heart condition, it is important for your doctor to know about it *before* you get pregnant.

Some heart problems, such as mitral-valve prolapse, may be serious during pregnancy and may require antibiotics at the time of delivery. Other heart problems, such as congenital heart problems, may seriously affect your health; your doctor may advise against any pregnancy. Consult your doctor about these heart conditions so they can be dealt with before you become pregnant.

Bladder and Kidney Problems   Bladder infections, commonly called *urinary-tract infections* or *UTIs*, may occur more often during pregnancy. If a urinary-tract infection is not treated, it can become severe and affect the kidneys, resulting in a condition called *pyelonephritis*.

Urinary-tract infections and pyelonephritis are associated with premature delivery. If you have had a history of pyelonephritis or repeated urinary-tract infections, it should be evaluated before you begin your pregnancy.

Kidney stones may also create problems during pregnancy. Because they cause pain, it may be difficult to diagnose them and differentiate them from other problems that can occur during pregnancy. Kidney stones can also cause an increased chance of urinary-tract infections and pyelonephritis.

If you have had kidney or bladder surgery or other major kidney problems in the past or know your kidney function is less than normal, tell your doctor about it. It may be necessary to do tests before you become pregnant to evaluate the function of your kidneys.

If you have had an occasional bladder infection, don't be alarmed. Discuss your bladder or kidney problems with

✧

your doctor. Let him or her help you decide whether further testing is necessary before you become pregnant.

Thyroid Problems   Thyroid problems can appear as either too much or too little thyroid hormone. Too much thyroid hormone is called *hyperthyroidism.* In this condition, the metabolism is faster and is usually caused by Graves' disease. It is usually treated by surgery or medication to reduce the amount of thyroid hormone in your system. If this problem is untreated during pregnancy, there is a higher risk of premature delivery and low birth weight. If treatment is necessary during pregnancy, there are safe medications that can be given.

Too little thyroid hormone is called *hypothyroidism.* This is usually caused by autoimmune problems; the thyroid gland is damaged by your own antibodies. Treatment for this problem is thyroid hormones. If hypothyroidism is not treated, you may suffer infertility or miscarriage.

If you have hypothyroidism or hyperthyroidism, you should be tested before pregnancy to determine the correct amount of medication for you. Pregnancy can change medication requirements, and you will need to be checked during pregnancy. Read more about thyroid disease, pages 236-238.

Anemia   Anemia means you do not have enough hemoglobin to carry oxygen to your body cells. There are several causes and several types of anemia. Symptoms of anemia include weakness, fatigue, shortness of breath and paleness of the skin.

While you are pregnant, there are great demands on you for iron and iron stores. If you have low iron levels at the beginning of pregnancy, anemia can make it even more difficult for you during your pregnancy. Ask for a CBC (complete blood count) as a part of your prepregnancy physical.

One specific type of anemia is *sickle-cell anemia,* a genetically transmitted anemia that mainly affects the black population. If you have sickle-cell anemia, your body may be deprived of oxygen. This may be very painful and may cause more infections and other problems during pregnancy.

There is no cure for sickle-cell anemia, and it can be passed to your baby. Women with sickle-cell anemia have a higher rate of miscarriages and a higher rate of urinary-tract infections. They may also have high blood pressure and painful sickle-cell crises.

Another specific anemia is *thalassemia,* a genetically inherited anemia found primarily in those of Mediterranean descent. If you have relatives with thalassemia or think you are at risk, check for it before you become pregnant. Read more about anemia on pages 208-212.

Lupus Systemic lupus erythematosus (SLE) is a collagen vascular disease (an autoimmune disease). This means you produce antibodies to your own organs, which may destroy or damage those organs and their function. Lupus can affect many parts of the body, including joints, kidneys, lungs and the heart.

This problem can be difficult to diagnose. Lupus occurs in about 1 in 700 women between 15 and 64 years. In black women, it occurs in 1 in 254 women. Lupus is found more commonly in women than in men, especially in women between the ages of 20 and 40.

There is no cure for lupus. Treatment is individual and usually involves taking steroids. It is best not to become pregnant while you are experiencing a flare-up. There is an increased risk of miscarriage in women with lupus. There is also an increased chance of stillbirth, which requires extra care during pregnancy.

Babies born to women with lupus may have a rash. They also may have heart block and heart defects. These babies may be born prematurely or experience intrauterine-growth retardation. Consult your doctor before you become pregnant if you have lupus. Also see pages 238-239.

Epilepsy and Seizures Epilepsy includes several different problems. There are different kinds of seizures, usually

✧

called *grand mal* and *petit mal* seizures. The cause of most seizures is unknown. Mothers with epilepsy have a 1 in 30 chance of having a baby with a seizure disorder. Babies also have a higher chance of birth defects, perhaps related to medications taken for epilepsy during pregnancy.

If you take medication for epilepsy, it is important to consult your doctor before you become pregnant. Discuss the amounts and the types of medication you are taking. Many medications taken for a seizure disorder or epilepsy are associated with problems during pregnancy, such as birth defects.

Some medications are safe to take for epilepsy during pregnancy. Most doctors will have you switch to pheno-barbital during the time you are trying to get pregnant and while you are pregnant.

Seizures can be dangerous to the mother and fetus. It is important for you to take your medication regularly and as prescribed by your doctor. Do not decrease or discontinue any medication on your own! Read pages 244-245.

Migraine Headaches　About 15 to 20% of all pregnant women suffer from migraine headaches. Many women notice an improvement in their headaches while they are pregnant. If you take medication for your headaches during pregnancy, check with your doctor ahead of time so you'll know whether the ones you take are safe to use during pregnancy.

Cancers　How a particular cancer will affect pregnancy depends on the organ involved with the cancer and the extent of the cancer. Breast cancer is the most common form of cancer in women. Having had breast cancer should not affect pregnancy nor will pregnancy cause breast cancer to occur.

Most doctors recommend waiting a few years after the breast-cancer treatment is completed before attempting to become pregnant. It is important to discuss any history of cancer or treatment of cancer with your doctor before pregnancy. This situation can become very complicated if you

✧

are pregnant and being treated for cancer. Many medications and treatments for cancer are not safe for use during pregnancy. Cancer in pregnancy is discussed further on pages 280-285.

Other Problems   There are many other specific chronic illnesses you may experience that need to be discussed with your doctor. If you have any chronic problems or take any medication on a regular basis, talk it over with your doctor. It is best not to stumble into pregnancy and take medication or have tests or treatments during the early stages of pregnancy.

Most of the organ development and early development of the baby occurs in the first trimester. This is an important time to keep your baby from being exposed to unnecessary medications or tests. You'll feel better and do better during pregnancy if you have these problems under good control *before* you try to get pregnant.

Current Medications

It's important for you and your doctor to consider the possibility of pregnancy each time you are given a prescription or told to take a medication. When you are pregnant, *everything* changes with regards to medications.

Medications that may have been safe when you were not pregnant may have harmful effects when you are pregnant. There may not be a precise answer to whether a medication is safe during pregnancy. You need to ask your doctor before changing any medication. Some effects of medications and chemicals are discussed on pages 100-102, and 164.

Some medications are intended for short-term use, such as antibiotics for infections. Others are for more chronic or long-lasting problems, such as high blood pressure or diabetes. Some medications are OK to take while you are pregnant and might even be important for you to take to help make your pregnancy successful. Other medications may not be safe to take during pregnancy.

During pregnancy, stay on the safe side with regards to medications. Some general guidelines to medication use during pregnancy, or if you are trying to get pregnant, include the following.

+ Do not stop birth control unless you want to be pregnant.
+ Take your prescriptions as they are prescribed.
+ Notify your doctor if you think you might be pregnant or if you are not using birth control when a medication is suggested.
+ Do not self-treat or use medications you were given in the past for other problems.
+ Never use someone else's medications to treat a current problem you are experiencing.
+ If you are unsure, ask your doctor.

About 2 to 3% of all birth defects can be traced to medication use during pregnancy. Researchers have even indicated medications can affect the sperm from your male partner, which may affect your pregnancy. In 1979, the FDA devised a rating system of medications using categories. These categories are A, B, C, D and X.

+ *Category A*—drugs or medications proved to be safe in human pregnancy. Examples are vitamins or thyroid hormone.
+ *Category B*—medications believed to be without significant risk, based on information from animal or human studies. An example would be an antibiotic such as amoxicillin or erythromycin.
+ *Category C*—medications that have been studied in animals. These studies show adverse affects on the fetus; there are no controlled studies in humans. These medications should be prescribed only if the potential benefits outweigh potential risks of the medication. Examples include Compazine® and theophyline.

✦ *Category D*—medications with evidence of human fetal risk. These medications should be used only if there is a life-threatening situation, when no other medication is available. An example of a category D medication is tetracycline.

✦ *Category X*—medications where studies in animals or humans show fetal abnormalities. The risk clearly outweighs any possible benefit. These medications should not be used in pregnant women. Examples include Accutane®, lithium and smallpox vaccination. Accutane is discussed on page 88.

Inoculations and Vaccinations

The same rule applies to vaccinations as X-rays. When you are planning to have vaccinations, use reliable contraception. Many vaccinations are safe during pregnancy; some are not. A good rule of thumb is to complete vaccinations at least 3 months before trying to get pregnant. The most critical time most vaccinations can be harmful to a pregnancy is in the first few weeks and throughout the first trimester. Also read pages 108-110.

Genetic Counseling

If you are planning your first pregnancy, you are probably not considering genetic counseling. However, there may be circumstances in which genetic counseling could help you and your partner in making informed decisions about child bearing.

Genetic counseling is an information session between you and your partner and a genetic counselor or group of counselors. Any information you share with or receive from a genetic counselor is confidential. This may involve one visit or several visits. Genetic counseling is available at most major universities. Your pediatrician or physician can guide you.

Through genetic counseling, you hope to understand the possibilities or probabilities of what might affect your future offspring or your ability to get pregnant. In genetic counseling, information you receive is not given in precise answers. The answer may only be "chances" or "odds of a problem." One of the most frustrating aspects of genetic counseling is that even when you learn about defects, they are rarely treatable.

In genetic counseling, a decision will not be made for you. You will be provided information on tests you might take and what the results of those tests indicate. When speaking with a genetic counselor, don't hide information you feel is embarrassing or hard to talk about. It is important to give him or her as much information as possible.

Ask your doctor if you should seek genetic counseling. Most couples who need genetic counseling do not find out they should have sought it until after they have a child born with a birth defect. Some groups of people who should seek genetic counseling include:

✦ Women over 35 at the time of delivery. (The age of 35 has been arbitrarily selected.) The general rule is that with increasing age, genetic counseling becomes more important.
✦ Any woman who has delivered a child with a birth defect.
✦ When either partner has a birth defect.
✦ If there is a family history of inherited diseases, including Down's syndrome, mental retardation, cystic fibrosis, muscular dystrophy, bleeding disorders, skeletal or bone problems, dwarfism, epilepsy, congenital heart defects or blindness.
✦ If you and your mate are related in any way.
✦ Women who have had recurrent miscarriages (usually 3 or more).
✦ If both partners are descended from Ashkenazi Jews.

Research indicates the age of the fetus's father is important. Medical information shows a father over 40 may have an increased chance of fathering a child with a birth defect.

Some of the information you need may be difficult to gather together, especially if you or your partner were adopted. You may know little or nothing of your previous family history. Discuss all of this with your doctor before you become pregnant; you will have a better idea of the chances of problems before getting pregnant, rather than becoming pregnant and then having to make choices. The primary goal in genetic counseling is the same as other goals in pregnancy—early diagnosis and/or prevention of problems.

Also read additional material on genetic counseling, page 150.

The Older Pregnant Woman

More couples are choosing to start their families at a later age. Today, physicians are seeing more first-time mothers over 35.

An older pregnant woman has two main concerns. She wants to know how the pregnancy will affect her and how her age will affect the pregnancy and developing baby. There are increased complications for the mother and baby when the mother is older. See pages 150-152.

We have discovered that with increasing age, parents have had increased exposure to potentially harmful toxins, sometimes called *teratogens*. These can increase the incidence of birth defects.

Down's Syndrome In the past, the picture painted for the woman over 35 has been a bleak one. Today, this isn't always the case. Numbers are quoted indicating incidents of Down's syndrome. For instance, a doctor might tell you that at age 25 your chance of a baby with Down's syndrome is 1 in 1,300, at age 30 it is 1 in 965, at age 35 it is 1 in 365, at age 40 it is 1 in 109 and at age 45 it is 1 in 32. The older you get, the higher the risk of having a baby with Down's syndrome. See pages 151-152.

Where does this leave you in your decision about becoming pregnant? Let's look at it another way. Using the above numbers, at age 35, you have a 99% chance of *not* having a baby with Down's syndrome. At age 40, it is almost the same chance but a little bit lower. At age 45, you still have a *97% chance of not having a baby with Down's syndrome!* Therefore, if you are 35 or older and considering pregnancy, it is more likely you will have a normal, healthy baby than a baby with Down's syndrome.

Father's Age   Research shows that the father's age may also be important. Chromosomal abnormalities that cause birth defects occur more often in older mothers, particularly in women over age 35, and in men over 40. Men over 55 have twice the normal risk of fathering a child with Down's syndrome than younger men. The chance of chromosomal problems increases with the increase in the age of the father. Some researchers recommend men father their children before age 40. However, there is still a great deal of controversy about this.

Maternal Problems   Maternal problems with increasing age include most of the chronic illnesses that increase as age increases. High blood pressure is one of the more common complications in pregnancy in women over 35. There is also a higher incidence of pre-eclampsia or toxemia of pregnancy in over-35 pregnant women.

The chance of diabetes, as well as complications of diabetes, increases with age. Researchers cite figures demonstrating that twice as many women over age 35 will have complications with diabetes.

A very broad simplification of this is that it is easier to be pregnant when you are 20 than it is when you are 40. In the past, hypertension and diabetes were major complications in any pregnancy. With today's advances, we can manage these complications of pregnancy quite well.

Tests for the Older Mother-to-be   Tests that may be considered in the older pregnant woman include ultrasound, amniocentesis, chorionic villus sampling and alphafetoprotein measurement.

✧

These tests are discussed later in the book. These tests provide information while the baby is still growing and developing inside you. An important consideration about these tests involves what you are you going to do with the information from these tests. Would you have an abortion? What if the test causes a miscarriage?

Your General Health   Important questions to consider before getting pregnant when you are older include those about your general health. How fit are you for pregnancy? Are you willing to take the risk that a pregnancy could accelerate blood-pressure problems, diabetes, back or joint problems and other medical problems? There is an increased incidence of Cesarean sections in women over 35. There is also a higher incidence of longer, harder labor in this age group.

If you are an older woman, you can maximize your chances of having a successful pregnancy by being as healthy as possible before you become pregnant. Most researchers recommend a mammogram be performed at age 35. It is important to have this done before you become pregnant so you do not complicate a pregnancy with a breast lump or early cancer of the breast. Paying attention to general recommendations for your diet and your health-care are also important keys in preparing for pregnancy, especially if you are 35 or older.

It is important to remember most pregnancies in older women are tolerated well by these women, and they have normal, healthy babies. If you become pregnant and you're older, focus on your health and what you can do to make your pregnancy as comfortable for you as it can be.

Nutrition Before Pregnancy

Most people feel better and work better when they eat a well-balanced diet. Planning a good diet and carrying through with it before pregnancy ensures that your developing fetus receives good nutrition during the first few weeks or months of pregnancy. A balanced diet is part of good general health.

Usually a woman takes good care of herself once she knows she is pregnant. By planning ahead, you will guarantee your baby a good healthy environment for the entire 9 months of your pregnancy, not just for 6 or 7 months. When you make your nutrition plan, you are preparing the environment in which your baby will be conceived and develop and grow.

It has long been recognized that good nutrition and a balanced diet are important in pregnancy. Why not apply this to the time before you try to get pregnant so it carries into the early weeks of pregnancy? Establish eating habits and a general nutrition plan to follow throughout your pregnancy.

Do *not* diet during pregnancy or while you are trying to conceive. Consult your doctor if you are considering a special diet for weight reduction or weight gain before you try to get pregnant. Dieting may cause temporary deficiencies in vitamins and minerals that may be important to your pregnancy.

Be Careful with Vitamins and Herbs   Don't self-medicate with large amounts or unusual combinations of vitamins or herbs. You can overdo it. In specific instances, certain vitamins can cause birth defects if used in excessive amounts. A good example is vitamin A; excessive use has been shown to increase birth defects. A good general rule to follow is to stop *all* supplementation at least 3 months before pregnancy. Eat a well-balanced diet and take a multivitamin or a prenatal vitamin. Most doctors are happy to provide you with prenatal vitamins if you are planning a pregnancy.

Begin Good Eating Habits   Your eating habits before pregnancy will carry on into your pregnancy. Many women eat on the run and pay little attention to what they eat most of the day. Before pregnancy, you may be able to get away with this without any problems. However, because of the increased demands on you and the requirements of your developing fetus, this won't work when you do become pregnant.

The key to good nutrition is *balance*. Going to extremes with either vitamins or specific diets can be harmful to you and your developing fetus. It could even make you feel worse than you need to during your pregnancy.

Specific Considerations Some specific factors to consider with relation to your nutrition before getting pregnant include medications you take, whether you follow a vegetarian diet, the amount of exercise you do, whether you skip meals, your diet plan (are you trying to lose or gain weight?) and any special diet needs you might have.

If you eat a special diet because of medical problems, consult your doctor about it. Much information is available through your doctor or your local hospital about good diets and nutrition.

Many diets go to extremes that *you* may be able to tolerate, but these extremes can be harmful to a developing fetus. It is important to discuss dieting with your doctor ahead of time and not find out when you are 8 weeks pregnant that you are malnourished because of dieting.

Exercise Before Pregnancy

Few would argue that exercise is good for you—before you become pregnant and during your pregnancy. However, exercise can be carried to extremes, which can be harmful and dangerous when you are pregnant.

Begin exercising regularly before you become pregnant. Making adjustments in your lifestyle to include regular exercise will benefit you. And if you are feeling good, have a problem-free pregnancy and an easier delivery, it will help your baby. The benefits to you may include weight control, a feeling of well-being and increased stamina or endurance, which will become important later in your pregnancy.

While you are trying to get pregnant, don't be involved in intense training or try to increase your exercise program.

This is not a good time to play competitive sports where you push yourself to the maximum.

It's important to find exercise you enjoy and will continue on a regular basis, in any kind of weather. Concentrating on improving the strength in your lower back and abdominal muscles may be helpful during your pregnancy, but it is hard to begin this type of program once you are already pregnant.

Some general guidelines for exercise before pregnancy and during pregnancy have been proposed by the American College of Obstetricians and Gynecologists (ACOG). Many hospitals and health clubs or spas have exercise programs for pregnant women. ACOG has tapes available on exercise during pregnancy and after pregnancy. Ask your doctor how you might be able to obtain these tapes or guidelines.

General Guidelines on Exercise   Below and on the next page are some general guidelines relating to exercise before and during pregnancy.

✦ Before beginning any exercise program, consult with your doctor about past medical problems and past problems with pregnancy.

✦ Begin any exercise program *before* you are pregnant.

✦ Include exercise on a regular basis.

✦ Begin exercising gradually.

✦ Wear comfortable clothing when you exercise, including clothing that is warm enough or cool enough, and good comfortable shoes.

✦ Avoid risky sports such as horseback riding or water skiing.

✦ Allow sufficient time to warm up and cool down.

✦ Do not get overheated.

✦ Start with 15-minute workout intervals, with 5-minute rest periods.

✦ Take your pulse every 15 minutes. Do *not* let it exceed 140 beats a minute. An easy way to calculate your pulse is to count the number of heartbeats by feeling your neck or wrist for 15 seconds. Multiply by four. If your pulse exceeds 140 beats a minute, rest until your pulse drops below 90.

+ Increase the number of calories you take in when you exercise.
+ When you are pregnant, be careful about getting up and lying down.
+ After the fourth month of pregnancy, do not lie on your back while exercising. This can decrease the blood flow to the uterus and placenta.
+ When you finish exercising, lie on your left side for 15 to 20 minutes.
+ Stop exercising and consult your healthcare provider if you experience any of the following: bleeding or loss of fluid from the vagina while exercising, shortness of breath, dizziness, severe abdominal pain or any other serious problem.
+ Because of medical problems, consult your doctor and exercise *only* under supervision if you experience any of the following: irregular heartbeat, high blood pressure, diabetes, thyroid disease, anemia or any other chronic medical problem.

Your Pregnancy History   Your pregnancy history is also important. Consult with your doctor about exercise if you have a history of three or more spontaneous abortions, an incompetent cervix, a history of intrauterine growth retardation, premature labor or any abnormal bleeding during pregnancy.

If you have other concerns about exercise before or during pregnancy, talk with your doctor ahead of time. The exercise you have tolerated well and easily before pregnancy may be difficult for you and potentially harmful to your pregnancy.

As with dieting during pregnancy, the best approach with exercise is a balanced approach. Regular exercise that is

❖

enjoyable will help you feel better and help you enjoy your pregnancy more. And it will provide your developing baby with a healthy environment.

Substance Use and Abuse Before Pregnancy

We have learned much about the use and abuse of drugs and alcohol in recent years. Some people ask—how much of a particular substance is OK to use during pregnancy. The safest approach to drug or alcohol use during pregnancy is *no use* at all.

It makes sense to solve these problems before pregnancy. By the time you realize you're pregnant, you may already be 8 or 10 weeks along. Your developing fetus goes through some of its most important stages in the first 12 weeks of pregnancy. You might use drugs and not realize you are pregnant. Few women would take these substances if they knew they were pregnant. Stop using any substance you don't need at least 3 months before trying to get pregnant!

In the past, little was understood about drug or alcohol abuse, and not a lot could be done to help a person with these problems. However, today health-care providers are able to give suggestions and provide care for those who use or abuse drugs, alcohol or other substances.

Doctors who specialize in caring for those with addictions are called *addictionologists.* Do not be embarrassed about confiding information about substance abuse to your doctor. Your doctor's concern is for you and your developing baby.

There is no doubt tobacco, drugs and alcohol can harm you and your pregnancy. The time to get help is *before* you conceive, rather than asking for help in quitting a habit once you are already pregnant. If you think it will not hurt anyone or anything for you to continue to abuse these substances during your pregnancy, you're only kidding yourself. And you may do irreparable harm to your baby.

Information continues to be gathered showing that use of drugs or alcohol during pregnancy affects a child's IQ and its attention span and learning ability. To date, *no* safe level of these substances has been identified. Also read pages 38-44.

Cigarette Smoking   We have known for a long time that smoking affects pregnancy and the development of the fetus. Low birth weight and growth retardation have been shown to be problems in babies whose mothers smoked during pregnancy. Ask for help in stopping smoking before you become pregnant; your doctor should be receptive to this request. See pages 41-42.

Alcohol   In the past, some believed a small amount of alcohol during pregnancy was OK. Today, we believe there is *no* safe amount of alcohol during pregnancy. Alcohol crosses the placenta and directly affects your baby. When you take a drink, so does your baby! Heavy drinking during pregnancy can result in fetal alcohol syndrome (FAS), discussed on pages 42, 44.

Cocaine   Cocaine has a very definite affect on pregnancy. It has been shown to affect the fetus all during a pregnancy. Women who use cocaine during the first 12 weeks of pregnancy have more miscarriages. Cocaine has been shown to cause birth defects. Women who use cocaine have a higher number of stillbirths and babies who later develop SIDS (Sudden Infant Death Syndrome).

     If cocaine use is a problem for you, get help before you stop birth control and before you try to get pregnant. In some parts of the country it is estimated that more than 10% of all pregnant women use cocaine at some time during their pregnancy. See pages 40, 61.

Marijuana   Marijuana (hashish) is a dangerous drug during pregnancy because it crosses the placenta and enters the baby's system. It can have long-lasting effects on babies exposed before birth. Research has shown a mother's use of marijuana during pregnancy can affect cognitive function, the ability to make decisions and future-planning ability in her child. Use

❖

can also affect a child's verbal reasoning and memory.

Drug use before pregnancy is serious business. Fortunately, there is help for those who use drugs. Get help before you become pregnant. Preparing for pregnancy may be a good reason for you and your partner to change your lifestyle and your drug habits.

Work and Pregnancy

One consideration in planning for your pregnancy is your job. Many women do not know they are pregnant until the early stages of the pregnancy are already behind them. Because this part of the pregnancy is so important to the development and growth of your fetus, it is wise to plan ahead. This should include learning about things you are exposed to at work.

Another important consideration related to work is the type of benefits or insurance coverage you have and your company's maternity-leave program. Most programs allow at least a few months off work. It makes sense to check into this before getting pregnant. With the expense of medical care and having a baby, it could cost you several thousand dollars if you don't plan ahead.

Some jobs might be considered dangerous or possibly harmful during pregnancy. Some substances, such as chemicals, inhalants, radiation or solvents that you might be exposed to at work, could be a problem during pregnancy. Much of this chapter has discussed your lifestyle and how you take care of yourself. It is important to consider things you are exposed to at work on a daily basis as part of your lifestyle. Continue reliable contraception until you know the environment at work is a safe one. See pages 59-61 and 134-135.

Attention has been paid to women who must spend a lot of time standing at work. Women who stand a large portion of the day have smaller babies. If you have had a premature delivery in the past or if you have an incompetent cervix, a job that requires you to be active and stand a great deal may not be the wisest choice for you during pregnancy. Talk to your doctor about your work.

Attitudes have changed about women working during pregnancy. Most doctors will encourage you to work during your pregnancy unless there are special circumstances. If you are concerned about things you are exposed to, talk to your doctor about this problem. Also see pages 59-61.

Sexually Transmitted Diseases

Infections or diseases passed from one person to another by sexual contact are grouped together and called *sexually transmitted diseases (STDs)*. These infections can affect your ability to get pregnant and can harm your developing baby. The type of contraception you use may have an effect on the likelihood of your contacting an STD. Condoms and spermicides can lower the risk of getting an STD. You are much more likely to get a sexually transmitted disease if you have more than one sexual partner.

If you have had an STD in the past or think you have one, discuss it with your doctor. The time to be treating a sexually transmitted disease is before pregnancy, not during the early parts of pregnancy. Also read pages 58-59 and 77-78.

Pelvic Inflammatory Disease The most common STDs are chlamydia and gonorrhea. These infections can be very serious and can cause pelvic inflammatory disease (PID). PID is serious because it can spread from the vagina and cervix through the uterus and involve the Fallopian tubes and ovaries. The result can be scarring and blockage of the tubes, making it difficult or impossible for you to become pregnant or making you more susceptible to a tubal or ectopic pregnancy. Later in pregnancy, gonorrhea and chlamydia can infect the fetus as it passes through the vagina during delivery, which can cause infection in the baby. Also see pages 78 and 275.

✧

Genital Herpes Genital herpes is an infection involving the vagina and labia. It is most often passed during sexual activity from a person who has active herpes sores. There is no cure for herpes, and it tends to be a recurrent problem. It disappears, then returns months or years later.

A baby can become infected with herpes during birth as it passes through the birth canal. This can cause severe infection in the baby. If you have ever had genital herpes, tell your doctor. It may be necessary to check frequently during your pregnancy for this problem. Herpes is also discussed later in this book. See page 77.

Genital Warts Human papillomavirus (HPV) is receiving greater attention as we learn more about it. It causes genital warts, also called *condyloma*. Warts are passed from person to person during sexual relations and oral and anal sex. These warts need to be treated. If warts are present during pregnancy, they may become much larger and can get in the way during delivery. Many researchers now believe this virus causes abnormal Pap smears and cervical cancer. Also see pages 78, 138-141.

Syphilis Syphilis, although not frequently seen, remains a serious STD. Syphilis can be passed through the bloodstream to the developing fetus; this sometimes causes miscarriage or stillbirth. Normally, a test for syphilis is done at the beginning of pregnancy.

HIV and AIDS HIV infection and AIDS have become increasing threats to women. HIV is the abbreviation for *human immune deficiency virus;* AIDS stands for *Acquired-Immune-Deficiency Syndrome.* HIV affects your immune system, your defense against disease, leaving you open to infections. When you have the HIV virus and get one of these serious infections, it is called *AIDS.* AIDS is nearly always fatal. It can be passed to your sexual partner as well as to a developing fetus.

An HIV-positive woman who is *not* late in the course of her illness can generally have an uneventful pregnancy, labor and delivery. Each baby from an HIV-positive woman has a 20-30% risk of being infected during the pregnancy, during birth or with breast-feeding. Research now indicates that a woman with AIDS has a greater chance of giving birth to an *uninfected* baby if she takes AZT during her pregnancy.

Because of the mother's antibodies in the baby's blood at birth, *all* babies will test positive for HIV. The test becomes accurate for the baby 15 to 18 months after birth.

Protecting Yourself from STDs   Part of planning and preparing for pregnancy includes protecting yourself against STDs. You can help protect yourself against STDs by using a condom, regardless of what other type of contraception you might be using, limiting your sexual partners and having sexual contact only with those you are sure do not have multiple sexual partners. Ask for treatment if you think you have a sexually transmitted disease. These infections are discussed later in this book, see pages 58-59 and 77-78.

Weeks *1 & 2*

Pregnancy Begins

Whether this is your first pregnancy or whether you've already had a child and you're expecting again, it's an exciting time for you. Having a growing baby developing inside you is an incredible experience. This book will help you understand and enjoy your pregnancy by providing an insight into what is going on in your body.

A main focus of this book is to help you see how your actions and activities affect your health and well-being and that of your growing baby. If you are aware of how a particular test at a particular time, such as an X-ray, will affect the growing fetus, you may decide on another course of action. If you understand how taking a certain drug can harm your baby or cause long-lasting effects, you may decide not to use it. If you know eating incorrectly or poorly can cause heartburn or nausea in you or delayed growth in your baby, you may choose to eat a nutritious diet. If you are aware of how much your actions impact on your pregnancy, you may be able to choose wisely, free yourself from worry and enjoy your pregnancy more.

Material in this book is divided into weeks of pregnancy. Illustrations with each week help you see clearly how you and your baby are changing and growing. General topics are discussed each week, such as how big your baby is and how big you are. Areas of special concern are also discussed.

The information in this book is *not* meant to take the place of any discussion with your physician. Be sure you discuss *any* and *all* concerns with him or her. Use this material as a beginning in your dialogue with your medical-care provider. It may help you put your concerns into words.

When Is Your Baby Due?

It may seem odd to begin this section by discussing how to determine when your baby is due *before* you're pregnant, but that's how your doctor figures it. The beginning of a pregnancy is actually figured from the *beginning* of your last menstrual period. That means for your doctor's computational purposes, you are pregnant 2 weeks before you actually conceive! This can be confusing, so let's examine it more closely.

Figuring Your Due Date   Most women don't know the exact date of conception, but they are usually aware of the beginning of their last period. This is the point from which a pregnancy is dated. For most women, the fertile time of the month (ovulation) is around the middle of their monthly cycle or about 2 weeks before the beginning of their next period.

Using this date, pregnancy lasts about 280 days or 40 weeks from the beginning of the last menstrual period. You can calculate your due date by counting 280 days from the first day of bleeding of your last period. Or add 7 days to the date of your last period and subtract 3 months. This also gives you the approximate date of delivery. For example, if your last period began on February 20, your due date (EDC—estimated date of confinement) is November 27.

Calculating a pregnancy this way gives the *gestational* age or *menstrual age*. This is how most doctors and nurses keep track of time during pregnancy. It is different from *ovulatory age* or *fertilization age*, which is 2 weeks shorter, dating from the actual date of conception.

Many people count the time during pregnancy by using weeks. It's really the easiest way. But trying to remember to

✧

begin counting from when your period starts and you don't become pregnant until about 2 weeks later can make things confusing. For example, if your doctor says you're 10 weeks pregnant (from your last period), conception occurred 8 weeks ago. You have 30 weeks to go to your due date for a total pregnancy of 40 weeks.

You may hear references to your stage of pregnancy by *trimester*. Trimesters divide pregnancy into three periods, each about 13 weeks long. This helps group together times of development. For example, most miscarriages (spontaneous abortions) occur during the first trimester. This is a time of great formation and development of the organ systems of your baby. During the third trimester, most problems with pregnancy-induced hypertension in the mother (toxemia or pre-eclampsia) occur.

You may even hear about *lunar months*, referring to a complete cycle of the moon, which is 28 days. Because pregnancy is 280 days from the beginning of your period to your due date, pregnancy lasts 10 *lunar months*.

40-Week Timetable In this book, pregnancy is based on a 40-week timetable. Using this method, you actually become pregnant during the *third week*. The details of your pregnancy are discussed week by week beginning with Week 3. Your due date (EDC) is the end of the 40th week.

Each week includes the actual age of your growing baby. For example, under Week 8 you'll see:

> **8th Week of Pregnancy** (*gestational age*)
> **Age of Fetus—6 Weeks** (*fertilization age*)

In this way, you'll know how old your developing baby is at any point in your pregnancy.

It's important to understand a due date is only an estimate, not an exact date. Only 1 out of 20 women delivers on her exact due date; 90% deliver the week before or the week after. It's a mistake to count on a particular day (your due date or an earlier date). You may see that day come and go and still not have your baby. Think of your due date as a *goal*—a time to look forward to and prepare for. It's helpful to know you're making progress. Understanding how time is recorded during your pregnancy helps.

No matter how you count the time of your pregnancy, nothing will make it go by any faster. It's going to last as long as it's going to last. But a miracle is happening—a living human being is growing and developing inside of you! Enjoy this wonderful time in your life.

Your Menstrual Cycle   For your calculations, your menstrual period probably ends at the beginning of the second week of pregnancy or a few days before. *Menstruation* is the normal, periodic discharge of blood, mucus and cellular debris from the cavity of the uterus. It occurs at more or less regular intervals beginning at an early age (12 or 13 years) and continues until menopause (around age 50). It is usually not interrupted other than during pregnancy or lactation.

The usual interval for menstruation is 28 days, but this can vary widely and still be considered normal. The duration and amount of menstrual flow is also variable; the usual duration is 4 to 6 days. Menstrual discharge is made up of fragments of endometrium (the lining of the uterine cavity) mixed with blood. Clots of blood may also appear. The average amount of blood lost during a normal period is estimated to be 1 to 2 ounces (25 to 60 milliliters). This can vary considerably from one woman to another woman or from one cycle to another.

Two important cycles actually occur at the same time— the ovarian cycle and the endometrial cycle. The *ovarian cycle* provides an egg for fertilization. The *endometrial cycle* provides a suitable site for implantation of the fertilized egg inside your uterus. Because endometrial changes are regulated by hormones made by the ovary, the two cycles are intimately related.

The normal regulation of the ovarian cycle and menstrual cycle (with production of one egg for fertilization) is the rule, not the exception. Some women have irregular cycles and egg production. These cycles can be *anovulatory* or *without ovulation.* This is rare compared to regular, predictable menstrual cycles and hormone changes.

Your body produces many hormones. These include follicle-stimulating hormone (FSH) and luteinizing hormone (LH), which come from the pituitary gland at the base of the brain, and estrogen, progesterone and androgens (testosterone), which are primarily produced in the ovary.

The ovarian cycle is aimed at producing an egg (ovum) for fertilization. There are about 2-million eggs in a newborn girl at birth. This decreases to about 400,000 in prepubertal girls. The maximum number of eggs is actually *before* birth. When the fetus is about 5 months old (4 months before birth), there are about 6.8-million eggs.

During any ovarian cycle, 20 or more follicles may start the process that leads to ovulation. But only one produces the egg. This follicle makes its way to the surface of the ovary in preparation for ovulation. As it approaches the surface of the ovary, the wall of the follicle becomes thinner. At ovulation, the egg is released from the follicle. The site of release is called the *stigma.*

Some women (about 25%) experience lower abdominal pain or discomfort on or about the day of ovulation, called *Mittelschmerz.* It is believed to be caused by irritation from fluid or blood from the follicle when it ruptures. It does not usually occur with each cycle. The presence or absence of this symptom cannot be considered as proof that ovulation did or did not occur.

Your Health Can Affect Your Pregnancy

Your good health is one of the most important factors in your pregnancy. Good nutrition, proper exercise, sufficient rest and attention to how you care for yourself all impact on your pregnancy. In Preparing for Pregnancy, Chapter 1, and throughout this book, I provide information on medications you may take, medical tests you may need, over-the-counter substances you may use and many other areas of concern to you. This information is presented so you will be aware of how your actions affect your health and the health of your developing baby. Please go back and read the first chapter, Preparing for Pregnancy, if you have not already read it.

The healthcare you receive can also affect your pregnancy and how well you tolerate being pregnant. Good healthcare is important to the development and well-being of your baby. It's important for you to be in good health *before* your pregnancy.

It is "ideal" to see your doctor before you get pregnant. This includes taking care of medical problems and routine checkups. If you do this, you'll know your Pap smear is normal, your breast exam is OK and any chronic illnesses, such as asthma or diabetes, are under control.

Before getting pregnant, discuss any medications you take with your doctor. He or she may need to adjust the doses or have you stop taking them over a period of time. Medications that aren't absolutely necessary can be discontinued before pregnancy. *Never* stop taking any medication on your own, without consulting your physician. Some medications can't and should not be stopped before or during your pregnancy, such as thyroid hormone.

Medical problems or considerations can be recognized and dealt with before pregnancy. By doing this, they won't become complications or greater problems during pregnancy. A good example is diabetes. Studies have shown diabetes can have far-reaching effects on a pregnant woman and her unborn baby. If diabetes is left uncontrolled during pregnancy, birth defects, stillbirths and other problems are possible.

Your Healthcare Provider   You have many choices when it comes time to choose your healthcare provider. An obstetrician is a doctor who specializes in the care of pregnant women, including delivering babies. Obstetricians are M.D.s (medical doctors who have graduated from an accredited medical school and have fulfilled the requirements for a

✧

medical license) or D.O.s (doctors of osteopathic medicine who have graduated from an accredited school of osteopathic medicine and have fulfilled the requirements for a medical license). Both have completed further training after medical school (residency).

Obstetricians who specialize in high-risk pregnancies are called *perinatologists*. Few women require a perinatologist (1 out of 10). Ask your doctor if you need a specialist if you are concerned about past problems. Some women choose a *family practitioner*, previously called a *GP* or *general practitioner*, because he or she is their family doctor. In some cases, an obstetrician may not be available because a community is small or remote. The family practitioner often serves as your internist, obstetrician/gynecologist and pediatrician. Many family practitioners deliver babies and are very experienced. If problems arise, a family practitioner may need to refer you to an obstetrician for your prenatal care. This also may be the case if a Cesarean section is required for delivery of your baby.

Certified nurse-midwives are sometimes chosen by pregnant women. A certified nurse-midwife is a trained professional who usually cares for women who are at low risk and delivers low-risk, uncomplicated pregnancies. These professionals are registered nurses with additional training and certification in nurse-midwifery. They require the immediate availability of a physician, in case complications arise.

Other midwives deliver babies, however, their qualifications and training vary. Don't be embarrassed to ask for credentials if you want to consider a nurse-midwife. You're dealing with your health and the well-being of your baby. Don't take a chance on the outcome of your pregnancy. Be sure your care provider is well-qualified. Most deliveries are routine, without complications. But when complications do occur, they can occur very quickly. Quick attention and qualified, skilled people are needed to provide the best care.

What About the Hospital? In picking a healthcare provider, you usually also pick a hospital. There are many considerations when choosing where to have your baby. Some are listed below.

+ Is the facility close by?
+ What are the policies regarding your partner and his participation?
+ Can he be present if you have a Cesarean section?
+ Can you have an epidural?
+ Is it a birthing center (if that's what you want)?
+ Does your HMO (health maintenance organization) or your insurance cover the doctor *and* the hospital?

Communication Is Important These and other questions are important. There may be no choice for you. The doctor's office or the hospital can help answer these and many other questions you may have. It's important to be able to communicate well with your healthcare provider. Pregnancy and delivery are very individual experiences. You need to be able to ask your doctor any questions you have.

+ What about natural childbirth? Does your doctor believe in it?
+ Are there routines he or she performs on every patient? Does everyone "get" an enema, fetal monitor or more?
+ Who covers for your doctor when he or she is away?
+ Are there other doctors you will meet or who will take care of you?

Express your concerns and talk about things that are important to you. Your doctor has experience involving hundreds or thousands of deliveries and is drawing on this for your well-being. Your doctor has to consider what is best for you and your baby while he or she tries to honor any "special" requests you may have. Don't be afraid to ask *any* question. Your doctor has probably already heard it. It is possible a request is unwise or risky for you. But it's important to ask and discuss various questions and concerns with your physician.

✧

You'll also want to feel secure in the care you receive. While you may be concerned with who will be at the birth, such as family or friends, or if you will have soft music and dim lights, your doctor is concerned about other things. He or she is watching for warning signs of problems as well as normal development and progression.

Finding the "Right" Caregiver for You   How do you find someone who "fits the bill"? If you already have an obstetrician you're happy with, you may be all set. If you don't, call your local medical society. Ask for references to professionals who are taking new patients for pregnancy.

An added credential is *board certification*. Not all doctors who deliver babies are board-certified. It is not a requirement. Board certification means your doctor has put in extra time preparing for and taking exams to qualify him or her to care for pregnant women and deliver their babies.

Board certification is administered by the American Board of Obstetrics and Gynecology, under the direction of the American College of Obstetricians and Gynecologists. If your doctor has passed his or her boards, it is often indicated by particular initials after the doctor's name—F.A.C.O.G. This means he or she is a Fellow of the American College of Obstetricians and Gynecologists. Your local medical society can also give you this information.

There are other ways to find a caregiver with whom you are happy. Ask friends who have recently had a baby about their experiences. Ask the opinion of a labor-delivery nurse. Various publications, such as the *Directory of Medical Specialties* or the *Directory of the American Medical Association*, are available at most U. S. libraries. Another doctor, such as a pediatrician or internist, may also provide a reference.

Your Actions Affect Your Baby's Development

It's never too early to start thinking about how your activities and actions can affect your growing baby. Many substances you normally use may have adverse effects on a

❖

fetus. Some of these substances include drugs, tobacco, alcohol and caffeine. Below is a discussion on drug abuse, cigarette smoking and alcohol use. Any of these activities can harm a developing fetus. Stop using any substance that could harm your baby *before* you decide to become pregnant.

Drug Use and Abuse Drug abuse is common today in our society, and drug abuse in pregnancy is occurring more frequently. Unfortunately, it affects a second, innocent party—the unborn fetus. A baby exposed to drugs before birth can be affected developmentally or "born with a habit."

"Drug abuse" most often refers to drugs prohibited by law. But it can also include the recreational use of legal substances, such as alcohol, caffeine and tobacco. Legal medications, such as benzodiazepines or barbiturates, may also have harmful effects, whether or not they are used for legitimate reasons.

Dependence on a particular drug may be physical, psychological or both. *Physical dependence* implies the drug must be taken to avoid unpleasant withdrawal symptoms. It does not necessarily mean addiction or drug abuse. For example, many caffeine users develop withdrawal symptoms if they stop drinking coffee but they are not considered drug abusers or addicts. *Psychological dependence* means the user has an emotional need for a drug or medication. This need can be more compelling than a physical need and can provide the stimulus for continued drug use.

Many drug abusers primarily desire the enjoyable or pleasurable effects of the drugs. Tolerance may occur after continued use, requiring higher and higher amounts of the medication.

Another trend in drug abuse is the use of more than one drug at a time. This is done in an attempt to heighten the effect of a particular agent or to avoid undesirable effects.

Can use of drugs impact on a pregnancy? The answer is

a definite "Yes!" We know certain drugs have damaging effects on a fetus. In some cases, a woman who abuses drugs is more prone to complications of pregnancy associated with her lifestyle. With use of certain substances, nutritional deficiencies are common. Anemia and fetal-growth retardation are also problems. There may also be an increased chance of toxemia or pre-eclampsia.

Opioids, agents derived from opium and synthetic compounds with similar actions, produce euphoria, drowsiness or sleepiness and decreased sensitivity to pain. Habitual use often leads to physical dependence. Morphine, heroin, Demerol® and codeine all belong to this group. These drugs are associated with a variety of congenital abnormalities and complications of pregnancy that are difficult to separate from poor nutrition and lack of prenatal care. Women who use opioids during pregnancy are often at high risk for premature labor, intrauterine growth retardation, pre-eclampsia and other problems. A baby born to a mother who uses opioids may experience withdrawal symptoms after birth.

Often, prostitution is part of the picture with drug abuse, which leads to a high incidence of sexually transmitted diseases and other infectious diseases. Intravenous use of drugs is associated with hepatitis, endocarditis and acquired-immune-deficiency syndrome (AIDS). Any of these can present serious problems during pregnancy. Women with drug problems may not seek prenatal care.

Hallucinogens, such as LSD, mescaline and peyote, are still used but not as commonly as several years ago. Phencyclidine (PCP; angel dust) is a powerful hallucinogen that can cause psychotic episodes. It causes abnormal development in some animals and possibly humans, although this has not definitely been proved.

Marijuana and hashish, which both come from *Cannabis sativa*, contain tetrahydrocannabinol (THC). Research has indicated that drug use by the mother-to-be can result in cognitive problems in the child. Use of central-nervous-system stimulants, such as amphetamines, during pregnancy has been associated with an increase in cardiovascular defects in babies.

Most studies with drugs have been done using animals. This information is then inferred, but not proved, to have the same results in humans.

Information about effects of a specific drug on a human pregnancy comes from cases of exposure before the pregnancy is discovered. These "case reports" help researchers understand possible harmful effects but leave gaps in our knowledge. For this reason, it is sometimes difficult or impossible to make exact statements about particular drugs and their effects.

Cocaine (and crack) has become a popular recreational drug and includes a large number of women among its users. It is an increasingly common complication of pregnancy. Often the drug is consumed over a long period of time, such as several days. During this time, very little is eaten or drunk. This can have dangerous consequences for an unborn fetus. Intoxication with cocaine may be associated with convulsions, arrhythmias, hypertension and hyperthermia in the mother-to-be. Continual or repeated use of cocaine can affect maternal nutrition and temperature control, which can be damaging to the baby. Cocaine use has been linked to spontaneous abortion, placental abruption and congenital defects. These are important reasons for concern about its use during pregnancy. Also see page 61.

Barbiturates may be associated with birth defects, although a cause-and-effect relationship has not been proved. Withdrawal in a newborn infant, along with poor feeding, seizures and other problems, has been seen.

Benzodiazepines include tranquilizing agents such as diazepam (Valium®) and chlordiazepoxide (Librium®), along with newer agents. Several studies have related the use of these drugs to an increase in congenital malformations.

What can be done? It is best to stop using drugs *before* conception. If you use drugs, be honest with your doctor.

Ask questions about drugs and drug use. Tell your doctor about any agent you take that may affect your baby.

The victim of drug withdrawal is your baby. This problem could present serious consequences that can be dealt with best if they are known about in advance.

Cigarette Smoking   Smoking has harmful effects on a pregnancy. A pregnant woman who smokes 20 cigarettes a day (one pack) inhales tobacco smoke more than *11,000 times* during an average pregnancy.

Scientific evidence has shown smoking during pregnancy increases the risk of fetal death or fetal damage. Smoking interferes with the absorption of vitamins B and C and folic acid. Lack of folic acid can result in neural-tube defects. It also increases the risk of pregnancy-related complications in the mother-to-be.

Tobacco smoke contains many harmful substances— nicotine, carbon monoxide, hydrogen cyanide, tars, resins and some cancer-causing agents (carcinogens), such as diazobenzopyrene. These substances may be responsible singly or together for causing damage to your developing fetus.

For more than 20 years, we have known infants born to mothers who smoke weigh less by about 7 ounces (200g). That is why cigarette packages carry a warning to women about smoking during pregnancy. Decreased birth weight is *directly* related to the number of cigarettes the mother-to-be smoked. The same effects don't appear in other babies if the mother doesn't smoke in later pregnancies. There is a direct relationship between smoking and impaired fetal growth.

Children born to mothers who smoked during pregnancy have been observed to have lower IQ scores and increased incidence of reading disorders than children of non-smokers. The incidence of minimal-brain-dysfunction syndrome (hyperactivity) has also been reported to be higher in children of mothers who smoked during pregnancy.

Cigarette smoking during pregnancy increases the risk of spontaneous abortion and fetal death or death of a baby

✧

soon after birth. The risk is also directly related to the number of cigarettes the mother-to-be smoked. It may increase as much as 35% in a woman who smokes more than one pack of cigarettes a day.

Smoking also increases the incidence of serious, potentially lethal complications in a mother-to-be. An example of this is *placental abruption,* discussed in detail on pages 308-312. The risk of developing placental abruption is increased by almost 25% in moderate smokers and over 65% in heavy smokers.

Placenta previa, discussed on pages 326-329, also occurs more frequently among smokers. The rate of occurrence increases by 25% in moderate smokers and 90% in heavy smokers.

Known or suspected harmful effects to general health from smoking are numerous. Effects include increased risk of pulmonary diseases such as chronic bronchitis, emphysema and cancer. There is also an increased risk of developing cardiovascular diseases including ischemic heart disease, peripheral vascular disease or arteriosclerosis. There is even an increased risk of developing bladder cancer or peptic-ulcer disease if you smoke. A smoker has an increased mortality rate that is 30 to 80% higher than non-smokers.

What can you do? The answer sounds simple but isn't— quit smoking. In more realistic terms, a smoking mother-to-be (and her developing baby) benefit from reducing or stopping use of cigarettes before or during pregnancy.

In some studies, evidence has been found to indicate a non-smoker and her unborn fetus exposed to cigarette smoke in the environment, also called *secondary smoke,* are exposed to nicotine and carboxyhemoglobin. Perhaps pregnancy can serve as good motivation for *everyone* in the family to stop smoking!

Alcohol Use in Pregnancy   Alcohol use by a pregnant woman carries considerable risk. Moderate use of alcohol has been linked to an increased chance of miscarriage. Excessive alcohol consumption during pregnancy often results in abnormalities in the fetus. Chronic use of alcohol in pregnancy can lead to abnormal fetal development called *fetal alcohol syndrome* (FAS).

FAS is characterized by growth retardation before and after birth, and defects in limbs, the heart and facial characteristics of children born to alcoholic women. Facial characteristics are very recognizable—the nose is upturned and short, the upper jawbone is flat and the eyes look "different." An FAS child may also have behavioral problems.

FAS children often have impaired speech, and their fine and gross motor functions are impaired. The perinatal (time before, during and after birth) mortality rate is 15 to 20%. In one study of FAS children at age 7, 45% who survived had IQs below 80. In a population of normal children they were compared to, only 9% had IQs below 80.

Most studies indicate 4 to 5 drinks a day are required for FAS to occur. But mild abnormalities have been associated with 2 drinks a day (1 ounce of alcohol). This has led many researchers to conclude there is *no* safe level of alcohol consumption during pregnancy. For this reason, all alcoholic beverages in the U. S. carry warning labels similar to those on cigarette packages. The warning advises women to avoid alcohol during pregnancy because of the possibility of problems in the fetus, including fetal alcohol syndrome.

If drugs are taken with the alcohol, the chances of damaging a fetus are increased. The drugs that cause the greatest concern include analgesics, anti-depressants and anti-convulsants.

Some researchers have suggested heavy alcohol consumption by the baby's father may produce fetal alcohol syndrome. Alcohol intake by the father has been blamed for intrauterine growth retardation.

As a precaution, be very careful about over-the-counter cough and cold remedies you may use. Many contain alcohol—some as much as 25%!

Some women want to know if they can drink socially. There is a great deal of disagreement about it because there is no known safe level of alcohol consumption during pregnancy. Why take chances? For the health and well-being of your developing baby, abstain from alcohol during pregnancy. The responsibility of causing FAS rests squarely on your shoulders!

Hepatitis in Pregnancy *Hepatitis* is a viral infection of the liver. It is one of the most serious infections that can occur during pregnancy. *Hepatitis A* is responsible for over 30% of the cases of hepatitis in the U.S. It is usually transmitted by person-to-person contact via poor hygiene or poor sanitation.

Hepatitis B is responsible for nearly 50% of the cases of hepatitis in the U.S. It is transmitted by sexual contact and reuse of needles. Those at risk for contacting Hepatitis B include those with a history of intravenous drug use, a history of sexually transmitted diseases or exposure to people or blood products that contain Hepatitis B. The "B" type of virus can be transmitted to a developing fetus of a pregnant woman.

Another form of hepatitis, called *Non-A, Non-B Hepatitis* (also called *Hepatitus C*), is responsible for about 10% of the cases in the United States. A person becomes infected with this type of hepatitis through multiple blood transfusions or the use of intravenous drugs. *Hepatitis D* is usually only seen in someone who is already infected with Hepatitis B.

Symptoms of hepatitis include nausea, flu-like symptoms and pain in the area of the liver or upper-right abdomen. A person with hepatitis may appear yellow or jaundiced, and urine may be darker than normal. Diagnosis of hepatitis is made by blood tests.

In most areas, women are tested for Hepatitis B at the beginning of pregnancy. If you test positive for hepatitis at the beginning of pregnancy, it may be necessary to give your baby immune globulin against hepatitis following delivery. It is now recommended that all newborns receive hepatitis vaccine shortly after birth. Discuss it with your pediatrician to see if this vaccine is available in your area.

Week 3

Age of Fetus — 1 Week

How Big Is Your Baby?

The embryo growing inside you is very small. It is only a group of cells, but it is multiplying and growing very rapidly. It is the size of the head of a pin and would be visible to the naked eye if you could see it. The group of cells doesn't look like a fetus or baby. It looks like the illustration on page 47. During this first week, the embryo is only about 0.006 inch (0.150mm) long.

How Big Are You?

In this third week of pregnancy, you won't notice any changes. It's too soon! Few women know they have conceived. Remember, you haven't even missed a period yet.

How Your Baby Is Growing and Developing

A great deal is happening, even though your pregnancy is in its very beginning stages. Ovaries lie free in your pelvis or peritoneal cavity. They are close to the uterus and Fallopian tube. At the time of ovulation, the end of the tube (fimbria) lies close to the ovary. Some researchers believe this opening of the tube covers the area on the ovary where the egg is released at the time of ovulation. Site of release on the ovary is called the *stigma*.

During intercourse, an average of 0.06 to 0.15 ounce (2 to 5ml) of semen is deposited in the vagina. Each milliliter contains an average of 70-million sperm; each ejaculation contains 140- to 350-million sperm. Only about 200 sperm actually reach the site of fertilization with the egg in the tube. Fertilization is the joining together of a sperm and an egg.

Fertilization of the Egg   Fertilization is believed to occur in the middle part of the tube called the *ampulla*, not inside the uterus. Sperm travel through the uterine cavity and out into the tube to meet the egg. This may explain how tubal or ectopic pregnancies occur. See pages 66-69 for further information.

When the sperm and egg join, the sperm must pass through the outer layer of the ovum, called the *corona radiata*. The sperm must then digest its way through another layer of the ovum, called the *zona pellucida*. Although several sperm may penetrate the outer layers of the ovum, usually only one sperm enters the ovum and fertilizes it.

After the sperm penetrates the ovum, the sperm head attaches to its surface. The membranes of the sperm and ovum unite, enclosing them in the same membrane or sac. The ovum reacts to this contact with the sperm by making changes in the outer layers so no other sperm can enter.

Once the sperm is in the cytoplasm of the ovum, it loses its tail. The head of the sperm enlarges, and it is called the *male pronucleus*. The ovum is called the *female pronucleus*. The male and female pronuclei come together in the center of the ovum where their chromosomes intermingle. When this happens, extremely small bits of information and characteristics from each partner unite. This chromosomal information gives each of us our particular characteristics. The usual number of chromosomes in each human is 46. Each parent supplies 23 chromosomes. Your baby is a combination of chromosomal information from you and your partner.

Will Your Baby Be a Boy or a Girl?   Your baby's sex is determined at the time of fertilization by the type of sperm (male or female) that fertilizes the egg. A Y-chromosome-bearing sperm produces a male, and an X-chromosome-bearing sperm produces a female.

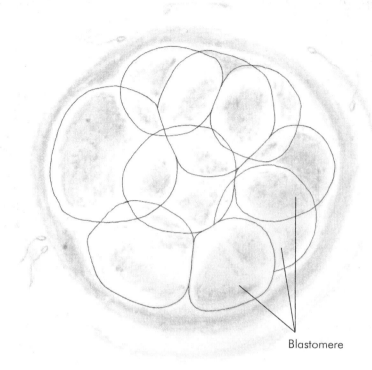

Blastomere

9-cell embryo 3 days after fertilization. The embryo is made up of many blastomeres. Together they form a blastocyst.

The developing ball of cells is called a *zygote*. The zygote passes through the uterine tube into the uterus as the division of cells continues. These cells are called a *blastomere*. As the blastomere continues to divide, a solid ball of cells is formed. It is called a *morula*. The gradual accumulation of fluid within the morula results in the formation of a *blastocyst*. The blastocyst is small—about 0.006 inch (0.150mm) in length. At the time of implantation in the uterine cavity, it is about 0.009 inch (0.23mm) long.

❖

During the next week, the blastocyst travels through the uterine tube to the cavity of the uterus (3 to 7 days after fertilization in the tube). The blastocyst lies free in the uterine cavity as it continues to grow and develop. About a week after fertilization, it attaches to the uterine cavity (implantation). The cells that implant into the uterine wall burrow into the lining of the uterus. Occasionally this causes a small amount of bleeding or spotting.

The distinction between an embryo and a fetus is somewhat arbitrary. For the first 8 weeks of development (10 weeks of gestation), it is called an *embryo*. During development of the embryo, the major organ systems are formed. After 8 weeks and until birth, the developing baby is called a *fetus*.

Changes in You

Some women can tell when and if they ovulate. They may feel mild cramping or pain, or they may have an increased vaginal discharge. Occasionally at the time of implantation of the fertilized egg into the uterine cavity, a woman may notice a small amount of bleeding.

It's too early for you to notice many other changes. Your breasts haven't started to enlarge, you won't be starting to "show" and you won't experience morning sickness. All of that is ahead of you in the weeks to come.

How Your Actions Affect Your Baby's Development

Exercise is an important part of life for many women. The more we learn about health, the more the advantages of regular exercise become evident. Regular exercise may decrease your risk of developing several medical problems, including cardiovascular disease, osteoporosis (softening of bones), depression, premenstrual syndrome (PMS) and obesity.

There are many types of exercise or physical activity to choose from. Each offers its own advantages. There may be many activities you can enjoy that fit your lifestyle. Aerobic exercise is one of the most popular with women today who want to keep in shape.

Aerobic Exercise For cardiovascular fitness, aerobic exercise is the best. Aerobic exercise must be performed at least 3 times a week at a sustained heart rate of 110 to 120 beats a minute and maintained for at least 15 continuous minutes. The rate of 110 to 120 beats a minute is an approximate target for people of different ages. Many tables show target heart rates. On page 51 is one I often use with my patients.

You exercise aerobically when you participate in many activities, including brisk walking, bicycling, running, jogging, swimming, aerobic dancing and cross-country skiing.

One of the benefits of aerobic exercise is an increase in the ratio of high-density lipoprotein cholesterol (HDL) to low-density lipoprotein cholesterol (LDL) and lowered levels of total cholesterol. These factors, along with a decrease in clotting or formation of blood clots, are believed to reduce heart attack and stroke.

Aerobic exercise also promotes weight loss and weight control by decreasing the appetite, using energy during exercise and accelerating metabolism for a short time after exercising.

Muscle Strength Some women exercise for muscle strength. To strengthen a muscle, there has to be resistance against the muscle. There are three different kinds of muscle contractions—isotonic, isometric and isokinetic. *Isotonic exercise* involves shortening the muscle as tension is developed, like lifting a barbell. *Isometric exercise* occurs when the muscle develops tension but doesn't change in its length, such as pushing against a stationary wall. *Isokinetic exercise* occurs when the muscle moves at a constant speed, such as when you swim.

Cardiac and skeletal muscles cannot usually be strengthened at the same time. Strengthening skeletal muscles

✧

requires lifting heavy weights. But you can't lift these heavy weights long enough to strengthen the cardiac muscle.

Weight-bearing exercise is the most effective at promoting increased bone density to help avoid osteoporosis. Other advantages of exercise include flexibility, coordination, improvement in mood and alertness. Stretching and warming up muscles before and after exercise help you improve flexibility and avoid injury.

Exercise During Pregnancy?   As a pregnant woman, you are probably concerned about the risks of exercise. Can you or should you exercise when you're pregnant or want to become pregnant?

It is desirable for a pregnant woman to have cardiovascular fitness. Women who are physically fit are more able to perform the work of labor and delivery. Exercise during pregnancy is not without some risk, however. Risks to the developing baby can include increased body temperature, a decreased blood flow to the uterus and possible injury to the mother's abdominal area.

You can exercise during pregnancy if you do it wisely. Avoid raising your body temperature above 102F (38.9C). Aerobic exercise can raise your body temperature higher than this, so take care. A rise in body temperature can be increased by dehydration. Avoid prolonged aerobic exercise, particularly during hot weather.

While exercising aerobically, blood can be diverted to the exercising muscle or skin and away from other organs, such as the uterus, liver or kidneys. A lower workload during pregnancy is advised to avoid potential problems. Most experts recommend you reduce your exercise level to between 70 and 80% of your prepregnancy level. Pregnancy is not the time to try to set any new records or train for an upcoming marathon! During pregnancy, keep your pulse below 140 beats a minute.

It is more desirable to become fit *before* pregnancy and continue exercising than to start after your pregnancy

| Target Heart Rates | | |
Age (years)	Target heart rate (beats/minute)	Maximum heart rate (beats/minute)
20	120-150	200
25	117-146	195
30	114-146	190
35	111-138	185
40	108-135	180
45	105-131	175
50	102-131	170
55	99-123	165
60	96-123	160
65	93-116	155
70	90-113	150

(U.S. Department of Health and Human Services)

begins. If you exercise aerobically before pregnancy, you can probably continue exercising at a somewhat lower rate. If you have any problems such as bleeding or premature labor, you and your doctor will have to choose another program.

It is unwise to start an aerobic exercise program during pregnancy or to increase training. If you haven't been involved in regular, strenuous exercise before pregnancy, walking or swimming is probably about as involved as you should get with exercise.

Before you begin, discuss exercising with your doctor. Together you can develop a program consistent with your current level of conditioning and your exercise habits.

You Should also Know

Bleeding During Pregnancy   Bleeding during pregnancy causes concern. During the first trimester, bleeding can make you worry about the well-being of your baby and the possibility of a miscarriage. Miscarriage is covered beginning on page 90.

❖

Bleeding during pregnancy is *not* unusual. Some researchers estimate that 1 in 5 pregnant women bleeds during the first trimester. Although it makes you worry about possible problems, not all women who bleed have a miscarriage.

Bleeding at the time of implantation is mentioned on page 48. This can occur as the blastocyst "burrows" into the uterine lining. At this point, you won't even know you are pregnant because you haven't missed a period. If this happens, you may just think your period is starting early.

As your pregnancy grows and the uterus grows, the placenta forms and vascular connections are made. Bleeding may occur at this time. Strenuous exercise or intercourse may also cause some bleeding. If this occurs, stop your activities immediately. Check with your doctor, who will advise you what to do.

If bleeding causes your doctor concern, he or she may order an ultrasound exam. Sometimes ultrasound can show a reason for bleeding, but during this early part of pregnancy, there may be no discernible reason for bleeding.

Most doctors suggest rest, a decrease in activity and avoidance of intercourse when bleeding occurs. Surgery and/or medication are *not* helpful and are unlikely to make a difference.

A lot of women have "spotting" or bleed a small amount of blood during pregnancy. It doesn't always mean something bad will happen. However, call your doctor if you experience any bleeding. He or she will advise you on a course of action.

Aspirin Use Almost any medication taken during pregnancy can have some kind of effect on your baby. This includes aspirin, a drug taken frequently for many reasons, either alone or in combination with other medications.

Aspirin has been shown to have harmful effects during pregnancy. Taking aspirin causes changes in your platelet

❖

function. Platelets are important in blood clotting. Aspirin use can increase bleeding. This is particularly important to know if you are bleeding during pregnancy or if you are close to delivery at the end of your pregnancy.

Read labels on any medication you take to see if they contain aspirin. Don't use them if they do. Avoid using aspirin or any products that contain aspirin during pregnancy without your doctor's knowledge.

If you need a pain reliever or a medication to reduce fever, and you cannot reach your physician for advice, acetaminophen (Tylenol®) is one over-the-counter medication you can use for a short while with little fear of complications or problems for you or your baby.

For further information on over-the-counter medication use during pregnancy, see pages 164-165.

Folic Acid Use and Neural-Tube Defects   Neural-tube defects are birth defects that occur with defective closures of the neural tube during early pregnancy. These birth defects occur in about 1 in 1,000 births in the United States; generally, the cause of these defects is unknown. These defects include *spina bifida*, when the base of the spine remains open, exposing the spinal cord and nerves, *anencephaly*, congenital absence of the brain and spinal cord, and *encephalocele*, a protrusion of the brain through a cranial fissure.

Recent studies indicate taking folic acid during pregnancy may help prevent or decrease the incidence of neural-tube defects. However, these studies are continuing.

Recommended dietary allowance of folic acid during pregnancy is 0.4mg a day. The American College of Obstetricians and Gynecologists recommends any woman who has had a child born with a neural-tube defect take 4mg of folic acid a day, preferably beginning 1 month *before* she plans to become pregnant. Continue taking this amount through the first trimester of pregnancy. It is unnecessary to supplement beyond the first trimester because the neural tube closes within 4 weeks after conception.

❖

If you have a family history of neural-tube defects, it is *not* necessary to take extra supplementation. The amount of folic acid (0.8mg or 1mg) in regular prenatal vitamins should be sufficient.

Week 4

Age of Fetus — 2 Weeks

How Big Is Your Baby?

Your developing baby is still very small. Its size varies from 0.014 inch to about 0.04 inch (0.36mm to about 1mm) in length. One millimeter is half the size of a letter "o" on this page.

How Big Are You?

At this point, your pregnancy isn't showing at all. You haven't gained any weight, and your figure hasn't changed. The illustration on page 57 gives you an idea of how small your baby still is. You won't notice any change yet.

How Your Baby Is Growing and Developing

Fetal development is still in very early stages, but many great changes are taking place! The implanted blastocyst is embedded more deeply into the lining of your uterus, and the amniotic cavity is starting to form. The area that will be the placenta is forming, and vascular networks are being established. These networks contain maternal blood.

Germ Layers Different layers of cells are developing. These layers, also called *germ layers*, develop into specialized parts of your baby's body, such as various organs. There are three germ layers—the ectoderm, endoderm and mesoderm.

The *ectoderm* will become the nervous system (including the brain), the skin and the hair. The *endoderm* develops into the lining of the gastrointestinal tract, the liver, pancreas and thyroid. From the *mesoderm* comes the skeleton, connective tissues, blood system, urogenital system and most of the skeletal and smooth muscles.

Changes in You

You are probably expecting a period around the end of this week. When it doesn't occur, pregnancy may be one of the first things you think of!

The Corpus Luteum   When you ovulate and the egg leaves the ovary, the area on the ovary where the egg comes from is called the *corpus luteum.* If you become pregnant, it is called the *corpus luteum of pregnancy.* The corpus luteum forms immediately after ovulation at the site of the ruptured follicle where the egg is released. The corpus luteum looks like a small cyst or sac of fluid on the ovary. It undergoes rapid development of blood vessels in preparation for producing hormones, such as progesterone, to support a pregnancy in its early stages before the placenta takes over.

The mature corpus luteum is usually 0.5 inch to 1.2 inches (1 to 3cm) in diameter, but it may be larger and it may be painful. A cyst may even form. It can rupture, causing further pain and internal bleeding. You may need surgery to correct the problem.

The importance of the corpus luteum is the subject of much debate. It is believed to be essential in the early weeks of pregnancy because it produces progesterone. The placenta takes over this function between 8 and 12 weeks of pregnancy. The corpus luteum lasts until about the sixth month of pregnancy, although normal corpus lutea have been found with some full-term pregnancies. Successful pregnancies have also occurred when the corpus luteum was removed because of a ruptured cyst as early as the 20th day after a menstrual period or about the time of implantation.

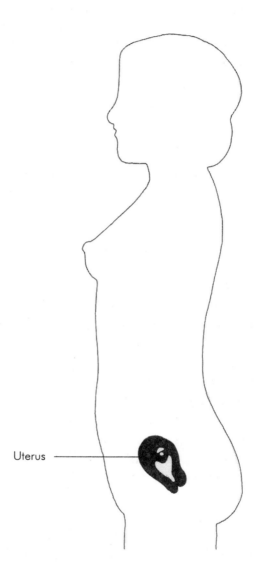

Uterus

Comparative size of uterus early in pregnancy at around 4 weeks (fetal age—2 weeks).

✧

How Your Actions Affect Your Baby's Development

HIV and AIDS Women make up one of the fastest growing groups that is infected with the human immunodeficiency virus (HIV). Most of the affected women are of childbearing age.

HIV is the causative agent of Acquired-Immune-Deficiency Syndrome (AIDS). The exact number of people infected with HIV is unknown. Currently it is estimated that up to 1.5-million people in the United States alone may be infected. About 8% of all AIDS patients are women, and this percentage is increasing. Infected women will be the source of thousands of future cases of pediatric HIV infections.

HIV infection can lead to a progressive debilitation of the immune system, which normally fights infection. This can leave the individual susceptible to various infections and unable to fight them.

Women at greatest risk include current or former I.V. drug users and women whose sexual partners have used drugs intravenously or engaged in bisexual activities. Women with sexually transmitted diseases, those who engage in prostitution or those who received blood transfusions before screening began are also at risk. If you are unsure about your partner's I.V. drug usage or past sexual activities, seek counseling about testing for the AIDS virus.

A woman infected with HIV may not have any symptoms. There may be a period of weeks or months when tests do not reveal the presence of the virus. In most cases, antibodies can be detected 6 to 12 weeks after exposure. In some cases, this latent period can be as long as 18 months after exposure. Once the test is positive, a person may remain without symptoms for a variable amount of time. For every patient with AIDS, there are 20 to 30 infected individuals who have no symptoms.

There is no evidence of transmission through casual contact with water, food or environmental surfaces. There is no evidence the virus can be transmitted with RhoGAM™. See page 156. There is a potential risk for a woman receiving donor insemination (artificial insemination). However, most women contract HIV through the use of intravenous drugs or sexual relations with I.V. drug users. HIV can be passed to a baby during its birth.

Pregnancy may hide some of the symptoms of AIDS, which makes the disease harder to discover. The presence of disease may alter possible methods of treatment. The prognosis for an infected child is poor. Children diagnosed with AIDS in the first 6 months of life rarely survive beyond their first year. Because the illness is a serious threat to an unborn child, counseling and psychological support are critical.

There *is* some positive news for women who suffer from AIDS. We know if a woman is in the early course of the illness, she can usually have an uneventful pregnancy, labor and delivery. Her baby has a 20-30% risk of being infected during pregnancy, birth or breast-feeding. Research has also shown that taking AZT during pregnancy decreases the risk of giving birth to a baby infected with AIDS.

There is no indication that one method of delivery (C-section versus vaginal delivery) is safer for mother or infant. We now know spreading the HIV infection during breast-feeding is possible. HIV-infected women are advised *not* to breast-feed.

Testing for AIDS   Testing includes two tests—the ELISA test and the Western Blot test. The ELISA is a screening test. If it is positive, it should be confirmed by the Western Blot test. Both tests involve testing blood to measure antibodies to the virus, not the virus itself. No test should be considered positive unless the Western Blot test has been done. It is believed to be more than 99% sensitive and specific.

You Should also Know

Environmental Poisons in Pregnancy   Environmental pollutants have been identified that can be harmful to a developing

❖

baby. This is particularly important to a pregnant woman. Avoiding exposure to these pollutants can be very important to the well-being of a growing baby.

Lead   The toxicity of lead has been known for centuries. In the past, most lead exposure came from the atmosphere. Today, exposure to lead may come from many sources, including some gasoline (now regulated), water pipes, solders, storage batteries, construction materials, paints, dyes and wood preservatives.

     Lead is readily transported across the placenta to the baby. Toxicity can occur as early as the 12th week of pregnancy.

     Avoid exposure to lead. Be concerned about where you work. If you might be exposed in your workplace, find out if there is a risk.

Mercury   Mercury also has a long history as a potential poison to the pregnant woman. Reports of fish contaminated with mercury have been linked to cerebral palsy and microcephaly. There was also an incidence of contamination of grain with mercury, which resulted in cerebral palsy.

PCBs   Our environment has been significantly contaminated with polychlorinated biphenyls (PCBs). PCBs are not single chemical compounds but mixtures of several compounds.

     Most fish, birds and humans now have measurable amounts of PCBs in their tissues. Some experts have suggested that pregnant women limit their intake of fish (to avoid exposure to mercury and PCBs), particularly if a woman is exposed to PCBs where she works.

Pesticides   Pesticides include a large number of agents used to control unwanted plants and animals. Human exposure is common because of the extensive use of pesticides. Those of most concern contain several agents—DDT, chlordane, heptachlor, lindane and others.

✧

What Can You Do? There is a lack of definitive information on the safety or lack of safety of many chemicals in our environment. The safest course of action is to avoid exposure whenever possible, whether by oral ingestion or through the air you breathe. It may not be possible to eliminate all contact.

If you know you will be around various chemicals, wash your hands well before eating. Not smoking cigarettes will also help.

One reassuring fact is that most of the chemicals tested have produced illness in the mother-to-be before damage to her growing baby occurred. An environment that is healthy for you will be healthy for your developing baby.

Cocaine Use in Pregnancy Cocaine is a drug that is used and abused by many people. It can be introduced into the body by three primary routes. When *smoked,* it is called *crack.* It may be sniffed or snorted up the nose. When it is injected directly into a vein, it is called *freebasing.*

Use of cocaine by a pregnant woman can be disastrous for the developing fetus. Cocaine acts as a stimulant and increases the user's heart rate and blood pressure. Women who use cocaine during pregnancy have a higher rate of placental abruption.

If you use cocaine during the first 12 weeks of pregnancy, you will have an increased risk of miscarriage. Cocaine is known to cause severe deformities in a fetus. What type of defect it causes depends on the point in the pregnancy when cocaine is used.

Infants born to mothers who use cocaine during pregnancy have been found to have lower IQs and long-term mental deficiencies. Sudden infant death syndrome (SIDS) is also more common in these babies. Many babies born to women who use cocaine are stillborn.

Stop using cocaine before you stop using birth control. Damage to the embryo (later the fetus) can occur as early as *3 days* after conception!

Week 5

Age of Fetus — 3 Weeks

How Big Is Your Baby?

Your developing baby hasn't grown a great deal larger. It's about 0.05 inch (1.25mm) long.

How Big Are You?

At this point, there are still no big changes in you. Even if you are aware you're pregnant, it will be awhile before others will notice your changing figure.

How Your Baby Is Growing and Developing

As early as this week, a heart-forming plate has developed. Formation of the central nervous system (brain) and muscle and bone formation are in early stages. During this time the basis of your baby's skeleton is also forming.

Changes in You

Many changes are occurring now. Some changes you may be aware of. Others will be evident only after some kind of test.

Pregnancy Tests Pregnancy tests have become more sensitive, which makes early diagnosis of pregnancy more common. Tests detect human chorionic gonadotropin (HCG). A pregnancy test can be positive before you have even missed a period! Many tests can provide positive results (pregnant) 10 days after you become pregnant. But it's usually best to wait until you have missed a period before investing money and emotional energy in pregnancy tests, whether done at a hospital, in a clinic or at home.

Most home tests range in price from $12 to $30. They vary in how effective they are in helping you "diagnose" your pregnancy. Their accuracy can vary widely. Many hospitals or clinics offer free testing for pregnancy. This may save you some money.

Signs and Symptoms of Pregnancy   Actual positive signs of pregnancy, in addition to a pregnancy test, include:

+ Seeing the embryonic heartbeat with ultrasound, possible 3 to 6 weeks after conception.
+ Hearing the fetal heartbeat, possible as early as 12 weeks (10 weeks after conception).
+ Feeling fetal movements through the abdomen, usually around the 18th week of pregnancy.

What signs and symptoms of pregnancy will you notice first? It's different for every woman, and the timing of different events can vary widely. Your period does not begin, which may or may not signal something to you. Sudden cessation of menstruation, if you're usually regular, is strong evidence of pregnancy.

Nausea and Vomiting   Another early symptom is nausea, with or without vomiting. This is often called *morning sickness*, whether it occurs in the morning or later in the day. It usually starts early in the day and improves during the day as you become active. Morning sickness usually begins around the 6th week of pregnancy and usually improves by the end of the first trimester (at around 13 weeks).

Many women have nausea; it rarely causes enough trouble to require medical attention. However, a condition called *hyperemesis gravidarum* (pregnancy-induced nausea and vomiting) causes a great deal of vomiting, with resulting lack of nutrients. The pregnant woman must be treated in the hospital with intravenous fluids and medications for nausea.

There is no completely successful treatment for the normal nausea and vomiting of pregnancy, although remedies are often tried to provide relief. These include eating small amounts at frequent intervals and avoiding foods with unpleasant odors. There are currently no approved medications for nausea of pregnancy.

This is an extremely important period in the development of your baby—don't expose your unborn baby to medication, herbs, over-the-counter treatments or any other "remedies" for nausea that neither you nor your doctor know to be safe during pregnancy. Ask about a medication or remedy *before* you take it.

Other Changes You May Notice   In early pregnancy, the need to *urinate frequently* may occur. It can continue during most of your pregnancy and become particularly annoying near delivery, as your uterus enlarges and puts pressure on your bladder.

You may also notice *changes in your breasts*. A common symptom is tingling or soreness in the breasts or nipples. You may also see a darkening of the areola or an elevation of the glands around the nipple.

Food cravings have long been considered a non-specific sign of pregnancy. Craving a particular food doesn't mean pregnancy, but when added together with many other signs, it might mean you're pregnant.

Another early symptom of pregnancy is *tiring easily*. This very common symptom may continue through pregnancy. Be sure to take your prenatal vitamins and any other medications prescribed by your doctor.

How Your Actions Affect Your Baby's Development

When Should You Visit the Doctor?   One of the first questions you may ask yourself when you suspect you're pregnant is "When should I see a doctor?"

Good prenatal care is necessary to deliver a healthy baby from a healthy mother. See your physician as *soon* as you are reasonably sure you're pregnant. This could be as early as a few days after a missed period.

It's helpful to be in good physical condition and have medical problems under control *before* you attempt to conceive. But many women are not prepared for a pregnancy. For various reasons, some women put off seeing their doctor or don't see one at all. For the health of your baby, as well as your own health and well-being, seek care early.

Getting Pregnant While Using Birth Control   If you're using some type of birth control, it's important to tell your doctor. Occasionally all methods fail, even oral contraceptives. If you are sure you're pregnant, stop taking the pill, and see your doctor as soon as possible. While it is not desirable for you to take the pill while you're pregnant, don't become overly alarmed if this happens to you. Talk to your doctor about it. While there is a small increase in some fetal problems, it isn't high enough to cause a great deal of worry. But be sure to discuss it with your physician.

Pregnancy can also occur with an IUD (intrauterine device) in place. If this happens to you, it's important to see your doctor immediately! Discuss whether you should remove the IUD or leave it in. In most cases, an attempt is made to remove the IUD. If left in place, there is an increased risk of miscarriage. The chance of miscarriage with removal is about 20%. This is a little higher than the normal miscarriage rate, which is about 15 to 20%.

Spermicides used alone or with a condom, sponge or diaphragm are frequently used when pregnancy occurs. They have not been shown to be harmful to your developing baby.

You Should also Know

Ectopic Pregnancy   As described earlier, fertilization occurs in the Fallopian tube. The fertilized egg travels through the tube to the uterine cavity for implantation into the uterus.

✧

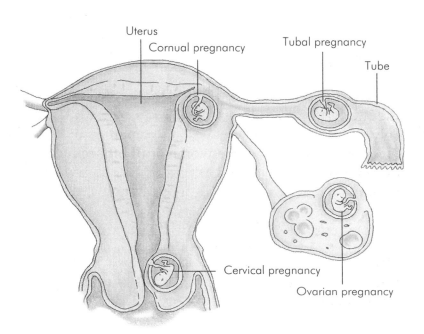

Possible locations of an ectopic (tubal) pregnancy.

An ectopic pregnancy occurs when implantation occurs outside the uterine cavity, usually in the tube itself. Ninety-five percent of all ectopic pregnancies occur in the tube (hence the term tubal pregnancy). Other possible sites of implantation are the ovary, cervix or other places in the abdomen. The illustration above shows some possible locations of an ectopic pregnancy. A tubal abortion occurs when a pregnancy is extruded (falls out) through the end of the tube back into the abdomen.

Ectopic pregnancy occurs in 1 out of every 100 pregnancies. Chances of an ectopic pregnancy occurring increase with damage to the Fallopian tube from pelvic inflammatory disease (PID) or from other infections, such as a ruptured appendix or abdominal surgery. If you have had a previous ectopic pregnancy, there is a 12% chance of recurrence. Use of an intrauterine device (IUD) also increases the chance of ectopic pregnancy.

✧

Diagnosing Ectopic Pregnancy Diagnosis of an ectopic pregnancy has improved with use of laparoscopy. With laparoscopy, surgery is performed through very small incisions in the bellybutton and lower-abdominal area. The inside of the abdomen and the pelvic organs can be viewed, and an ectopic pregnancy can be seen.

Some doctors do the surgery through the laparoscope, without making a larger incision (laparotomy) in the abdomen. The type of surgery used and the type of incision depend on whether the ectopic pregnancy is ruptured or unruptured.

An attempt is made to diagnose a tubal pregnancy *before* it ruptures and damages the tube, which could make it necessary to remove the entire tube. Early diagnosis also attempts to avoid the risk of internal bleeding from a ruptured, bleeding tube.

With an ectopic pregnancy, a pregnancy test is positive, even though the pregnancy is developing abnormally outside the uterus. Pregnancy tests detect a hormone produced early in pregnancy—human chorionic gonadotropin (HCG). HCG is found in your blood or urine.

Testing for Ectopic Pregnancy Pregnancy tests are reported as positive (pregnant) or negative (not pregnant). HCG can also be measured as an exact number, called a *quantitative HCG,* which may be useful in diagnosing an ectopic pregnancy or a miscarriage. The level of HCG increases very rapidly in a normal pregnancy. It doubles in value about every 2 days. If HCG levels do not increase as they should, an abnormal pregnancy is suspected.

Ultrasound testing, also called *sonography* or *sonogram,* is helpful in diagnosing an ectopic pregnancy. Ultrasound is discussed in detail beginning on page 116. A tubal pregnancy may be seen in the tube during ultrasound examination. The doctor looks for a pregnancy in the uterus (normal) consistent in size for the HCG level. In the case of an ectopic pregnancy, the woman may have a high HCG level, with no sign of a

✧

pregnancy inside the uterus. In an ectopic pregnancy, blood may be seen in the abdomen from rupture and bleeding, or a mass may be seen in the area of the Fallopian tube or the ovary.

With an ectopic pregnancy, the doctor's goal is to remove the pregnancy and preserve fertility. This is often difficult because diagnosing an ectopic pregnancy is difficult. Symptoms include vaginal bleeding, pain in the abdomen and other signs such as tender breasts or nausea, that can also occur in normal pregnancies.

Most ectopic pregnancies are detected around 6 to 8 weeks of pregnancy, but they may be detected earlier or later. The key in early diagnosis involves communication between you and your doctor about symptoms and their severity. Ectopic pregnancy can be very serious with internal hemorrhage and loss of fertility.

What Will Your Baby Be?   You can guess the sex of your child as well as your doctor—often better! As I have already mentioned, the sex of your baby is determined at the time of fertilization by the baby's father.

Many couples ask for ways to "get a boy" or "get a girl" before they try to get pregnant. In a few cases, sperm separation is used. Male and female sperm are separated and artificial insemination deposits the selected sperm in the woman. It's not a foolproof method, and it is expensive.

Health of the Baby's Father   Some women are concerned about the health of the father of the baby. Can his general health and his drug or alcohol use affect the health of the developing baby?

In recent years, more attention has been given to the paternal contribution in pregnancy. We now believe if a father's age is over 50, it may have an effect of increased risk of Down's syndrome, although there is not a great deal of evidence to support this theory. A father's drug habit may also influence the outcome of your pregnancy. Again, evidence is scanty, but there does appear to be an effect.

Artificial Sweetener Use During Pregnancy   Many women use artificial sweeteners. Aspartame and saccharin are the two most common artificial sweeteners added to foods and beverages. But are they safe to use during pregnancy?

Aspartame (sold under the brand names Nutrasweet® and Equal®) may be the most popular and widely used artificial sweetener. It is used in many "low-calorie" foods and beverages to help reduce their calorie content. Aspartame is a combination of two amino acids—phenylalanine and aspartic acid.

In studies that have been done, no adverse effects have been reported in healthy pregnant women. Foods and beverages that contain aspartame do not appear to be hazardous. They may be consumed in moderation. However, pregnant women who suffer from phenylketonuria must follow a low-phenylalanine diet or their babies may be born mentally retarded and suffer from delayed development. The phenylalanine in aspartame contributes to phenylalanine in the diet.

Saccharin is another artificial sweetener that is used in many foods and beverages. Although it is not used as much today as in the past, it is still found in many foods. The Center for Science in the Public Interest reports testing of saccharin does not indicate safety for use during pregnancy. Without further evidence, it would probably be better to avoid using this product while you are pregnant.

It would be wise during pregnancy not to use *any* kind of artificial sweetener or food additive you can avoid. I recommend eliminating any substance you don't really need from the foods you eat and the beverages you drink. Do it for the good of your baby.

Weight Gain During Pregnancy   The amount of weight women gain during pregnancy varies greatly. It may actually range from a loss of weight to a total gain of 50 pounds or more.

✧

We know complications arise at the extremes of these weight changes. Because of this, it is difficult to set one figure as the "ideal" weight gain during pregnancy. How much weight you gain is affected by your weight before you became pregnant. Many quote a weight-gain figure of 2/3 of a pound (10 ounces) a week until 20 weeks, then 1 pound a week from 20 to 40 weeks.

Other researchers have divided weight-gain amounts acceptable for underweight, normal weight and overweight women. See the chart below.

Weight Gain During Pregnancy	
Body Type	*Acceptable Gain (pounds)*
Underweight	28 to 40
Normal Weight	25 to 35
Overweight	15 to 25

If you have any questions about your weight gain during pregnancy, discuss them with your physician. He or she will advise you and guide you about how much weight you should gain during your pregnancy.

Dieting during pregnancy is *not* a wise idea. But that doesn't mean not watching your caloric intake. You should! It's important for your baby to get proper nutrition from the foods you eat. You must choose your foods for the nutrition they provide for you and your growing baby.

Week 6

Age of Fetus — 4 Weeks

How Big Is Your Baby?

The crown-to-rump length of your growing baby is 0.08 to 0.16 inch (2 to 4mm). *Crown-to-rump* is the sitting height or distance from the top of the baby's head to its rump or buttocks. This measurement is used more often than the crown-to-heel length because the baby's legs are most often bent, making this determination difficult.

Occasionally, with the proper equipment, a heartbeat can be seen on ultrasound by the 6th week. Ultrasound is discussed in more detail beginning on page 116.

How Big Are You?

You may have gained a few pounds or possibly even lost a few pounds by now. If you have been nauseated and not eating well, you may have lost weight. You have been pregnant for 1 month, which is enough time to notice some changes in your body. If this is your first pregnancy, your abdomen may not have changed much. Or you may notice your clothes are getting a little tighter around the waist. You may be gaining weight in your legs or other places, such as your breasts.

If you have a pelvic exam at this time, your uterus usually can be felt and a change in size noted.

❖

How Your Baby Is Growing and Developing

This is the beginning of the *embryonic period,* from 6 to 10 weeks of pregnancy (4 to 8 weeks of development). It is a period of *extremely* important development in your baby. At this time, the embryo is *most susceptible* to factors that can interfere with its development. Most malformations originate during this critical period.

The germ layers continue to develop—the ectodermal, mesodermal and endodermal layers. They later become various tissues and organ systems. From this organ formation, the major features of the body and its form are established.

The *ectodermal germ layer* becomes many things, including the central nervous system, peripheral nervous system, skin, hair, nails, tooth enamel, pituitary gland, mammary gland, sweat glands and sensory epithelium of the ear, nose and eye.

The *mesodermal germ layer* becomes muscle, cartilage, blood vessels, kidneys, gonads and spleen. The *endodermal germ layer* later becomes the gastrointestinal tract, respiratory tract, urinary bladder, tonsils, thyroid, parathyroids, thymus, liver and pancreas.

As the illustration shows, the result of this rapid growth is a body form showing the head and tail area. Around this time, the neural groove closes, and early brain chambers form. The optic vesicles and lens in the eyes are also forming. Limb buds can be seen.

The heart tubes are fused, and contractions of the heart begin. This can be seen on ultrasound.

Changes in You

Suffering from Heartburn   Discomfort from heartburn *(pyrosis)* is one of the most common complaints of pregnancy. It may begin early, although it generally becomes more severe later in pregnancy. It is usually caused by reflux of gastric and duodenal contents into the esophagus. This occurs

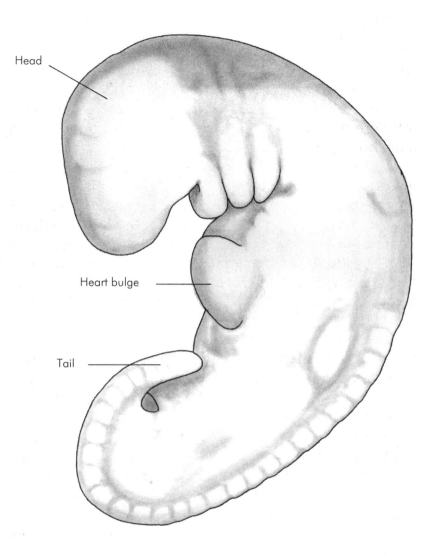

Head

Heart bulge

Tail

Embryo at 6 weeks of pregnancy (fetal age—4 weeks).
It is growing rapidly.

more frequently during pregnancy because of two factors—decreased gastrointestinal motility and compression of the stomach by the uterus as it enlarges and moves up into the abdomen.

For most women, symptoms are not severe. They improve with frequent small meals and avoidance of some positions, such as bending over or lying flat. One sure way to get heartburn is to eat a large meal and then lie down!

Antacids can provide considerable relief; follow your doctor's orders or the instructions on the package relating to pregnancy. Don't overdo it taking antacids! Some antacids, such as aluminum hydroxide, magnesium trisilicate and magnesium hydroxide (Amphojel®, Gelusil®, Milk of Magnesia® and Maalox®), may be used effectively. However, excessive overuse of any antacid that contains magnesium may cause magnesium poisoning. Avoid sodium bicarbonate because of the possibility of water retention with excessive sodium intake.

Try to find foods (and amounts of foods) that don't give you heartburn. But don't go overboard on them. If you find chocolate malts don't cause problems, don't have one for every meal! Cravings for certain foods during pregnancy can be good and bad. Eliminate foods that aren't good for you. Add foods that benefit you and your growing baby. Some women find they can't stand foods they usually enjoy.

Constipation   It is common during pregnancy for your bowel habits to change. Most women notice an increase in constipation, often accompanied by irregular bowel movements. This includes an increase in the occurrence of hemorrhoids.

You can do some things to help avoid constipation problems during pregnancy. Increase your fluid intake. Exercise may also be beneficial. Many doctors suggest a mild laxative, such as Milk of Magnesia or prune juice, if you have problems. Certain foods, such as bran and prunes, can increase the bulk in your diet. This may help relieve your constipation.

Do *not* use laxatives, other than those mentioned, without your doctor's OK. If constipation is a continuing problem, discuss treatment with your doctor.

❖

How Your Actions Affect Your Baby's Development

Sexually transmitted diseases (STD) are always important to treat. During pregnancy, a sexually transmitted disease can harm your growing baby. Any STD must be taken care of as soon as possible!

Genital Herpes Simplex Infection   Usually a herpes infection during pregnancy is a reinfection not a primary infection. Infection early in pregnancy may be associated with an increase in spontaneous abortion and, rarely, fetal malformations. Infection in the mother is associated with an increase in premature delivery and low-birth-weight infants. We believe an infant can get the infection from traveling through the birth canal. When membranes rupture, the infection may also travel upward to the uterus.

There is no safe treatment during pregnancy for genital herpes. When a woman has an active herpes infection late in pregnancy, a Cesarean section is done to prevent the infant from traveling through the infected birth canal. Infected newborns have a mortality rate of about 50%.

Monilial Vulvovaginitis   Monilial (yeast) infections are more common in pregnant women than in non-pregnant women. They have no major negative effect on pregnancy, but they may cause discomfort and anxiety.

Yeast infections are sometimes harder to control when you're pregnant. They may require frequent retreatment or longer treatment (10 to 14 days instead of 3 to 7 days). Creams used for treatment are safe during pregnancy. Your partner does not need to be treated.

A newborn infant can get thrush after passing through a birth canal infected with monilial vulvovaginitis. Treatment with nystatin is effective.

Trichomonal Vaginitis   This infection has no major effects on pregnancy. However, a problem in treatment may arise because metronidazole, the drug of choice, shouldn't be

✧

taken in the first trimester of pregnancy. Its use is also controversial during later stages of pregnancy.

Condylomata Acuminatum This condition is commonly called *venereal warts*. If you have extensive venereal warts, a Cesarean delivery may be necessary to avoid heavy bleeding.

Warty skin tags often become enlarged during pregnancy. They have been known to block the vagina at the time of delivery. Infants have also been known to get laryngeal papillomas (small benign tumors on the vocal cords) after delivery.

Gonorrhea A woman may contract gonorrhea at any time. The disease presents risks to her, her partner and her baby as it passes through the birth canal. The result to the baby is *gonorrheal ophthalmia*. Eyedrops are used in newborns to prevent this problem. Other infections may also result.

Gonorrheal infections are easily treated with penicillin or other medications that are safe to use during pregnancy.

Syphilis Detection of a syphilis infection is important for you, your partner and your infant. Fortunately this infection is rare, and it is also very treatable.

If you notice any ulcerative lesion on your genitals during pregnancy, have your doctor check it out. Syphilis can be treated effectively with penicillin and other medications that are safe in pregnancy.

You Should also Know

Your First Visit to the Doctor Your first visit to your doctor may be your longest visit. There's a lot to be accomplished. If you saw your doctor before you got pregnant, you may have already discussed some of your concerns.

Feel free to ask questions and get an idea of how this person will relate to you and your needs. This is important as your pregnancy progresses. During pregnancy, there should be an exchange of ideas, not a one-sided discussion from you or your doctor. Consider what your doctor suggests to you and why. It's important to share your feelings and ideas. You also need to remember your doctor has experience that can be valuable for you during pregnancy.

What Will Happen?   What should you expect at this first visit? First, you will be asked for a history of your past medical health. This includes general medical problems and any problems relating to your gynecological and obstetrical history. You will be asked about your periods and recent birth-control methods. If you've had an abortion or a miscarriage, tell your doctor. If you've been in the hospital for surgery or for some other reason, it's important information.

If you have old medical records, bring them with you. Your doctor also needs to know about any medication you take or any medications you are allergic to. Your family's past medical history may be important, such as the occurrence of diabetes or other chronic illness.

Your doctor will want to know if you were exposed to DES (diethylstilbestrol) when your mother was pregnant with you. At one time, DES was given to pregnant women to prevent miscarriage. This practice was discontinued years ago, but many babies were exposed. Many women who were exposed *in utero* have been found to have structural abnormalities of their reproductive organs. This is usually of no significance. However, abnormalities can be more severe and cause problems, such as miscarriage and premature birth. If you know you were exposed to DES before birth, tell your doctor.

A physical exam, including a pelvic exam and Pap smear, will be performed. An important part of this exam is to determine if your uterus is the appropriate size for how far along in your pregnancy you are.

Laboratory tests may be done at this first visit or on a subsequent visit. Lab tests are discussed in depth beginning on page 93.

✧

If you have questions, ask them. If you think you may have a "high-risk" pregnancy, discuss it with your doctor.

In most cases, you are asked to return every 4 weeks for the first 7 months, then every 2 weeks until the last month, then every week. If problems arise, more-frequent visits may be necessary.

Week 7

Age of Fetus — 5 Weeks

How Big Is Your Baby?

Your baby has an incredible growth spurt this week! At the beginning of the 7th week, the crown-to-rump length of your growing baby is 0.16 to 0.2 inch (4 to 5mm). This is about the size of a BB pellet. By the *end* of the week, your baby has grown to 0.44 to 0.52 inch (11 to 13mm); about the size of a green pea.

How Big Are You?

Although you may be quite anxious to show the world you're pregnant, there still may be no change. Changes will come soon, though.

How Your Baby Is Growing and Developing

Leg buds are beginning to appear as short fins. As you can see on page 83, arm buds have grown longer; they have divided into a hand segment and an arm-shoulder segment. The hand and foot have a digital plate where the fingers and toes will develop.

The heart bulges from the body. By this time, it has divided into separate right and left heart chambers. The primary bronchi are present in the lungs. *Bronchi* are the passageways in the lungs.

The cerebral hemispheres, which make up the brain, are also growing. The eyes and nostrils are developing.

The intestines are developing and the appendix is present. The pancreas, which produces the hormone insulin, is also present. Part of the intestine bulges into the umbilical cord. Later in your baby's development, it will return to the abdomen.

Changes in You

Changes are occurring gradually. You still probably won't "show," and people around won't be able to tell you're pregnant unless you tell them. You may be gaining weight throughout your body, but you should have gained only a couple of pounds this early in your pregnancy.

If you haven't gained weight or if you have lost a couple of pounds, it isn't unusual. It will go the other direction in the weeks to come. You may still experience morning sickness and other symptoms of early pregnancy.

How Your Actions Affect Your Baby's Development

Good Nutrition Is Important   Many factors can influence the development of your baby. What you eat is an important contributing factor. If your diet is deficient, it may affect the development of your baby.

Increase the number of calories you consume during pregnancy by 300 to 800 calories a day. These extra calories are needed to provide extra energy for tissue growth in both you and your baby. This includes an increase in the amount of body fat you need during pregnancy and after your baby's birth for nursing.

Your baby is using the energy you provide to create and store protein, fat and carbohydrates, and to provide energy for its body processes to function. If enough calories aren't available, protein may be metabolized as a source of energy instead of being used for growth and development.

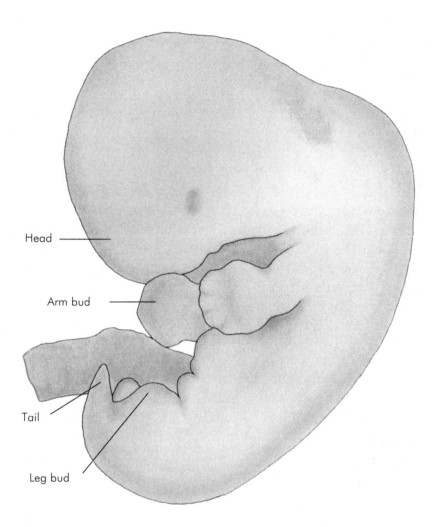

Head

Arm bud

Tail

Leg bud

Your baby's brain is growing and developing. The heart has divided into right and left chambers.

Below is a discussion of how your body uses protein, fats and carbohydrates during pregnancy. Discuss your questions with your doctor. Good nutrition and a healthy nutrition plan are essential for you and your growing baby.

Protein The non-pregnant woman needs protein to repair tissues. During pregnancy, your body also needs protein for growth and repair of the embryo/fetus, placenta, uterus and breasts. Most protein should come from animal sources, such as meat, milk, eggs, cheese, poultry and fish. These protein sources supply amino acids in the best combinations. The recommendation during pregnancy is 6 to 7 ounces (168 to 196g) of protein a day.

Carbohydrates There are no recommended dietary allowances (RDAs) for carbohydrate intake during pregnancy. Calories from carbohydrates should make up about 60% of the total number of calories in your diet. Adequate carbohydrate intake can help avoid formation of ketones, which accumulate when carbohydrate intake is low. High levels of ketones may be harmful to the growing baby.

Fat There are no recommended daily amounts for fat intake during pregnancy. There is rarely concern over inadequate fat intake; usually fat intake is excessive.

Cholesterol levels have recently gained much attention. Elevated cholesterol levels are a risk factor for heart disease. However, pregnancy and nursing are *not* times to evaluate your blood cholesterol. Cholesterol levels increase during pregnancy and nursing because of increased hormone levels. Sometimes this increase can be as much as 25%.

Minerals There is good evidence that only one mineral, iron, provides any benefit when provided as a supplement to pregnant women. Nearly all diets that supply a sufficient number of calories for appropriate weight gain contain enough minerals (except iron) to prevent mineral deficiency.

⟡

During pregnancy, you have an increased iron requirement. Very few women have sufficient iron stores for the demands of pregnancy. The average woman's diet seldom contains enough iron to meet the increased demands of pregnancy. During a normal pregnancy, blood volume increases by about 50%. This requires a large amount of iron to produce additional blood cells.

Iron needs are most important in the *latter half* of pregnancy. Usually iron supplements are not needed during the first trimester. If prescribed at this time, they can make symptoms of nausea and vomiting worse. Some doctors also prescribe calcium supplements, but it is probably unnecessary in most women.

The value of fluoride and fluoride supplementation in a pregnant woman is unclear. Some researchers believe fluoride supplementation during pregnancy results in improved teeth in the child. Not everyone agrees with this. Some prenatal vitamins contain fluoride. No harm to the baby has been shown from fluoride supplementation in a pregnant woman.

Prenatal Vitamins   Prenatal vitamins are usually prescribed for a pregnant woman by her doctor. Prenatal vitamins contain recommended daily amounts of vitamins and minerals for you during pregnancy. For your good health and your baby's benefit, do *not* consider them a substitute for food.

Your prenatal vitamins are different from regular multivitamins because of their iron and folate contents. Prenatal vitamins are probably the most important supplement for you in your pregnancy. They contain folic acid, which can help prevent neural-tube defects, and zinc, which can help a thin woman have a healthy infant.

These special vitamins are usually best tolerated if you take them with meals or at night before bed. The iron content can be irritating to your stomach and may also cause constipation.

You Should also Know

Sexual Intimacy During Pregnancy   Many couples question whether it is wise or permissible to have sexual intercourse

✧

during pregnancy. Whenever miscarriage or premature labor are threatened, it is best to avoid intercourse. Otherwise, sexual relations are acceptable for a healthy pregnant woman. Some doctors recommend abstinence from intercourse during the last 4 weeks of pregnancy, but not all physicians agree with this. Discuss it with your doctor.

Most doctors recommend you do *not* douche. Douching could be dangerous because of possible infection, bleeding or even rupture of membranes. Any of these can be a serious complication of pregnancy.

Week 8

Age of Fetus — 6 Weeks

How Big Is Your Baby?

By your 8th week of pregnancy, the crown-to-rump length of your baby is 0.56 to 0.8 inch (14 to 20mm). This is about the size of a pinto bean.

How Big Are You?

Your uterus is getting bigger, but it still probably isn't big enough for you to be showing, especially if this is your first pregnancy. You will notice a gradual change in your waistline and the fit of your clothes. Your doctor will see that your uterus is enlarged if you have a pelvic exam.

How Your Baby Is Growing and Developing

Your baby is continuing to grow and change rapidly during these early weeks. Compare the illustration on page 89 with the illustration for the 7th week of pregnancy on page 83. Can you see the incredible changes?

Eyelid folds are forming on its face. The tip of the nose is present. Internal and external ears are forming.

In the heart, the aortic and pulmonary valves are present and distinct. Tubes leading from the trachea to the functioning part of the lungs, called *bronchi*, are branched, like the branches of a tree. The body's trunk area is getting longer and straightening out.

Elbows are present, and the arms and legs extend forward. Arms have grown longer. They bend at the elbows and curve slightly over the heart. The digital rays, which

❖

become the fingers of the hand, are notched. Hands are far apart. Toe rays are present on the feet.

Changes in You

Changes in Your Uterus   Before pregnancy, your uterus was about the size of your fist. After 6 weeks of growth, it is about the size of a grapefruit. As the uterus grows, you may feel cramping or even pain in your lower abdomen or your sides. Some women feel tightening or contractions of the uterus.

The uterus tightens or contracts throughout pregnancy. If you don't feel this, don't worry. However, when contractions are accompanied by bleeding from the vagina, it's natural to worry about a miscarriage.

Sciatic-Nerve Pain   Many women experience an occasional excruciating pain in their buttocks and down the back or side of their legs as pregnancy progresses. This is called *sciatic-nerve pain* because the sciatic nerve runs behind the uterus in the pelvis to the legs. Pain is believed to be caused by pressure on the nerve from the growing and expanding uterus.

The best treatment for the pain is to lie on your opposite side. This helps relieve the pressure on the nerve.

How Your Actions Affect Your Baby's Development

Some women notice an improvement in their acne during pregnancy. But this doesn't happen for everyone.

Accutane® (isotretinoin) is commonly prescribed for the treatment of acne. Don't take Accutane during pregnancy! If it's taken during the first trimester, there is a higher frequency of miscarriage and malformation of the fetus.

If you are pregnant or think you might be pregnant, *don't* take Accutane. Use reliable birth control to avoid pregnancy if you do take Accutane.

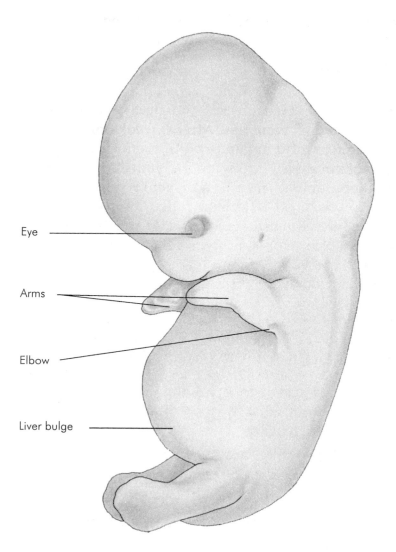

Eye

Arms

Elbow

Liver bulge

Embryo at 8 weeks (fetal age—40 to 42 days). Crown-to-rump length is about 0.8 inch (20mm). Arms are longer and bend at the elbows.

❖

You Should also Know

Miscarriage   The term *miscarriage* is used by lay people; the medical term is *abortion*. Abortion is differentiated into spontaneous abortion (or miscarriage) and voluntary, elective or therapeutic abortion, which is performed at the request of the woman. Voluntary abortion, legalized by the U. S. Supreme Court in January, 1973, is not discussed here.

In most places, if "delivery" (termination of a pregnancy) by spontaneous abortion or elective abortion occurs before 20 weeks, the fetus is called an *abortus*. After 20 weeks, a birth certificate is usually prepared. Delivery before 38 weeks of pregnancy is called *premature delivery* or *immature delivery.*

The exact incidence of spontaneous abortion is difficult to determine. Figures range from 10 to 25% of all pregnancies. It may be possible to be a week late for a period, have a heavy period and be unsure whether it was a late period or an early miscarriage.

What Causes a Miscarriage?   We don't usually know and are unable to find out what causes a miscarriage. By the time a pregnancy has miscarried, it has probably been dead for several weeks. Tissue has changed, and little or nothing can be done to determine the cause.

The most common finding in early miscarriages is an abnormality of the development of the early embryo. Sometimes called a *blighted ovum,* the term is used to describe a pregnancy in which the embryo died several weeks earlier, or no embryo is seen. Studies indicate more than half of these miscarriages have chromosomal abnormalities.

Many factors may affect the embryo and its environment, including radiation, chemicals (drugs or medications) and infections. These factors may cause miscarriage or malformation. Called *teratogens,* they are discussed in depth beginning on page 98.

Some maternal factors are believed to be important in some miscarriages. Unusual infections, such as listeria,

◇

toxoplasma and syphilis, have been implicated in spontaneous abortions.

We have no concrete evidence that deficiency of any
particular nutrient or even moderate deficiency of all nutrients causes abortion. Women who smoke have a higher rate
of spontaneous abortion. Alcohol is also blamed for an
increased rate of miscarriage.

The trauma of an accident or major surgery has been related to an increase in spontaneous abortion, although this is
difficult to verify. An incompetent cervix, see page 228, is a
cause of pregnancy loss after the first trimester. Many women
have blamed emotional upset or trauma for a spontaneous
miscarriage. This is very difficult to prove.

Below is a discussion of different types and causes of
miscarriage (abortion). It is included to alert you about what
to watch for if you have any symptoms of a miscarriage.
Discuss your questions with your doctor.

Threatened Abortion   A threatened abortion may be pre-
sumed when there is a bloody discharge from the vagina
during the first half of pregnancy. Bleeding may last for
days or even weeks. There may or may not be any cramping
or pain. Pain may feel like a menstrual cramp or a mild
backache. Bed rest is about all you can do, although being
active does not cause miscarriage. No procedures or medication can keep a woman from miscarrying.

Threatened abortion is a common diagnosis because 1
out of 5 women experience bleeding during early pregnancy; but not all miscarry. It is estimated that 15% of all pregnancies end in miscarriage.

Inevitable Abortion   An inevitable abortion occurs with the
rupture of membranes with dilatation of the cervix and passage of blood clots and even tissue. Abortion is almost certain under these circumstances. Contraction of the uterus
usually occurs, expelling the fetus.

Incomplete Abortion   The entire pregnancy may not come
out together. Part of the pregnancy is passed while part of it

✧

remains in the uterus. Bleeding may be heavy and continues until the uterus is empty.

Missed Abortion   A missed abortion can occur with prolonged retention of an embryo that died earlier. There may be no symptoms or bleeding. The time period from when the pregnancy failed to the time the miscarriage is discovered is usually weeks.

Habitual Abortion   This term usually refers to three or more consecutive spontaneous abortions.

If You Have Problems   If you threaten to abort, notify your doctor *immediately!* Bleeding usually comes first, followed by cramping. The possibility of tubal or ectopic pregnancy must be considered. A quantitative HCG may be useful in identifying a normal pregnancy, but a single value usually won't help. Your doctor needs to see an increase in the HCG over a period of days.

Ultrasound may help if you are more than 5 gestational weeks into your pregnancy. You may continue to bleed, but seeing your baby's heart beat and normal-appearing pregnancy may be very reassuring. It may be necessary to wait a week or 10 days then repeat the ultrasound to look for fetal growth if the first ultrasound is not reassuring.

The longer you bleed and cramp, the more likely you are to be having a miscarriage. If you pass all of the pregnancy (sometimes called *products of conception* when no embryo or fetus is present) and bleeding stops and cramping goes away, you may be done with it.

However, everything may not be expelled, and it is necessary to perform a D&C (dilatation and curettage). This is a minor surgery that empties the uterus. It is preferable to do this surgery so you won't bleed for a long period of time and risk anemia and infection.

Some women are given progesterone to help them keep a pregnancy. The use of progesterone to prevent miscarriage is controversial. It may cause possible harmful effects on the baby.

Rh-Sensitivity and Miscarriage If you're Rh-negative and you have a miscarriage, you will need to receive RhoGAM™. This applies *only* if you are Rh-negative. RhoGAM is given to protect you from making antibodies to Rh-positive blood. This is discussed on page 156.

If You Have a Miscarriage One miscarriage can be traumatic; two in a row can be very difficult to deal with. Repeated miscarriages occur due to chance or "bad luck" in most cases.

Most doctors don't recommend testing to try to find a reason for miscarriage unless you have three or more. Various tests, such as chromosome analysis, can be done to investigate the possibility of infections, diabetes and lupus.

Don't blame yourself or your partner for a miscarriage. It is usually impossible to look back at everything you've done, eaten or been exposed to and find the cause of a miscarriage.

Lab Tests Your Doctor May Order At your first or second visit, routine lab tests are performed. You will have a pelvic exam, including a Pap smear. Other tests include a CBC (complete blood count), urinalysis and urine culture, serologic test for syphilis (VDRL or ART), and cervical cultures as indicated. Many doctors test for blood sugar (to look for diabetes), rubella antibody titers (immunity against rubella), blood type and Rh-factor. Other tests are done as needed. Tests are not performed at each visit; they are done at the beginning of pregnancy and as needed. Tests for hepatitis are now standard.

Another blood test is the *maternal alphafetoprotein (mAFP)*. This test is required in some states but not all. It is designed to detect babies with spina bifida or meningomyelocele (neural-tube defects) before birth. Some researchers have also found a correlation between this test and Down's syndrome. Some couples may consider abortion for this reason. If abortion is not chosen, it is helpful to know about these problems before birth.

This blood test is done on *you* to determine an abnormality in your *baby!* It is usually performed between 16 and 20 weeks of pregnancy and must be correlated with your age, weight and gestational age. If the test is abnormal, an ultrasound and amniocentesis may be done. Ask your doctor about this test if he or she does not mention it to you.

If you have rubella (German measles) during pregnancy, it can be responsible for miscarriage or fetal malformation. It's a good idea to be checked for immunity to rubella *before* you get pregnant. Because there is no known treatment for rubella, the best approach is prevention. If you're not immune, you can receive the vaccine while you take reliable birth control. Do not have a vaccination shortly before or during pregnancy because of the possibility of exposing the baby to the rubella virus.

Toxoplasmosis If you have a cat, you may be worried about toxoplasmosis. *Toxoplasma gondii* is a protozoa that can cause infection in you and your baby. It is spread by eating raw, infected meat or by contact with infected cat feces. It can be passed across the placenta to your baby. Usually an infection in the mother has no symptoms.

Infection during pregnancy can lead to spontaneous abortion or an infected infant at birth. Antibiotics, such as pyrimethamine, sulfadiazine and erythromycin, can be used to treat toxoplasmosis, but the best plan is prevention. Hygienic measures prevent transmission of the protozoa.

Avoid exposure to cat feces (get someone else to change the kitty litter). Wash your hands after contact with meat and soil, and cook meat adequately.

Week 9

Age of Fetus — 7 Weeks

How Big Is Your Baby?

The crown-to-rump length of the embryo is 0.9 inch to 1.2 inches (22 to 30mm). This is close to the size of a medium green olive.

How Big Are You?

Each week your uterus grows larger with the baby growing inside it. You may begin to see your waistline growing thicker by this time. A pelvic exam will detect an enlarged uterus a little bigger than a grapefruit.

How Your Baby Is Growing and Developing

Your baby is forming its organ systems during this time. This process is called *organogenesis*. If you could see inside your uterus, you'd see many changes in your baby. The illustration on page 99 shows some of them.

Your baby's arms and legs are longer. Hands are flexed at the wrist and meet over the heart area. They continue to extend in front of the body. Fingers are longer, and the tips are slightly swollen where the touch pads are developing. The feet are approaching the midline of the body and may be long enough to meet in front of the torso.

The head is more erect, and the neck is more developed. The eyelids almost cover the eyes; up to this time, the eyes have been uncovered. External ears are evident and well-advanced in form.

✧

Your baby now moves its body and limbs. This movement may be seen during an ultrasound exam.

The baby looks more recognizable as a human being, although it is still extremely small. It still may be impossible to distinguish a male from a female. External organs (external genitalia) of the male and female appear very similar and will not be distinguishable for another few weeks.

Changes in You

Weight Gain   Most women are very interested in their weight during pregnancy; many watch their weight gain very closely. As strange as it may seem, your weight gain is an important way to monitor the well-being of your developing baby. Even though your weight gain may be small at this point, your body is changing and parts of you *are* growing.

Changes to your body (increased size of the uterus, breast tissue, blood volume and body fluid) account for the largest part of your weight gain. To support a pregnancy, your body stores nutrients and increases the volume of blood and other fluids it produces. One reason for the extra fat is to prepare you to produce milk for breast-feeding. See chart on the next page.

Increased Blood Volume   An interesting change that occurs during pregnancy is the change in your blood (hematologic) system. Your blood volume increases greatly during pregnancy—about 45 to 50% more than before you became pregnant. However, this amount varies from one woman to the next.

Increased blood volume is important in meeting the demands of your enlarged, growing uterus. This increase does not include the blood in the embryo, whose circulation is separate. Fetal blood does *not* mix with your blood. Increased blood volume is important in protecting you and your baby from harmful effects when you lie down or stand up. It is also a safeguard during labor and delivery when blood is lost.

✧

How is Pregnancy Weight Distributed?

7 pounds	Maternal stores (fat, protein and other nutrients)
4 pounds	Increased fluid volume
2 pounds	Breast enlargement
2 pounds	Uterus
7½ pounds	Baby
2 pounds	Amniotic fluid
1½ pounds	Placenta (tissue connecting mother and baby that brings nourishment and takes away waste)

(Modified from: A.C.O.G. *Guide to Planning for Pregnancy , Birth and Beyond;* 1990, American Collage of Obstetricians and Gynecologists.)

The increase in blood volume starts during the first trimester. The largest increase occurs during the second trimester. It continues to increase at a slower rate during the third trimester.

Blood is composed of fluid (plasma) and cells (red blood cells and white blood cells). Plasma and cells have an important role in your body's function.

Fluid and cells increase to different degrees. Usually there is an initial rise in plasma volume followed by an increase in red blood cells. An increase in red blood cells causes an increased demand for iron.

Your hematocrit, sometimes called *hemoglobin concentration,* is used as a measure of anemia. *Hematocrit* is a comparison of the number of red blood cells to the amount of plasma. A normal hematocrit for a woman is between 37 and 44. Although red blood cells and plasma both increase during pregnancy, plasma increases more. This can and often does cause a decrease in your hematocrit and can cause you to be anemic, called *pregnancy anemia.* A hematocrit below 37 indicates anemia. If you're anemic, especially during pregnancy, you may feel tired, fatigue easily or experience a general feeling of ill health.

Anemia Anemia in the mother has been associated with an increase in maternal mortality during pregnancy. A heavy blood loss at the time of delivery in an anemic woman can be very serious. If you have anemia, it can also affect your baby. Anemia has been associated with an increased risk of premature labor, fetal distress and perinatal death.

The average blood loss at delivery is about 15 ounces (450ml). The amount may double with a Cesarean section. It's beneficial if you're not anemic at the time of delivery. If you are severely anemic when it's time to deliver, it could place you in a serious situation. You may even need a blood transfusion.

Iron Supplementation Iron supplementation through diet (spinach, liver) or in prenatal vitamins or extra iron tablets may be the most important vitamin supplement for you during pregnancy.

In tablet form, the usual amount of iron prescribed is 60mg of elemental iron per day. This is the amount usually found in prenatal vitamins. An *anemic* pregnant woman may need twice this amount or more. Discuss it with your doctor. Do *not* self-medicate!

Iron may not be well-absorbed and may cause stomach upset or constipation. Work with your doctor to correct these problems because you need iron if you are anemic.

How Your Actions Affect Your Baby's Development

During pregnancy, nearly every woman worries about whether her baby will be perfect. Most women worry unnecessarily. Major birth defects are apparent in only about 3% of *all* newborns at birth. But in the 3% of the babies born with birth defects, are causes of these abnormalities known? Could they have been prevented?

Abnormal Fetal Development *Teratology* is the study of abnormal fetal development. An exact cause or reason for a birth defect is found in less than 50% of all cases.

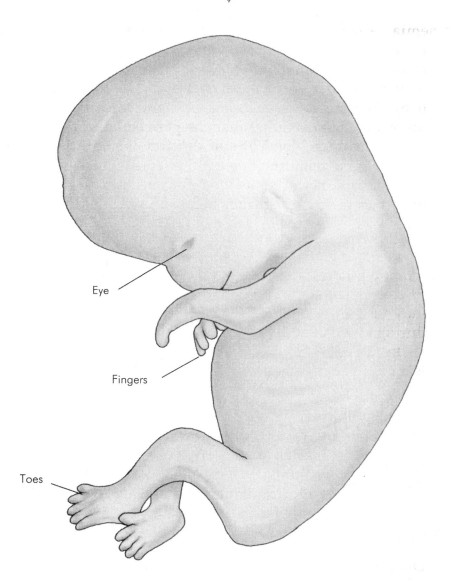

Embryo at 9 weeks of pregnancy (fetal age—46 to 49 days). Toes are formed, and feet are more recognizable. Crown-to-rump length is 1 inch (25mm).

Obstetricians and other doctors providing care to pregnant women are often asked about possible teratogenic substances. We believe some agents may be harmful, but researchers have not been able to prove this. However, some agents *have* been proved to be harmful.

✧

Some agents cause major defects if exposure occurs at a specific, critical time in fetal development. But they may not be harmful at other times. Once major development has been completed in the fetus, usually by the 13th week, the effect of a substance may be only growth retardation or smaller organ size rather than large, structural defects. One example is rubella. It can cause many anatomical defects, such as heart malformations, if the fetus is infected during the first trimester of pregnancy. But infection is less serious if it occurs later in pregnancy because fewer problems occur.

Individual Response to Medications   There is a great deal of individual variation in response to the size of a dose of an agent and to particular agents. Alcohol is a good example. Large amounts appear to have no effect on some fetuses, while other fetuses may be harmed by low amounts. See pages 42-44.

Animal studies have been the source of much of our information about possible teratogens. This information can be helpful but is not always directly applicable to humans. For example, the drug thalidomide did not cause malformations in rats and mice. However, severe malformations were later seen in human babies after use of the drug by the mother in pregnancy.

Other information comes from situations in which women were exposed who did not know they were pregnant or who did not know a particular medication could be harmful. Information can be gathered from these instances, but it is difficult to apply directly to a particular pregnancy.

It is always easier if you ask about a medication or possible teratogen *before* you take it. A good rule to follow is *avoid all medications during pregnancy unless you have discussed them with your doctor and know they are safe.*

A list of known teratogens and the effects they may have on an embryo or fetus follows. If you have taken any of these substances, *don't* panic. Discuss them as soon as possible with your doctor for your peace of mind and for any testing or follow-up that may be necessary.

Effects of Medications and Chemicals on Your Baby There are many substances that can affect the development of your baby during this critical time. Below is a list of some medications and chemicals and the effects they may have on a developing baby.

Drugs and Chemicals	Effects on Fetus
Alcohol	Growth and mental retardation Microcephaly Various major malformations
Androgens *(male hormones)*	Ambiguous genital development (depends on dose given and time given)
Anti-coagulants *(warfarin)*	Bone and hand abnormalities Intrauterine growth retardation Central-nervous-system and eye abnormalities
Anti-thyroid drugs *(propylthiouracil,iodide, methimazole)*	Hypothyroidism Fetal goiter
Chemotherapeutic drugs *(methotrexate, aminopterin)*	Increased risk of spontaneous abortion
Diethylstilbestrol (DES)	Abnormalities of female reproductive organs Female and male infertility
Isotretinoin *(Accutane®)*	Increased abortion rate Nervous-system defects Facial defects Cleft palate
Lead	Increased abortion and stillbirth rates
Lithium	Congenital heart disease
Organic mercury	Cerebral atrophy Mental retardation Spasticity Seizures Blindness

(continued on next page)

✧

DRUGS AND CHEMICALS	EFFECTS ON FETUS *(continued)*
Phenytoin *(Dilantin®)*	Growth retardation Mental retardation Microcephaly
Streptomycin	Hearing loss Cranial-nerve damage
Tetracycline	Hypoplasia of tooth enamel Discoloration of permanent teeth
Thalidomide	Severe limb defects
Trimethadione	Cleft lip Cleft palate Growth retardation Spontaneous abortion
Valproic acid	Neural-tube defects
X-ray therapy	Microcephaly Mental retardation Leukemia

(Modified from A.C.O.G. Technical Bulletin #84, *Teratology*, February, 1985, American College of Obstetricians and Gynecologists.)

Effects of Infections on Your Baby   Some infections and illnesses can also affect the development of your baby during this time of growth. Below is a list of some infections and diseases and what effects they may have on a developing baby.

INFECTIONS	EFFECTS ON FETUS
Cytomegalovirus (CMV)	Microcephaly Brain damage Hearing loss
Rubella *(German measles)*	Cataracts Deafness Heart lesions Can involve all organs
Syphilis	Fetal death Skin defects
Toxoplasmosis	Possible effects on all organs
Varicella	Possible effects on all organs

Week *10*

Age of Fetus — 8 Weeks

How Big Is Your Baby?

By the 10th week of pregnancy, the crown-to-rump length of your growing baby is about 1.25 to 1.68 inches (31 to 42mm).

At this time, we can start measuring how much the baby weighs. Before this week, the weight was too small to measure weekly differences. But now that the baby is starting to put on a little weight, weight will be included. The baby now weighs close to 0.18 ounce (5g). It is the size of a small plum.

How Big Are You?

Changes are gradual, and you may still not show much growth at this time. You may be thinking about and looking at maternity clothes, but you don't need them yet.

Molar Pregnancy   A condition that can make you grow too big too fast is called a *molar pregnancy*. It is sometimes called *gestational trophoblastic neoplasia (GTN)* or *hydatidiform mole*. In some countries, particularly the Orient, the condition occurs in about 1 in 100 pregnancies. It is less common in the United States and Canada, where it occurs in about 1 in every 1,000 pregnancies.

GTN can be serious; there is a 15% chance of cancer developing from a molar pregnancy. This type of cancer is called *choriocarcinoma*. GTN is divided into three categories:

+ Benign GTN or hydatidiform mole.
+ Malignant GTN, non-metastatic (low risk).
+ Malignant GTN, metastatic (high risk).

❖

The occurrence of GTN can be easily monitored by checking HCG hormone levels. See pages 68-69 for a more thorough discussion. Molar pregnancy can be cured with medications or by surgery.

When a molar pregnancy occurs, an embryo does not usually develop. Other tissue grows, which is abnormal placental tissue. The most common symptom is bleeding during the first trimester. Another symptom is the discrepancy between the size of the mother-to-be and how far along she is supposed to be in her pregnancy. Half the time, a woman is too large. Twenty-five percent of the time, she is too small. Nearly a quarter of the women are normal size. Excessive nausea and vomiting are other symptoms. Cysts may also occur on the ovaries.

The most effective way to diagnose a molar pregnancy is by ultrasound. This test shows a very distinctive pattern that usually does not include an embryo or fetus. Instead, the test has a "snowflake" appearance. This is usually found when ultrasound is done early in pregnancy to determine the cause of bleeding or rapid growth.

When a molar pregnancy is diagnosed, a D&C (dilatation and curettage) should be done as soon as possible. Other problems that may occur with a molar pregnancy include anemia, infection, hyperthyroidism and toxemia.

After a molar pregnancy occurs, effective birth control is important to be sure the molar pregnancy is completely gone. Most doctors recommend oral contraceptives if you can take them. It's important to be sure there is no tissue left. This is done by doing HCG measurements—they should decrease to normal amounts when a molar pregnancy is completely gone. If the HCG plateaus or rises, additional therapy may be necessary.

Nearly 80% of all molar pregnancies will be gone after D&C. Most doctors recommend a 1-year interval using birth control before pregnancy is attempted again.

A *malignant mole* or *malignant GTN* includes invasive moles and choriocarcinoma. Half of these occur after normal

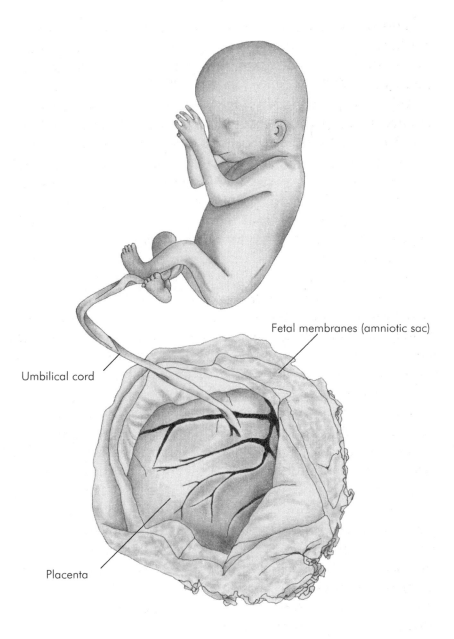

Umbilical cord

Fetal membranes (amniotic sac)

Placenta

Baby is shown attached to the placenta by its umbilical cord. Eyelids are fused and remain closed until week 27 (fetal age—25 weeks).

pregnancy, ectopic pregnancy, spontaneous abortion or induced abortion. Spread of the cancer can occur to almost any body organ, although 75% of the reported cancers occur in the lungs.

In addition to D&C, hysterectomy may be considered when childbearing is concluded. Ovaries are usually left untouched. Some medications, such as Methotrexate® and Actinomycin D®, are effective. This treatment is called *chemotherapy*. If cancer spreads to other parts of the body, a combination of medications may be necessary.

The good news about molar pregnancy is that treatment is very effective. Cure rates are close to 100%!

How Your Baby Is Growing and Developing

The end of week 10 is the end of the *embryonic period*. At this time, the *fetal period* begins. It is characterized by rapid growth of the fetus when the three germ layers are established. See pages 55-56 for further information. During the embryonic period, the embryo was most susceptible to things that could interfere with its development. Most congenital malformations occur before the end of week 10.

By the end of the 10th week, development of organ systems and the body are well under way. Your baby is beginning to look more human. See the illustration on the previous page. Problems can still occur, such as inadequate nutrition or drug exposure. But a critical part of your baby's development is safely behind you.

Changes in You

Pregnancy Brings Many Changes When your pregnancy is confirmed by an exam or a pregnancy test, you may be affected in many ways. Pregnancy can change many of your expectations. Some women see pregnancy as a sign of womanhood. Others consider it a problem to be dealt with. Still others feel they are blessed.

✧

You will experience many changes in your body. You may wonder if you are still attractive. Will your partner still find you interesting? (In reality, many men feel pregnant women are very beautiful.) Clothing becomes a new issue or a problem. You don't fit into anything, and you know there are more changes ahead. Can you look attractive? Can you learn to adapt? Will your partner help you?

If you aren't immediately excited about pregnancy, don't feel alone. A very common feeling and response to pregnancy is to question your condition. Some of this is because you're not sure of what lies ahead.

Learning to cope with being pregnant can be difficult. You won't always feel good. Changes in your lifestyle and your actions will be necessary.

When and how you begin to regard the fetus as a person is different for everyone. For some women, it is when their pregnancy test is positive. For others, it occurs when they hear the fetal heartbeat, usually around 12 weeks. For some, it happens when they first feel their baby move, at about 16 to 20 weeks.

These are also times of worry. Many things may make you worry about your baby and its development—bleeding, medical problems, medications you must take. This can produce stress for you.

You may also find you are very emotional about many things. You may feel moody, cry at the slightest thing or go off in daydreams. These emotional swings are very normal, and they will continue to some degree throughout your pregnancy. If you don't worry about these changes, they may not be as bad as you expect.

Dealing with These Changes What can you do? One of the most important things you can do for yourself is to get good prenatal care. Follow your doctor's recommendations. Keep *all* your appointments. Establish a good communication system with your doctor and his or her office staff. Ask questions. If something bothers you or worries you, discuss it with someone reliable.

❖

How Your Actions Affect Your Baby's Development

Vaccinations and Immunizations   Many vaccines are available that help prevent illness. A *vaccine* is a substance given to provide protection for you against foreign substances (infection). A vaccine is usually given by injection or taken orally. Four types of vaccines or agents are used for immunization—*toxoid killed-bacterial, killed-viral vaccine, live-virus vaccine* and *immune globulin preparation.*

A toxoid is a preparation of chemically altered bacterial poison or exotoxin made by bacteria. Killed vaccine contains microorganisms inactivated by heat or chemicals. Live-virus vaccine is made of strains of virus that produce protection but are not strong enough to produce the disease. Immune globulin preparation is a protein made from human blood that can produce a passive or temporary antibody protection in the person who receives the globulin. *Hyperimmune globulin* is made from donors with very high amounts of antibodies to a particular agent. It may be useful against various infections, such as Hepatitis B, rabies and varicella. *Pooled immune globulin* is useful in providing protection against Hepatitis A and measles (rubeola).

Most women of childbearing age in the United States and Canada should be immune to measles, mumps, rubella, tetanus and diphtheria. Most people born before 1957 were exposed to and infected naturally with measles, mumps and rubella and can be considered immune. They have antibodies and therefore are protected.

For women born after 1957, it may not be quite so clear. A physician-diagnosed case of measles, documentation of vaccination with measles vaccine or a positive blood test for measles is necessary to determine immunity. The clinical diagnosis of rubella is not reliable because many other illnesses may look like rubella with similar signs and symptoms. Physician-diagnosed mumps or mumps vaccination on or after the first birthday is necessary evidence of immunity to mumps. Vaccination for measles, mumps and rubella (MMR) should be administered *only* when a woman is

✦

practicing birth control. She must continue to use contraception for at least 3 months after receiving this immunization!

A woman is considered immune to tetanus and diphtheria if she has received at least three doses of each toxoid and if the last dose was given at least a year after the previous dose. A booster dose is required every 10 years.

Other vaccines are recommended for pregnant women in North America *only* under special circumstances.

Risk of Exposure   The risk of exposure to various diseases is an important consideration. Try to decrease any chance of exposure to disease and illness. Avoid visiting areas known to have prevalent diseases. This includes travel to areas with yellow fever or plague unless you are vaccinated *before* pregnancy. Avoid people (usually children) with known illnesses.

It's impossible to avoid all exposure to disease, such as measles, mumps and rubella. Sometimes influenza can't be avoided. Once your doctor determines you have been exposed, or exposure is unavoidable, the risk of the disease must be balanced against the potential harmful effects of vaccination.

After risk is assessed, a vaccine must be evaluated in terms of its effectiveness and its potential for complicating pregnancy. There is little information on harmful effects on the developing fetus from vaccines. In general, killed vaccines are safe. There is no evidence they affect the fetus or increase the risk of abortion.

Live-measles vaccine should *never* be given to a pregnant woman. Pooled immune globulin can help prevent or modify measles in the person exposed if given within a few days after exposure.

The only immunizing agents that are recommended for use during pregnancy are tetanus and diphtheria. Measles, rubella and mumps vaccine should be given *before* pregnancy or right after delivery. A pregnant woman should receive primary vaccination against polio *only* if her risk of exposure to the disease is high. Only inactivated polio vaccine should be used.

Protection against rubella is important because of the possible devastating effects of the infection on a developing baby. Measles can increase the risk of abortion and premature birth. Tetanus can be transferred to the fetus inside the uterus, causing neonatal tetanus.

You Should also Know

Chorionic Villus Sampling   A test done in some areas is *chorionic villus sampling*. This test is used to detect genetic abnormalities before delivery. Sampling is done early in pregnancy, usually between the 9th week and the 11th week.

There are different ways to perform chorionic villus sampling. An instrument is placed through the cervix or abdomen to remove fetal tissue from the area of the placenta. This can be helpful in detecting genetic problems. There is a small risk of miscarriage after this procedure. This test should be performed *only* by someone experienced in the technique.

Chorionic villus sampling is done for many reasons. The test helps discover and identify problems related to genetic defects, such as Down's syndrome.

This test offers a large advantage over amniocentesis because it is done much earlier in pregnancy. Results are available in about 1 week. If an abortion is going to be done, it can be performed earlier in the pregnancy and may carry fewer risks to the woman.

If your doctor recommends you have chorionic villus sampling, ask about its risks. The risk of miscarriage is small —between 1 and 2% with the test.

Fetoscopy   Fetoscopy is another test you may hear about. It is a test that is done on the fetus and placenta while they are still inside your uterus. It provides a view of baby and placenta; in some cases, abnormalities and problems can be detected and corrected.

The goal of the fetoscopy is to correct a defect before the problem worsens, which could prevent a fetus from developing into a normal baby. With fetoscopy, a doctor can see the problem more clearly than with ultrasound.

The test is done by placing a scope, like the one used in laparoscopy or arthroscopy, through the abdomen. The procedure is similar to amniocentesis, but the fetoscope is larger.

If your doctor suggests fetoscopy to you, discuss the possible risks, advantages and disadvantages of the procedure with him or her. The test should be done *only* by someone experienced in the technique. Risk of miscarriage is 3 to 4% with this procedure. It is not available everywhere.

Dieting During Pregnancy?   Don't diet to lose weight during pregnancy! You should be gaining weight during pregnancy; it can be harmful to your baby if you don't. A woman of normal weight can expect to gain between 25 and 35 pounds during pregnancy. Expect to gain about 10 pounds during the first 20 weeks and about 1 pound a week for the rest of the pregnancy. Your doctor will be watching your weight gain as an indication of the well-being of you and your baby.

Pregnancy is *not* a time to experiment with different diets or cut down on calories. However, this doesn't mean you have the go-ahead to eat anything you want, any time you want.

Exercise and a proper nutrition plan, without "junk food," will help you manage your weight. Be smart about your food choices. It's true you're eating for two—however, you must eat *wisely* for both of you!

Week 11

Age of Fetus — 9 Weeks

How Big Is Your Baby?

By this week, the crown-to-rump length of your baby is 1.75 to 2.4 inches (44 to 60mm). Fetal weight is about 0.3 ounce (8g). Your baby is about the size of a large lime.

How Big Are You?

While big changes are occurring in your baby, things may be happening more slowly with you. You are almost at the end of the first trimester; your uterus has been growing along with the fetus inside it. It is almost big enough to fill your pelvis and may be felt in your lower abdomen above the middle of your pubic bone.

You won't be able to feel your baby moving yet. If you think you feel your baby move at this time, you either have gas or are farther along in your pregnancy than you thought.

How Your Baby Is Growing and Developing

Fetal growth at this time is rapid. The crown-to-rump length of your baby *doubles* in the next 3 weeks. As you can see in the illustration on page 115, the head is almost half the entire length of your baby. As the head extends (uncurls or tips backward toward the spine), the chin raises from the chest and the neck develops and lengthens. Fingernails also appear.

❖

Distinguishing features of the external genitalia are beginning to appear. The development of the fetus into a male or female is complete in another 3 weeks. If a miscarriage occurs after this point, it may be possible to tell if it is male or female.

All embryos begin looking very much the same, as far as outward appearances are concerned. Development into a male or female is determined by the genetic information contained in the embryo. This was determined at the time of fertilization. If a male sperm fertilized the egg, you will have a son. If a female sperm fertilized the egg, you will have a daughter. The process of differentiation is accomplished by hormones produced by the fetus that affect the developing genital areas.

Changes in You

Some women notice changes in their hair, fingernails or toenails during pregnancy. This doesn't happen to everyone, but it may happen to you. It's not an indication of anything harmful, so don't worry about it unnecessarily. Some fortunate women notice an increase in hair and nail growth during pregnancy. Others note a loss of hair during this time. Explanations for these changes vary widely.

Some doctors believe changes occur during pregnancy because of increased circulation throughout your body. Others give credit to the hormonal changes occurring in you. Still others explain these differences with a change in "phase" of the growth cycle of the hair or nails.

In any event, rest assured. These differences are rarely permanent, and there is little or nothing you can do about them.

How Your Actions Affect Your Baby's Development

Travel Pregnant women frequently ask whether travel during pregnancy can hurt their baby. If your pregnancy is uncomplicated and you are not at high risk, travel is usually

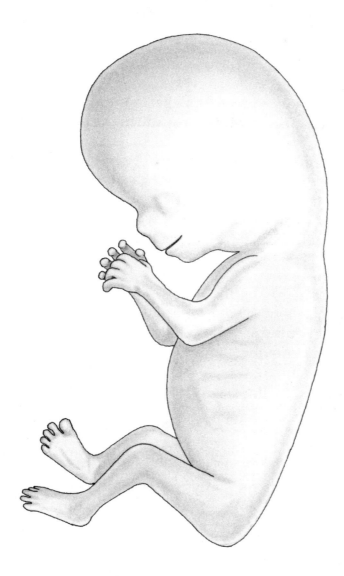

By week 11 of gestation (fetal age—9 weeks), fingernails are beginning to appear.

acceptable. Transportation in a pressurized airplane is believed to be within safe limits.

Whether you travel by car, bus, train or airplane, it's wise to get up and walk at least every 2 hours. Regular visits to the bathroom may take care of this requirement.

The biggest risk of traveling during pregnancy is development of a complication while you are away from those who know your medical and pregnancy history.

If you do decide to take a trip, be sensible in your planning. Don't overdo it. Take it easy!

Ask your doctor about any travel you are considering *before* making firm plans or buying tickets.

Bathing   Some women believe they cannot bathe during pregnancy. They have the impression they can only take showers. There's no medical reason to choose one over the other while you're pregnant. In your third trimester, you may need to be more careful than usual. Your balance will be different; you might fall and hurt yourself getting in and out of the bathtub. If balance is a problem for you, it may be wiser to shower.

You Should also Know

Ultrasound and Pregnancy   By this point in your pregnancy, you may have discussed ultrasound with your doctor. Or you may already have had an ultrasound test. *Ultrasound* (also called *sonography* or *sonogram*) is one of the most valuable methods for evaluating a pregnancy. Although doctors, hospitals and insurance companies (yes, they get involved in this) don't agree as to when ultrasound should be done or if every pregnant woman should have an ultrasound test during pregnancy, it remains a valuable tool. The test has been shown to be useful in improving the outcome in pregnancy. It is a non-invasive, safe test. There are no known risks.

Ultrasound involves the use of high-frequency soundwaves that are made by applying an alternating current to a transducer. The transducer is applied to the abdominal wall over the uterus. A lubricant is placed on the skin to improve contact with the transducer. Soundwaves are projected from the transducer through the abdomen and into the abdomen and pelvis. The soundwaves bounce off tissues they are directed toward and bounce back to the transducer. The reflection of soundwaves can be compared to "radar" used by airplanes or ships.

Different tissues of the body reflect ultrasound signals differently, and we can distinguish between them. Motion can be distinguished, so we can detect motion of the fetus or parts of the fetus, such as the heart. Through the use of ultrasound, a fetal heart can be seen beating as early as 5 or 6 weeks of pregnancy.

Your doctor can use ultrasound in many valuable ways in relation to your pregnancy. These include:

+ Helping in the early identification of an intrauterine pregnancy.
+ Showing the size and rate of growth of the embryo or fetus.
+ Identifying the presence of two or more fetuses.
+ Measuring the fetal head, abdomen or femur to determine the duration of pregnancy.
+ Identifying some fetuses with Down's syndrome.
+ Identifying fetal abnormalities, such as hydrocephalus and microcephaly, and abnormalities of internal organs, such as the kidneys or bladder.
+ Measuring the amount of amniotic fluid, which can be a clue to the well-being of the fetus.
+ Identifying the location, size and maturity of the placenta.
+ Identifying abnormalities of the placenta, such as molar pregnancy (see page 103-106).
+ Identifying uterine abnormalities or tumors.
+ Detecting an IUD or retained placenta inside the uterus after delivery.
+ Differentiating between miscarriage, ectopic pregnancy and normal pregnancy.

✦ In connection with amniocentesis, to select the correct place to position the needle to remove amniotic fluid from around the baby.

Ultrasound is useful for detecting fetal motion. Movement of your baby's body and limbs can be seen as early as 7 weeks of embryonic growth (9th week of pregnancy).

If you have had an ultrasound exam, one of the main things you may remember is how uncomfortable you were with your bladder full to overflowing! Your bladder is in front of your uterus. When your bladder is empty, your uterus is harder to see because it is farther down inside the pelvic bones. Bones disrupt ultrasound signals and make the picture harder to interpret. With your bladder full, your uterus rises out of the pelvis and is seen more easily.

The bladder acts as a window to look through to see the uterus and the fetus inside the uterus.

The ultrasound *vaginal probe* can be used in early pregnancy to get a better view of the baby and placenta. A probe is placed inside the vagina, and the pregnancy is viewed from this angle. You don't have to have your bladder full for this one!

Often you are able to get a "picture" of your baby before birth from the ultrasound test. Some facilities have equipment to make a video movie of the ultrasound.

Some women ask for ultrasound to determine whether they are carrying a boy or girl. If the baby is in a good position and it is old enough for the genitals to have developed and you can see them clearly, determination *may* be possible. However, many doctors feel this reason alone is not a good reason to do an ultrasound exam. Discuss it with your doctor. Understand ultrasound is a test, and tests can occasionally be wrong.

Dental Care   Don't avoid your dentist while you're pregnant. It's a good idea to see your dentist at least once during your pregnancy. Tell your dentist you're pregnant. If you need dental work, postpone it until after the first 12 weeks, if possible. If you have an infection, you may not be able to wait.

✧

Care should be taken with regard to anesthesia for dental work during pregnancy. Avoid general anesthesia. If general anesthesia is necessary, make sure it is given by an experienced anesthesiologist who *knows* you are pregnant.

Antibiotics or pain medications may be necessary. If medication is necessary, consult with your physician before taking anything.

Your gums may change during pregnancy; gums may be affected by the hormones of pregnancy. They can become sensitive and bleed more easily. Floss and brush regularly. You can use mouthwash and gargles during pregnancy.

Don't ignore your teeth. Problems could get worse. If infection occurs, it could be harmful to you and your baby.

Bringing Children to an Office Visit Some women bring their children with them to an appointment. However, it's more beneficial for you to be able to talk to your doctor and ask questions without having to take care of your children. Most office personnel don't mind if you bring your children with you occasionally and understand it may not always be possible to find someone to watch them. But you have important things to discuss with your doctor. Trying to keep your children happy while you talk with the doctor may be a very unpleasant experience for all involved.

A doctor's visit isn't the time to be taking care of other people's children either. Some women bring their children and the neighbor's children to their regular obstetrical appointments!

Involve your children and make them a part of your pregnancy, but think twice about bringing them to the office. If a child is sick, has just gotten over chicken pox or is getting a cold, leave him or her home. Don't expose everyone else in the waiting room.

Some women like to bring one child per visit if they have more than one child. That makes it special for you and them. If you are having problems or have a lot to discuss with your doctor, don't bring your child. Crying or complaining children can create a difficult situation. Ask your doctor when it's good to bring family members with you *before* they accompany you.

Week *12*

Age of Fetus — 10 Weeks

How Big Is Your Baby?

Your baby weighs between 0.3 and 0.5 ounce (8 to 14g). The crown-to-rump length is almost 2.5 inches (61mm). As you can see on page 131, your baby's size has almost doubled in the past 3 weeks! Length of the baby is a better measure of how far along you are than fetal weight.

How Big Are You?

Your weight may have stayed the same or you may have gained a few pounds during these first 12 weeks. If morning sickness has been a problem, you may have even lost a couple of pounds.

Average weight gain during pregnancy is 25 to 35 pounds (11.4kg to 15.9kg). Most weight comes in the *last* part of pregnancy. For these first 12 weeks, a weight gain of 4 to 8 pounds (1.8 to 3.6kg) is normal.

By the end of 12 weeks, your uterus is too large to remain completely in your pelvis. You may feel it above your pubic bone (pubic symphysis). The uterus has a remarkable ability to grow during pregnancy. It returns to its usual size within a few weeks after delivery! During pregnancy, the uterus grows upward to fill the pelvis and abdomen.

Before pregnancy, your uterus is almost solid. It holds about 0.3 ounce (10ml) or less. The uterus changes during pregnancy into a comparatively thin-walled, muscular container big enough to hold the fetus, placenta and amniotic fluid. It may hold a total volume of 5 to 10 quarts (about 5 to 10 liters) by the end of your pregnancy. The uterus achieves a capacity of 500 to 1000 times greater during pregnancy!

The weight of the uterus also changes. When your baby is born, your uterus weighs almost 40 ounces (1100g) compared to 2.5 ounces (70g) before pregnancy.

Growth of the uterine wall during the first few months of pregnancy is a result of stimulation by two hormones—estrogen and progesterone. Later in your pregnancy, the growth of the baby and the placenta stretch and thin the uterine wall.

How Your Baby Is Growing and Developing

Few, if any, structures in the fetus are formed *after* the 12th week of pregnancy. However, the structures already formed continue to grow and develop.

At your 12-week visit (or close to that time), you'll probably be able to hear your baby's heartbeat! It can be heard with a special listening machine (not a stethoscope) called a *doppler*. It magnifies the sound of your baby's heartbeat enough so you can hear it.

The skeletal system, which began developing earlier, now has centers of bone formation (ossification) in most bones. Fingers and toes have separated, and nails are growing. Scattered rudiments of hair appear on the body. External genitalia are beginning to show definite signs of male or female sex characteristics.

The digestive system (small intestine) is capable of producing the contractions that push food through the bowels. It is also able to actively absorb glucose or sugar.

At the base of your baby's brain, the pituitary gland is beginning to make many hormones. *Hormones* are chemicals that are made in one part of the body, but their action is exerted on another part of the body. Hormones produced

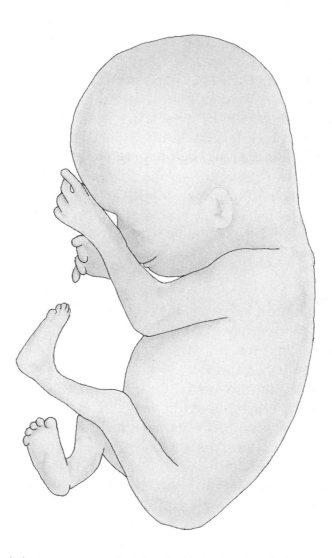

Your baby is growing rapidly. It has doubled in length in the last 3 weeks.

✧

include growth hormone, corticotropin (ACTH), prolactin, luteinizing hormone (LH) and follicle-stimulating hormone (FSH).

Other things are also happening. The nervous system has developed further. Your baby is moving inside your uterus, but you won't probably feel it for another month or two. Local stimulation to the fetus may cause squinting, opening of the mouth, and finger or toe movement.

The amount of amniotic fluid is increasing. The volume is now about 1.5 ounces (50ml). At this time, the fluid is similar to maternal plasma (the non-cellular portion of your blood), except it has a much lower protein concentration.

Changes in You

You are probably starting to feel better than you have for most of the pregnancy. At this point, morning sickness often begins to improve. You aren't extremely big and are probably still quite comfortable.

You may or may not be wearing maternity clothes. If it's your first pregnancy, you may still be wearing regular clothes. If you've had other pregnancies, you may start to show earlier and feel more comfortable in looser clothing.

You may be getting bigger in other places besides your tummy. Your breasts are probably getting larger. They may have been sore for some time. You may also notice weight gain in your legs and at your sides.

Skin Changes Changes in your skin may also occur. In many women, the midline of the skin of the abdomen becomes markedly darker or pigmented with a brown-black color. It forms a vertical line called the *linea nigra.*

Occasionally irregular brown patches of varying size appear on the face and neck. These are called *chloasma* or *mask of pregnancy.* Fortunately these disappear or get lighter after delivery. Oral contraceptives may cause similar pigmentation changes.

✧

There may also be vascular changes to the skin. These are called *vascular spiders*, *telangiectasias* or *angiomas.* They are small, red elevations on the skin, with branches extending outward. They are most commonly found on the face, neck, upper chest and arms. They develop in about 65% of white women and 10% of black women during pregnancy.

A similar condition is redness of the palms, called *palmar erythema.* It is seen in 65% of white women and 35% of black women.

Vascular spiders and palmar erythema often occur together. Symptoms are temporary and disappear shortly after delivery. The occurrence of either condition is probably caused by high levels of estrogen during pregnancy.

How Your Actions Affect Your Baby's Development

Some women have the false notion they can eat all they want during pregnancy. Don't fall into this trap! First, it's unhealthy for you and your baby if you gain a great deal of weight during pregnancy. It makes carrying your baby more uncomfortable, and delivery may be more difficult. Second, it may be difficult to get extra pounds off after pregnancy. After the baby is born, most women are anxious to return to "normal" clothes and to look the way they did before pregnancy. Having to deal with extra weight can interfere with reaching this goal.

Junk Food   Is junk food your kind of food? Do you eat it several times a day? Pregnancy is the time to break that habit!

Now that you are pregnant, your dietary habits affect someone else besides just yourself—your growing baby! If you're used to skipping breakfast, getting something "from a machine" for lunch, then eating dinner at a fast-food restaurant, it could be harmful to your pregnancy.

What and when you eat becomes more important when you realize your actions impact on your baby. Proper nutrition takes some planning on your part. You can do it!

If you work, take healthy foods with you that you like. Stay away from fast food and junk food.

Late-Night Snacks   Late-night nutrition snacks for some women are beneficial. However, for many women, snacking at night is unnecessary. If you're used to ice cream or other goodies before bed, you may pay for it during pregnancy with excessive weight gain. Food in your stomach late at night may also cause you more distress if you suffer from heartburn or nausea and vomiting.

Avoiding late-night splurges can help you keep your weight under control. It can also make you feel better.

You Should also Know

End of First Trimester   The end of the 12th week marks the end of the first trimester. It should be a reassuring feeling to hear the baby's heart beating. Reassurance may be taken in knowing most miscarriages happen *before* the 12th week.

Auto Safety During Pregnancy   Women often ask about automobiles and use of seat belts and shoulder harnesses during pregnancy. Wearing safety restraints substantially decreases the incidence of injury in an accident. Over 50,000 deaths and 2-million injuries are directly related to auto accidents every year. Wearing a seat belt and shoulder harness can decrease these losses.

During pregnancy, many women believe using a safety restraint might be harmful to their pregnancy. Here are some commonly given excuses or myths about using seat belts and shoulder harnesses in pregnancy.

"Using a safety belt will hurt my baby."

There is no evidence their use will increase the chance of fetal or uterine injury. You have a better chance of survival with a seat belt than without one. Your survival is important to your unborn baby.

"I don't want to be trapped in my car."

✧

Few automobile accidents result in fires. Even if a fire did occur, you could undo the restraint and escape if you were conscious. *Ejection* from a car accounts for about 25% of all deaths in automobile accidents.

"I'm a good driver."

Defensive driving helps, but it doesn't prevent any accident.

"I don't need to use a safety belt; I'm just going a short distance."

Most injuries occur within 25 miles of home.

A few studies have been done on pregnant women who used seat belts. In one California study, only 14% of all pregnant women used seat belts compared to 30% of non-pregnant women. However, we know the lap/shoulder system is safe to wear during pregnancy.

The Proper Way to Wear a Lap Belt and Shoulder Harness Is there a proper way for you to wear a seat belt during pregnancy? Yes. Place the lap-belt portion *under* your abdomen and *across* your upper thighs. It should be as snug as is comfortably possible. The shoulder belt should also be snug but comfortable. Adjust your position so the belt crosses your shoulder without cutting into your neck. Position the shoulder belt between your breasts. This belt should not be slipped off your shoulder. If it's a long trip, adjust the belt as needed for comfort.

Infant-Restraint Seats This isn't too early to think about infant- and child-restraint systems. Some people believe they can hold their baby safely in an accident. Others say their child won't sit still in a restraint.

In an accident, an unrestrained child becomes a missilelike object in a car. The force of a crash literally pulls the child out of an adult's arms! One study showed more than 30 deaths a year occur to unrestrained infants *going home from the hospital* after birth! In nearly all cases, if the baby had been in an approved infant-restraint system, he or she would have survived the accident.

✧

Start early to teach your child safety. If you *always* place your child in a restraint system in the car, it will become a natural thing to do. And you can increase your child's acceptance of a restraint if you wear seat belts, too!

Many states now have infant-restraint laws. Call your local police department or hospital for further information.

Many hospitals now *require* you to take your baby home from the hospital in an approved infant-restraint system. If you want any additional information, your pediatrician or the American Academy of Pediatrics can provide a list of safe child- and infant-restraint systems. Consumer magazines rate them quite frequently. Check your local library.

Week 13

Age of Fetus — 11 Weeks

How Big Is Your Baby?

Your baby is growing rapidly! Its crown-to-rump length is 2.6 to 3.1 inches (65 to 78mm). Its weight is 0.5 to 0.7 ounce (14 to 20g). It is about the size of a peach.

How Big Are You?

Your uterus has grown quite a bit. You can probably feel its upper edge above the pubic symphysis in the lowest part of your abdomen, about 4 inches (10cm) below your bellybutton. At 12 to 13 weeks, your uterus fills your pelvis and starts growing upward into your abdomen. It feels like a soft, smooth ball.

You have probably gained some weight by now. If morning sickness has been a problem and you've had a hard time eating, you may have lost a few pounds or not gained much weight. As you feel better and as your baby rapidly starts to gain weight, you'll gain weight.

How Your Baby Is Growing and Developing

Around this time, the *fetal period* begins, following the period of organ development that concluded in the last week or two. The fetal period of development is characterized by rapid growth and maturation of the tissues and organs that have already formed in your baby.

Few malformations occur during the fetal period. However, drugs and other harmful exposures, such as severe stress or radiation (X-ray), can destroy fetal cells during any portion of pregnancy. Continue to avoid them.

Fetal growth is particularly striking from this time through about 24 weeks of pregnancy. The fetus has doubled in *length* since the 7th week. By comparison, changes in fetal *weight* are tremendous during the *last* 8 to 10 weeks of your pregnancy.

One interesting change is the relative slowdown in the growth of your baby's head compared to the rest of its body. In week 13, the head is about half the crown-to-rump length. By week 21, the head is about one-third of the fetal body. At birth, your baby's head is only one-fourth the size of its body! The change occurs because fetal body growth accelerates as fetal head growth slows.

Your baby's face is beginning to look more human-like. Eyes, which started out on the side of the head, move closer together on the face. The ears come to lie in their normal position on the side of the head.

External genitalia have developed enough so a male can be distinguished from a female if examined outside the womb.

Intestines initially develop in a large swelling in the umbilical cord outside the fetal body. About this time, they withdraw into the fetal abdominal cavity. If this doesn't occur and the intestines remain outside the fetal abdomen at birth, a condition called an *omphalocele* occurs. It is rare and occurs in only 1 of 10,000 births. The condition can usually be repaired with surgery, and babies do well afterward.

Changes in You

You are losing your waist! Clothing is snugger. It's time to start wearing loose-fitting clothing.

Stretch Marks   Stretch marks, called *striae distensae*, are seen often and in varying degrees during pregnancy. They may

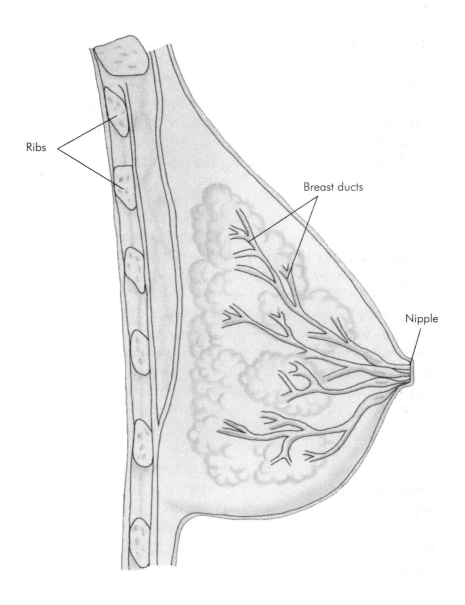

Development of the maternal breast by end of the first trimester (13 weeks pregnancy).

❖

appear early in your pregnancy, usually on the abdomen, breasts, and hips or buttocks. After pregnancy, they may fade to the same color as the rest of your skin, but they won't go away.

There is *no* known prevention or cure for stretch marks. Women have tried many kinds of lotions with ingredients ranging from lanolin to aloe vera to mineral oil. It doesn't hurt to try lotions, but it probably won't make a difference.

If you use steroid creams, such as hydrocortisone or topicort, to treat stretch marks during pregnancy, you absorb some of the steroid into your system. The substance can then pass to your developing fetus. Don't use steroid creams during pregnancy *unless it is absolutely necessary.* See page 248 for further discussion.

Itching   Itching *(pruritus gravidarum)* is a common symptom during pregnancy. There are no bumps or lesions on the skin; it just itches. Nearly 20% of all pregnant women suffer from itching, usually in the latter weeks of pregnancy, but it can occur at any time. It may occur with each pregnancy and may also be experienced when you use oral contraceptives. The condition doesn't present any risk to you or your baby.

Treatment for the itching consists of antihistamines or cooling lotions containing menthol or camphor. Often no treatment is needed.

Changes in Your Breasts   You have probably noticed your breasts are changing. See the illustration on the previous page. The mammary gland (another name for the breast) got its name from the Latin term for breast—*mamma.* Mammary glands begin to develop in the 6-week-old embryo. By the time of birth, milk ducts are present.

Your breast is made up of glands, connective tissue to provide support and fatty tissue to provide protection. The *alveoli* are milk-producing sacs that connect with the ducts leading to the nipple. After birth, a newborn's breasts may be swollen and may even secrete a small amount of milk.

❖

This can occur in both male and female infants. It is caused by secretion of estrogen, which is a hormone.

When you are not pregnant, each breast weighs about 7 ounces (200g). During pregnancy, your breasts increase in size and weight. Near the end of pregnancy, each breast may weigh 14 to 28 ounces (400 to 800g). During nursing, each breast may weigh 28 ounces (800g) or more!

Size and shape of women's breasts vary greatly. Breast tissue usually projects under the arm. Glands that make up the breast open up into ducts in the nipple. Each nipple contains nerve endings, muscle fibers, sebaceous glands, sweat glands and about 20 milk ducts.

The nipple is surrounded by the *areola,* a circular, pigmented area. Before pregnancy, the areola is usually pink. It turns brown or red-brown and enlarges during pregnancy and lactation. Darkening of the areola may act as a visual signal for the breast-feeding infant.

There are many changes in the breasts during pregnancy. During the early weeks, a common symptom of pregnancy is tingling or soreness of the breasts. After about 8 weeks of pregnancy, your breasts may grow larger and become nodular or lumpy from the growth and development of the glands and ducts inside the breasts.

As your breasts change during pregnancy, you may notice veins just beneath the skin. During the second trimester, a thin yellow fluid called *colostrum* begins to form. It can sometimes be expressed from the nipple by gentle massage. If the change in size of your breasts is very large, you may notice stretch marks on your breasts similar to those on your abdomen.

The breast develops from a line of glandular tissue called the *milk line.* It is not unusual to see "extra" mammary glands, called *hypermastia* or *accessory mammary glands,* left from early development of breasts. A nipple or even a small breast may be seen under the regular breast following the milk line. There may be a nipple only *(hyperthelia)* or the nipple may be absent with mammary tissue only *(hyperadenia).*

How the extra mammary gland responds during pregnancy depends on how much tissue is present. Tissue swelling during lactation may cause pain.

How Your Actions Affect Your Baby's Development

Today, many women work outside the home, and many continue to work during pregnancy. An important issue in this regard is disability and pregnancy. It is now common for employers and patients to ask doctors about work and pregnancy.

"Is it safe?"

"Can I work the entire pregnancy?"

"Am I in danger of harming my baby if I work?"

More than half of all women either work or are seeking work. In the United States alone, more than 1-million babies are born to women who have been employed at some time during pregnancy. There is increased concern about safety and occupational health.

The U. S. *Pregnancy Discrimination Act* prohibits job discrimination on the basis of pregnancy, childbirth or related disability. It states pregnancy and related conditions should be treated the same as any other disability or medical condition. A doctor may be asked to certify a pregnant woman can work without endangering herself or her pregnancy. Pregnancy-related disability comes from:

✦ The pregnancy itself.
✦ Complications of pregnancy, such as toxemia, premature labor or medical problems.
✦ Job exposures to chemicals, inhalants, gases, solvents or radiation.

It may be difficult to know the exact risk of a particular job. In most cases, studies have not been done on specific agents to determine damage or possible damage to a developing fetus.

The goal is to minimize the risk to the mother and fetus while still enabling the woman to work without concern. A

✧

normal woman with a normal job should be able to work throughout her pregnancy. However, modifications or changes may be necessary, such as the amount of standing. It has been determined that women who stand in the same position for prolonged periods have an increased risk of premature delivery and low-birth-weight babies.

Work with your doctor and your employer. If problems arise, such as premature labor or bleeding, listen to your doctor. If bed rest at home is suggested, follow your doctor's advice. As your pregnancy progresses, you may have to work fewer hours or do lighter work. Be flexible. It does not help you or your baby if you "wear yourself out" and make complications of pregnancy worse.

You Should also Know

Caffeine is a central-nervous-system stimulant. It is found in many beverages and foods, including coffee, tea, cola drinks and chocolate. It is also found in some medications, particularly diet aids and headache medications. More than 200 over-the-counter medications, foods and beverages contain caffeine.

As little as 4 cups of coffee (800mg of caffeine) a day has been associated with a decreased birth weight and a smaller head size in newborns. An exact toxic amount has not been determined for caffeine.

No benefits for you or your unborn fetus have been found with the use of caffeine. Drinking up to 8 cups of coffee (1600mg of caffeine) a day has been associated with a decrease in a woman's ability to get pregnant (fertility). Some researchers say there is an association between caffeine ingestion and miscarriage, low birth weights and premature labor. Caffeine consumption by a mother-to-be may cause an increase in newborn breathing problems.

Caffeine crosses the placenta to the baby and is found in breast milk. This can cause irritability and sleeplessness in a breast-fed baby. An infant or fetus metabolizes caffeine

✧

slower than an adult, and caffeine can be collected in the infant. It can affect the calcium metabolism of the mother and the fetus.

Caffeine effects on you during pregnancy may include irritability, sleeplessness, jitteriness and possibly a decrease in fertility. Smoking may cause an increase in the stimulant effect of caffeine.

Limit the amount of caffeine you consume. Read labels on over-the-counter medications for caffeine. Eliminate as much caffeine as you can from your diet. It is healthy for your baby, and you'll probably feel better, too.

Week 14

Age of Fetus — 12 Weeks

How Big Is Your Baby?

The crown-to-rump length is 3.2 to 3.5 inches (80 to 89mm). Your baby is about the size of your fist. It weighs about 0.9 ounce (25g).

How Big Are You?

Maternity clothes may be a "must" by now. Some women try to get by for a while by not buttoning or zipping their pants all the way or by using rubber bands or safety pins to avoid having to wear maternity clothing. Others wear their partner's clothing, but that works only for a while. The inevitable is coming. You're going to get even bigger. You'll enjoy your pregnancy more and feel more comfortable with clothing that fits and provides room to grow.

A common complaint from women with previous pregnancies is they show earlier, carry the pregnancy lower and feel bigger. Nearly all women notice these changes with each additional pregnancy.

How your body responds is influenced by previous pregnancies and the changes your body experienced then. Remember how big you got? Your skin and muscles stretched to accommodate your uterus, placenta and baby. Your abdominal skin and muscles are never exactly the same again. They may be unable to hold things in the way they did before. Skin and muscles may give way faster to accommodate your growing uterus and baby. This causes you to show sooner and feel bigger.

✧

A similar feeling may occur when you stand up and look down at your abdomen. Below your umbilicus you may feel there's a lot of loose skin "hanging" there. You may not see it when you lie down, but when you stand up, it's there! You probably notice it more than anyone else. No matter how hard you try or how many situps you do, you may not be able to get rid of this problem. This may be true during *and* after pregnancy. Extra skin is one reason women seek a tummy tuck or other plastic surgery when childbearing is over.

How Your Baby Is Growing and Developing

As you can see in the illustration, by this week the ears of your baby have moved from the neck to their more normal position on the sides of its head. Eyes have been moving gradually to the front of the fetal face from the side of the head. The neck continues to get longer. The chin no longer rests on the chest.

Sexual development continues. The external genitalia are developing more definitely. It is becoming easier to determine male from female by looking at external genitalia.

Changes in You

Skin Tags and Moles   Pregnancy can make skin tags and moles change and grow. *Skin tags* are small tags of skin; they may appear for the first time or may get larger during pregnancy. *Moles* are important any time, but they may appear for the first time during pregnancy, or existing moles may grow larger and darker during pregnancy. Moles that change need to be checked. If you notice any changes in a mole, show it to your doctor.

Venereal Warts   If you have warts in the area of the birth canal, around the vagina or near the rectum, discuss it with your doctor. Warts in this area are called *venereal warts*. Venereal

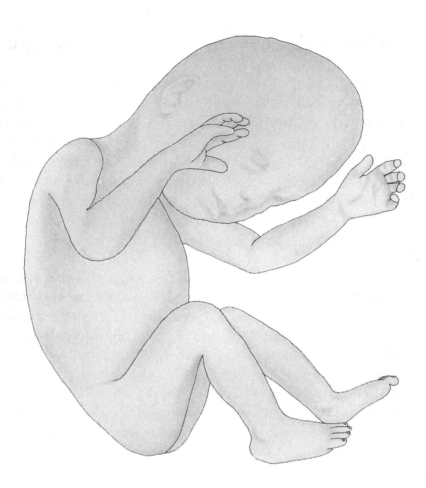

Your baby continues to change. Ears and eyes move to a more normal position by this week.

warts are caused by a virus from the papovavirus family—the human papilloma virus. They can complicate pregnancy.

Papilloma viruses cause warts in rabbits, cattle and humans. These warts in the genital area are called *condyloma acuminata* (venereal warts). They are important for several reasons. Condylomas flourish and can grow to very large sizes during pregnancy, probably from hormone changes, changes in the immune system or increased circulation during pregnancy. Occasionally they can grow large enough to block the birth canal and get in the way during labor and delivery. Cesarean deliveries have been necessary because a growth of skin was so large. However, this is a very unusual complication.

Condylomata can be very fragile and bleed easily, which can be a problem at delivery. Another problem at delivery is transmission of the virus to the newborn. There are reports of warts on vocal cords of newborns. They are believed to be a result of delivery through a vagina infected with warts containing the papilloma virus. This is an undesirable complication but not serious.

There are different views on the complications caused by venereal warts in the birth canal at the time of delivery. Not all doctors agree as to whether the presence of venereal warts is a reason for Cesarean delivery to avoid exposure for the baby. Discuss it with your doctor if you have venereal warts.

Condyloma are treatable. Treatment methods include painting warts with medication, laser removal, surgical removal and freezing or burning them off. It's best to take care of warts *before* pregnancy because some treatment methods are not advisable during pregnancy. Another reason to get rid of warts before pregnancy is they often cause an abnormal Pap smear. An abnormal Pap smear is more easily dealt with before pregnancy than during pregnancy. For more information about Pap smears, see page 146.

The papilloma virus is important for other reasons. There is evidence indicating a relationship between the papilloma virus, abnormal Pap smears and cervical cancer.

If you think you have venereal warts or have had them in the past, talk with your doctor.

How Your Actions Affect Your Baby's Development

X-Rays, CT Scans and MRIs During Pregnancy Some women are concerned about tests that use radiation during pregnancy. Can they hurt your baby? Can you have them at any time in pregnancy? What kind of problems can tests on you cause your baby?

Let's examine X-rays first. X-rays should be used with caution in pregnant women. If you think you're pregnant or there's any chance you *might* be pregnant, tell your doctor or dentist, or have a pregnancy test *before* any X-ray.

There is no known safe amount of radiation or X-ray for a developing fetus. Dangers to your baby include an increased risk of mutations and an increased risk of cancer later in life. Some doctors believe the only safe amount of X-ray during pregnancy is none.

Some doctors believe there is an increase in childhood leukemia in children exposed to X-rays before birth. If you have had a problem for several weeks or months and decide to have an evaluation, plan X-rays while you are on reliable birth control or right after your period ends. In this way, the likelihood of pregnancy will be very low.

When you do have X-rays, such as at the dentist, ask for a shield over your abdomen. You have all the eggs you will ever have, and you don't make new ones. Shielding you with the proper cover will decrease the exposure of your ovaries (and eggs) to radiation from various X-rays.

The need for X-rays must be determined on an individual basis. There are medical reasons for X-rays, but the need must be weighed against the risk to your pregnancy. Because pregnancy can occur at varying times during your menstrual cycle, reliable birth control is the best safeguard. No time of the cycle can be considered *completely* safe. Ask about risk, whether or not you know you are pregnant.

✧

If you have an X-ray or series of X-rays then discover you are pregnant, talk to your doctor about the possible risk to your baby. He or she will be able to advise you.

In the past, X-rays of the birth canal, called *pelvimetry,* were performed to determine the size of the birth canal or the possible need for Cesarean delivery. This is not often done now. Most doctors have found this procedure provides little additional information to help in determining the need for a Cesarean section. Fetal monitoring has helped: see the discussion that begins on page 353. The risk of radiation to the baby and possible risk of leukemia later for your child has decreased the use of pelvimetry to almost zero.

There *are* medical reasons for X-ray during pregnancy. Problems such as pneumonia or appendicitis can and do occur in pregnant women. Discuss the need for X-rays with your doctor. You bear some of the responsibility in letting your doctor and others involved in your healthcare know you are pregnant or may be pregnant before you undergo *any* medical test. It's easier to deal with the questions of safety and risk *before* a test is performed rather than after the fact.

Computerized tomographic scans, also called *CT scans,* are a form of very specialized X-ray. This technique involves the use of X-ray, with computer analysis. Many researchers believe the amount of radiation received by a fetus from a CT scan is much lower than that received from a regular X-ray. However, these tests should be undertaken with caution until we know more about the effects of even this small amount of radiation on a developing fetus.

Researchers are becoming more aware of the potential dangers of radiation to a developing fetus. Risk to the fetus from radiation appears to be greatest between 8 and 15 weeks gestation (between the fetal age of 6 weeks and 13 weeks). Some believe the only amount of *safe* radiation exposure for a fetus is *no* exposure.

✧

Magnetic resonance imaging, also called *MRI*, is another diagnostic tool that is being widely used today. It is a very expensive test to perform. At this time, no harmful effects in pregnancy have been reported from the use of MRI. However, it is advised that you avoid MRI during the first trimester of pregnancy.

You Should also Know

It's important to involve your partner in the miracle that is happening in your body. He can be a big support to you. It helps if you try to make him feel part of what is going on. Some men get jealous of all the attention given to the woman and her developing baby. New maternity clothes, baby toys and equipment, and conversations with friends or family often center around the pregnancy, making him feel left out.

This can be a time of communication and growth in your relationship. It may be the beginning of your family. But you may have to work a little to make your partner feel he is part of what's happening to you.

Take your partner with you to an appointment with your doctor. It's nice for your partner and doctor to meet before labor begins. Maybe your mother or the other grandmother-to-be would like to go with you to hear their grandchild's heartbeat. Or you may want to take a tape recorder, and record the heartbeat for others to hear. Things have changed since your mother carried you; many grand-mothers-to-be enjoy this type of visit.

It's a good idea to wait until you have heard your baby's heartbeat before bringing other people. You don't always hear it the first time, and this can be frustrating and disap-pointing for everyone. Wait until you have heard it before bringing anyone else along.

Week *15*

Age of Fetus — 13 Weeks

How Big Is Your Baby?

The fetal crown-to-rump length by the 15th week of pregnancy is 3.7 to 4.1 inches (93 to 104mm). The fetus weighs about 1.75 ounces (50g). It's close to the size of a softball.

How Big Are You?

You can easily tell you're pregnant by the changes in your lower abdomen, which alter the way your clothes fit. You may be able to feel your uterus about 3 or 4 inches (7.6 to 10cm) below your umbilicus.

Pregnancy may not be obvious to other people when you wear regular street clothes. But it may become obvious if you have to start wearing maternity clothes or put on a swimming suit.

It's still a little early to feel movement, although you should feel your baby move in the next few weeks!

How Your Baby Is Growing and Developing

Rapid growth of your baby continues. Its skin is very thin. Blood vessels can be seen through the skin at this point in its development. Fine hair called *lanugo hair* covers the baby's body.

By this time, your baby may be sucking its thumb. This has been seen with ultrasound examination. Eyes continue to move to the front of the face but are still widely separated.

External ears are continuing to develop. As you can see in the illustration, they now look more like normal ears. In fact, your baby looks more human all the time.

Bones that have already formed are getting harder and retaining calcium (ossifying) very rapidly. If an X-ray were performed at this time, the fetal skeleton would be visible.

Changes in You

Having a Pap Smear During Pregnancy   During your first visit to your doctor, you received a Pap smear. A Pap smear is usually done at the beginning of pregnancy. By now, the result is back, and you have discussed it with your doctor, particularly if it was abnormal.

The Pap smear (short for Papanicolaou smear) is a screening test done at the time of a pelvic exam. It identifies cancerous or precancerous cells coming from the cervix, which is located at the top of the vagina. Through the use of Pap smears as a screening device, there has been a decrease in mortality from cervical cancer because of early detection and treatment.

Some have suggested that on the basis of cost effectiveness, a Pap test is required only once every 3 years instead of every year. Most doctors would not agree with this suggestion, especially for women at high risk for abnormal Pap smears or cervical cancer. The first Pap smear should be performed when a woman becomes sexually active or at the age of 18, whichever comes first. If the first Pap test is negative, a yearly test is suggested.

Women considered at high risk for abnormal Pap smears include those with a history of early sexual intercourse or multiple sexual partners or someone who has had a previous abnormal Pap smear. As discussed earlier, women with venereal warts are at higher risk for cervical cancer and abnormal Pap tests. See page 138.

Getting a Pap smear is usually inexpensive, and it is widely available. Although most women do not "enjoy" having a Pap smear, few report it is painful.

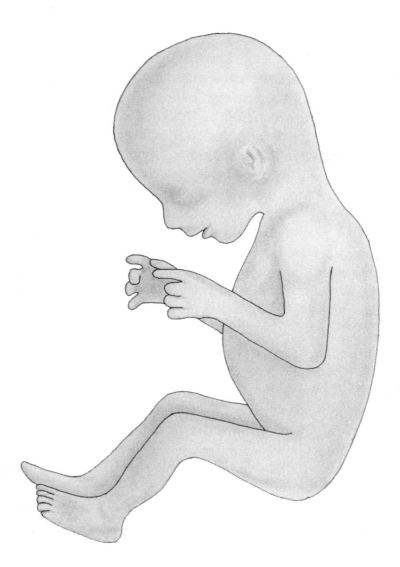

By week 15 of pregnancy (fetal age—13 weeks), your baby may suck its thumb. Eyes have moved to the front of the face but are still widely separated.

⬧

There are special cases to consider in deciding the frequency of Pap smears. Women exposed to diethylstilbestrol (DES) while their mothers were pregnant require special screening. For those women, a Pap smear should be done at the beginning of menstruation or by the age of 14, whichever comes first. Tests should be done every 6 months for the first few years, then every year if they are normal.

If a woman has had a hysterectomy, Pap smears may not be required every year. If the hysterectomy was done for cancer, testing must be individualized. Otherwise a Pap test every 3 years is considered adequate.

You can help get a "good" Pap smear by following certain guidelines before your test. Do not use any lubricants or douches before going to the doctor. It is best if you are not having your period and if you do not have a vaginal infection when your Pap smear is done.

An Abnormal Pap Smear If you have had an abnormal Pap smear or have been treated for an abnormal Pap test, continue to get checked as your doctor suggests.

What is an abnormal Pap smear? What does it mean? Below is a list of possible results of a Pap smear that range from normal to cervical cancer.

+ No abnormal cells.
+ Test was unsatisfactory (usually a reason is given, such as specimen dried out).
+ Mild squamous atypia.
  ⬧ Metaplasia
  ⬧ Inflammation (frequent and may be from infection)
  ⬧ Regeneration and repair
  ⬧ Viral effect
+ Cytologic findings consistent with dysplasia.
  ⬧ Mild
  ⬧ Moderate
  ⬧ Severe
  ⬧ Carcinoma-in-situ

✦ Cytologic findings consistent with invasive squamous-cell carcinoma.

Pap smears are screening tests. If a test is abnormal, findings must be verified and treated by your doctor. Most doctors will suggest a biopsy of the cervix if your Pap smear is abnormal.

When Is a Biopsy Necessary? A biopsy of the cervix is done in your doctor's office, without anesthesia, with colposcopy. *Colposcopy* is a procedure that uses an instrument like a pair of binoculars or a microscope to look at the cervix. This allows your doctor to see where abnormal areas are so biopsies can be taken. Most obstetricians/gynecologists are able to do this procedure without sending you to a specialist.

A biopsy provides a better idea of the nature and extent of the problem. If there is a possibility of spread to other parts of the body of abnormal cells, a *cone biopsy* may need to be done. A cone biopsy precisely determines the extent of more severe disease and removes abnormal tissue. This surgery is done with anesthesia. It is not usually done during pregnancy.

Treating Abnormal Cells There are several ways to treat abnormal cells on the cervix. Most treatment methods cannot be performed during pregnancy. These treatments include cutting off the abnormal spot (if it can be seen), electric cautery to remove or "burn" small abnormal spots, cryocautery to freeze small lesions, laser treatment to destroy abnormal areas on the cervix, cone biopsy for more-involved lesions and hysterectomy for women who do not want any more children.

An abnormal Pap smear during pregnancy must be handled individually. When abnormal cells are "not too bad" (premalignant or not as serious), it may be possible to watch them during pregnancy with colposcopy or Pap smears. The cervix bleeds easily during pregnancy because of changes in circulation. This situation must be handled carefully.

✧

How Your Actions Affect Your Baby's Development

Genetic Counseling   For some couples, genetic counseling may be important. If you have reasons for concern, genetic counseling can help you make informed decisions about childbearing.

Couples who may be advised to seek genetic counseling include those who have had a malformed infant, those with a family history of inherited diseases, women who have had recurrent miscarriages (usually 3 or more) and any woman whose age will be 35 or more at the time of birth.

Questions asked may include things about both partner's family histories of Down's syndrome, spina bifida, hemophilia and muscular dystrophy. If either partner is black, screening for the sickle-cell trait may be suggested. If both partners are descended from Ashkenazi Jews, they may be tested to see if they are carriers for the trait for Tay-Sachs disease.

Technology and research are expanding our medical knowledge. Yet, in the delicate process of the development and growth of an embryo and fetus, things do not always work out right. Earlier I discussed teratogens, which can affect a developing embryo. The susceptibility of an embryo to a teratogen may be a combination of genetic predisposition and outside effects, such as exposure to teratogens at the wrong time in development. Agents capable of causing problems at one time of pregnancy may be harmless at other times.

You Should also Know

Pregnancy After 35   Today, many women are waiting until they have finished college and worked awhile before they get married and decide to start their families. There is a higher risk of abnormalities and problems in babies born to women over 35. Problems in pregnancy for a woman over 30 include premature labor, pelvic pressure and pelvic pain.

Pregnancy after 35 carries even higher risks for the pregnant woman. These include risks of:

+ Down's syndrome.
+ High blood pressure.
+ Cesarean delivery.
+ Multiple births.
+ Pre-eclampsia.
+ Placental abruption.
+ Bleeding and other complications.

It's also harder to *be* pregnant at 35 than 25. At 35, chances are you have a job or other children taking your time. You may find it harder to rest, exercise and eat right.

Each pregnancy stretches your abdomen, skin and muscles to some degree. You may find it harder to get back in shape.

The Possibility of Down's Syndrome   Until a woman is 30 years old, the risk of Down's syndrome is less than 1 in 800. It increases to 1 in 100 by the age of 40 and 1 in 32 by age 45. The actual number of pregnancies affected by Down's syndrome is actually higher, but many of these pregnancies result in early abortions or stillbirths.

The risk of giving birth to a Down's syndrome infant by the mother's-to-be age is shown in the table below.

Maternal age	Frequency of Down's syndrome infants
25 years	1 in 1,300 births
30 years	1 in 965 births
35 years	1 in 365 births
40 years	1 in 109 births
45 years	1 in 32 births
49 years	1 in 12 births

Down's syndrome is the most common chromosomal defect detected by amniocentesis. See page 157 for more information about amniocentesis. If you are concerned about the risk of Down's syndrome because of your age or family history, discuss it with your doctor.

Week *16*

Age of Fetus — 14 Weeks

How Big Is Your Baby?

The crown-to-rump length of your baby by this week is 4.3 to 4.6 inches (108 to 116mm). Weight is about 2.8 ounces (80g).

How Big Are You?

As your baby grows, your uterus and placenta are also growing. Six weeks ago, your uterus weighed about 5 ounces (140g). Today, it weighs about 8.75 ounces (250g). The amount of amniotic fluid around the baby is also gradually increasing. There is now about 7.5 ounces (250ml) of fluid. You can easily feel your uterus about 3 inches (7.6cm) below your umbilicus.

How Your Baby Is Growing and Developing

There is fine lanugo hair on your baby's head. The umbilical cord is attached to the abdomen; this attachment has moved lower on the body of the fetus than before.

Fingernails are well formed. The illustration on page 155 shows the legs are longer than the arms. The arms and legs are moving. Movement can be seen easily during an ultrasound examination. It may also be possible to feel your baby move.

If you haven't felt your baby move yet, don't worry. Fetal movement, also called *quickening,* is usually felt between 16 and 20 weeks of pregnancy. The time is different for every woman. It can also be different from one pregnancy to another. One baby may be more active than another and produce more movement.

Many women describe these early feelings of movement as a "gas bubble" or "fluttering." Often, it's something you have noticed for a few days or more, but you didn't realize what you were feeling. Then it occurs to you it's the baby you're feeling moving inside you!

Changes in You

Alphafetoprotein Testing As your baby grows inside of you, it produces alphafetoprotein. This protein is found in increasing amounts in the amniotic fluid coming from the fetal urine. Some of the alphafetoprotein crosses fetal membranes and enters your circulation. The amount of this protein found in your blood is much lower than in the fetus or the amniotic fluid, but it does increase as your pregnancy progresses.

It is possible to measure the amount of alphafetoprotein in the amniotic fluid (by amniocentesis) and in maternal blood (by drawing your blood). The level of alphafetoprotein can be meaningful during pregnancy. A maternal alphafetoprotein (mAFP) test is usually done around 16 to 18 weeks of gestation. The timing of the test can be important and has to be correlated to the gestational age of your pregnancy and your weight.

An elevated level of alphafetoprotein can indicate important problems with the fetus, such as spina bifida (spinal-cord problem) or anencephaly (serious central-nervous-system defect). Some researchers have even found an association between a low level of alphafetoprotein and Down's syndrome. In the past, a test for Down's syndrome could only be done with amniocentesis. Now, by drawing your blood, a serious defect may be found at an early time in pregnancy.

If the level of alphafetoprotein is abnormal, it may be confirmed with another alphafetoprotein test or by

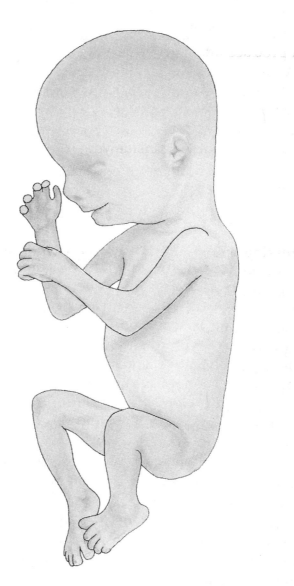

By this week, fine lanugo hair covers the baby's body and head.

✧

amniocentesis. A careful ultrasound examination is also done to look for spina bifida or anencephaly (also called *neural-tube defects*) and to determine how far along in the pregnancy you are.

This test is not done on all pregnant women, although it is required in some states in the United States. If the test isn't offered to you, ask about it. This has relatively little risk or trauma to you, and it tells your doctor how your fetus is growing and developing.

Rh-Sensitivity   In the lab tests you've already had, your blood type and Rh-factor were determined. You may know this information by now. Your blood type, such as O, A, B, AB, and the Rh-factor are important. In the past, Rh-negative women who carried an Rh-positive child faced complicated pregnancies resulting in a very sick child.

Your blood is separate from your baby's blood. If you are Rh-positive, you don't have to worry about any of this. If you are Rh-negative, you need to know about it.

If you are Rh-negative and your baby is Rh-positive or if you have had a blood transfusion or received blood products of some kind, there's a risk you could become Rh-sensitized or isoimmunized. *Isoimmunized* means you could make antibodies that circulate inside your system that don't harm you, but they can attack the blood of an Rh-positive person (your growing baby).

In the case of pregnancy, an Rh-negative woman may carry an Rh-positive baby. (If your baby is Rh-negative, there is no problem.) Antibodies from you can cross the placenta and attack your baby's blood. This can cause hemolytic disease of the fetus or newborn. It can make your baby very anemic while still inside the uterus and can be very serious.

Fortunately, this can be prevented. The use of RhoGAM™ (Rh-immune globulin) has alleviated many of the problems. It is given during pregnancy at 28 weeks gestation to prevent sensitization before delivery. Very few women are seen today who are sensitized. If you are

❖

Rh-negative and have a pregnancy, RhoGAM should be part of your pregnancy. RhoGAM is a product that is extracted from human blood. If you have religious or cultural concerns about using blood or blood products, consult with your physician or minister.

RhoGAM is also given to you within 72 hours after delivery if your baby is Rh-positive. If your baby is Rh-negative, you don't need RhoGAM after delivery and you didn't need the shot during pregnancy. But it's better not to take that risk and to have the RhoGAM injection during pregnancy.

If you have an ectopic pregnancy and are Rh-negative, you should receive RhoGAM. This applies to miscarriage or abortions as well. If amniocentesis is performed during pregnancy and you are Rh-negative, you should receive RhoGAM.

All of this attention is to prevent you from forming antibodies to Rh-positive blood. These antibodies can be harmful to your baby.

How Your Actions Affect Your Baby's Development

Amniocentesis   If it is necessary, amniocentesis is usually performed for prenatal evaluation around 16 to 18 weeks of pregnancy. By now, your uterus is large enough and there is enough fluid surrounding the baby to make the test possible. Doing the procedure at this time allows the woman enough time to make a decision about terminating the pregnancy, if that is what she desires.

In an amniocentesis test, ultrasound is used to locate a pocket of fluid where the fetus and placenta are not in the way. The abdomen over the uterus is cleaned. Skin is numbed, and a needle is placed through the abdomen into the uterus. Fluid is withdrawn from the amniotic cavity (area around the baby) with a syringe. About 1 ounce (30ml) of amniotic fluid is needed to perform various tests.

Fetal cells that float in the amniotic fluid can be grown in cultures. They are the cells that are used to identify fetal abnormalities. We know of over 400 abnormalities a child can be born with—amniocentesis identifies 40 (10%) of them. Abnormalities that can be identified include the following.

+ Chromosomal problems, particularly Down's syndrome. This is done by looking at fetal chromosomes. This same method can be used to determine the sex of the baby, although amniocentesis is not done for this reason alone.
+ Skeletal diseases, such as osteogenesis imperfecta.
+ Fetal infections, such as herpes or rubella.
+ Central-nervous-system diseases, such as anencephaly.
+ Hematologic (blood) diseases, such as erythroblastosis fetalis.
+ Inborn errors of metabolism (chemical problems or deficiencies of enzymes), such as cystinuria or maple syrup urine disease.

Risks from amniocentesis include trauma to the fetus, placenta or umbilical cord, infection, abortion or premature labor.

The use of ultrasound to guide the needle helps avoid complications but doesn't eliminate risk. There can be bleeding from the fetus to the mother. This can be important because fetal and maternal blood are separate and can be different types. As I've just discussed, this is important to an Rh-negative mother carrying an Rh-positive baby. This type of bleeding can cause isoimmunization. An Rh-negative woman should receive RhoGAM at the time of amniocentesis to prevent isoimmunization.

Fetal loss from amniocentesis complications is estimated to be about 0.5 to 3%. The procedure should be done *only* by someone who has experience doing it.

Saunas and Hot Tubs   Some women are concerned about using saunas, hot tubs and spas during pregnancy. They want to know if it is permissible to relax in this way.

Your baby relies on you to maintain the correct body temperature. Tests have shown if your body temperature is elevated a few degrees and stays there for several minutes, it may possibly cause damage to your baby if it occurs at critical times in its development. Don't take a chance with a hot tub or sauna until more medical research can tell us it won't hurt your baby.

Tanning Booths The effects on the growing fetus of a pregnant woman lying in a tanning booth have not been studied by medical researchers.

Until medical studies indicate it's safe to get in a tanning booth, it's best to avoid using them while you're pregnant.

You Should also Know

Change Sleeping Positions Now Some women have questions and concerns about their sleeping positions and sleep habits while they're pregnant. Some want to know if they can sleep on their stomachs. Others want to know if they should stop sleeping on their waterbed. If this is your first baby, your sleeping habits may never be the same again.

As you grow during pregnancy, you'll find it more difficult to find comfortable positions to sleep. Try not to lie on your back when you sleep. As your uterus gets larger, lying on your back can place the uterus on top of important blood vessels (inferior vena cava and aorta) that run down the back of your abdomen. This can decrease circulation to your baby and parts of your body. Some pregnant women also find it harder to breathe when lying on their backs.

Lying on your stomach isn't a good idea either. It puts a lot of pressure on your growing uterus. This will become a problem of comfort. The bigger you get, the harder it will be to lie on your stomach.

Start early to learn to sleep on your side. It will pay off later as you get bigger. Sometimes it helps to use a few extra pillows. Put one behind you so if you roll onto your back, you won't lie flat. Put another pillow between your legs, or rest your "top" leg on it. Some manufacturers now make a "pregnancy pillow" that provides support for your entire body. A pregnancy pillow could provide the support easily and effectively.

Try to find comfortable ways to sleep. As time passes and you grow larger, it will become more difficult and important to you.

Some women have commented their favorite thing after delivery was to be able to sleep on their stomachs again!

Week *17*

Age of Fetus — 15 Weeks

How Big Is Your Baby?

The crown-to-rump length of your baby is 4.4 to 4.8 inches (110 to 120mm or 11 or 12cm). Fetal weight has doubled in 2 weeks and is about 3.5 ounces (100g). By this week, your baby is about the size of a hand when it is spread open wide.

How Big Are You?

Your uterus is 1.5 to 2 inches (3.8 to 5cm) below your umbilicus. When your partner gives you a hug, he may feel the difference in your lower abdomen.

You are showing more now and have an obvious "swelling" in your lower abdomen. By this time, stretchy or maternity clothing is a must for comfort's sake.

The rest of your body is still changing. You may be gaining weight. A 5- to 10-pound gain (2.25 to 4.5kg) by this time is normal.

How Your Baby is Growing and Developing

If you look at the illustration on page 163 and then look at earlier chapters, it's obvious very big changes are occurring.

Fat begins to form during this week and the weeks that follow. Fat is important in heat production and metabolism. It is also called *adipose tissue.*

❖

At 17 weeks of development, water makes up about 3 ounces (89g) and fat 0.018 ounce (0.5g) of the content of your baby. In a newborn baby at term, fat makes up about 5.25 *pounds* (2.4kg) of the total average weight of 7.7 pounds (3.5kg).

You can feel your baby move, or you will soon. You may not feel it every day. As pregnancy progresses, movements become stronger and probably more frequent.

Changes in You

You're getting bigger too! Feeling your baby move can be reassuring that things are going well with your pregnancy. This is especially true if you have had previous problems, such as bleeding or pain.

As your pregnancy advances, the top of the uterus becomes almost spherical. It increases more rapidly in length (upward into your abdomen) than in width, so the uterus becomes more oval than round. The uterus fills the pelvis and starts to grow into the abdomen. Your intestines are pushed upward and to the sides. The uterus will eventually reach almost to your liver.

The uterus is not fixed in one place. Most attachments are around the cervix (lower part of the uterus) and by the lower part of the body of the uterus, called the *cardinal ligaments*. The uterus doesn't float around, but it is not firmly attached in one spot.

When you stand, the uterus touches the abdominal wall in the front. It may be felt most easily in this position. When you lie down, it can fall backward onto your spine and blood vessels (vena cava).

Round ligaments are attached to each side of the uterus at the upper part. These ligaments attach from the uterus to the pelvic side wall, inside the uterus. During pregnancy and the growth of the uterus, these ligaments are stretched and pulled. They become longer and thicker. Your sudden or mild movements can stretch and pull these ligaments.

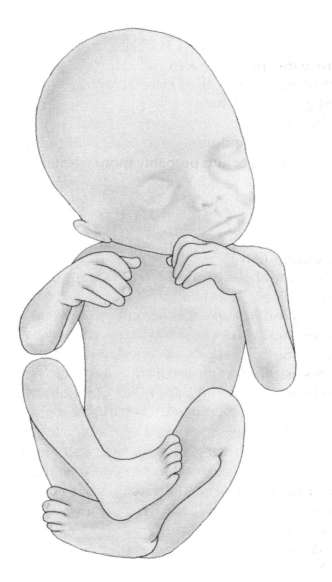

Your baby's fingernails are well formed. The baby is beginning to accumulate a little fat.

✧

This can cause pain or discomfort, called *round-ligament pain*. It doesn't signal a problem; it indicates your uterus is growing. Pain may occur on one side only or both sides. It may be worse on one side than another. This pain does not harm you or the baby.

It may feel better to lie down and rest. Some women try to keep busy and ignore the pain. Talk to your doctor about the pain if it gets severe or other symptoms arise. Warning signs of more serious problems include bleeding from the vagina, loss of fluid from the vagina or severe pain.

How Your Actions Affect Your Baby's Development

Using Over-the-Counter Medications and Preparations

Many people don't consider over-the-counter preparations as medication and take them at will, pregnant or not. Some researchers believe non-prescription or over-the-counter medication usage increases during pregnancy.

Over-the-counter medications and preparations may *not* be safe during pregnancy. They should be used with as much caution as any other drug! Many over-the-counter preparations are combinations of medications. For example, pain medication can contain aspirin, caffeine and phenacetin. Cough syrups or sleep medications can contain as much as 25% alcohol. This is no different than drinking wine or beer during pregnancy.

Don't use aspirin during pregnancy. Using aspirin can increase bleeding. This can be detrimental to you if you are bleeding during pregnancy or if you are close to term.

Another medication to be careful with is ibuprofen, a popular product that is available in prescription and non-prescription forms. Experience with this medication during pregnancy is limited; it hasn't been in use that long. There are no known benefits during pregnancy. There have been reports of possible harmful effects. Why take a chance? Ibuprofen products include Advil®, Motrin® and Rufen®.

✧

A new over-the-counter product is Aleve®, which is used for pain relief or to reduce fever. Experience with this medication during pregnancy is limited; it hasn't been in use that long. It is best to use this medicine *only* under your doctor's supervision.

Talk to your doctor about using *any* medication *before* you use it! Read package labels about safety during pregnancy. Nearly all medications contain this information. Some antacids contain sodium bicarbonate, which increases your intake of sodium (which can be important if you have water-retention problems) and can cause constipation and increased gas. Some antacids contain aluminum, which can cause constipation and affect metabolism of other minerals (phosphate). Others contain magnesium; excessive overuse of these may cause magnesium poisoning.

Some over-the-counter medications and preparations *can* be used safely during pregnancy, if you use them wisely. This means don't take the substance for longer than 48 hours without consulting your doctor. If the problem does not resolve, your doctor may offer alternative treatments.

Over-the-counter medications and preparations you may safely use for a short period of time include acetaminophen (Tylenol®), some antacids (Amphogel®, Gelusil®, Maalox®, Milk of Magnesia®), throat lozenges (Sucrets®), some decongestants (Sudafed®) and some cough medicines (Robitussin®).

If you think your symptoms or discomfort are more severe or worse than they should be, call your doctor. Follow the advice of your healthcare provider. In addition, take good care of yourself. Exercise, eat right and have a positive mental attitude about your pregnancy.

You Should also Know

Having a Baby Costs Money! Every couple wants to know what it will cost to have a baby. There are really two answers to that question—it costs a lot, and cost varies from one part of the country to another.

❖

In determining how much it costs to have a baby in your part of the country, there are different factors to consider. It makes a big difference whether or not you have insurance. If you don't, you will pay for everything.

If you do have insurance, there are some things you need to check out.

✦ Does it have maternity benefits?
✦ Does it pay for everything or only some things?
✦ Does it pay only if you have complications?
✦ Does your insurance specify which hospital or doctor you can go to?
✦ Does your insurance cover "extras" such as lab tests or ultrasound exams?
✦ How long will your insurance allow you to stay in the hospital?
✦ If a specialist is needed, who pays for this?
✦ Will your present doctor see you for pregnancy with your present insurance?

Believe it or not, your insurance dictates a lot of these costs and decisions for you.

Having a baby generates a couple of different areas of cost. One is the hospital. Much of the covered amount for the hospital is determined by the length of stay and what "services" you use. In some cases, having an epidural or Cesarean section adds to this bill. Your doctor's bill is separate from this except under some plans. A pediatrician usually examines the baby, does a physical and sees the baby each day in the hospital. This is another bill.

When my first daughter was born in 1974, a normal delivery and 2-day hospital stay for my wife (no C-section, anesthesia or complications) cost a total of $600 for hospital, doctor, nursery and pediatrician. When my youngest daughter was born in 1985, a similar stay (again no anesthesia, C-section or complications) cost about $3,500—an increase of almost 600% in 11 years! Across the United States, 1994 prices for a delivery range from $4,000 to $12,000, depending on complications and type of delivery.

It would be nice to think about costs before pregnancy and be sure to have insurance to help out. Unfortunately, many pregnancies are surprises or happen before they are planned.

What can you do? First, find the answers to your questions. Talk to your insurance carrier. Someone in your doctor's office handles insurance claims. This person may have answers or resources you haven't thought about. Don't be embarrassed to ask about it. You will be happier to get these things resolved early. Pregnancy is *not* the time to cut corners to save money.

Call around so you can compare hospitals and prices. Sometimes it is worth spending a little more money to get a little more. When you call, ask for specifics about what is included in the prices you are quoted. You may get a price that seems lower and better than others but really doesn't cover everything you will want and need.

You want to be prepared well in advance. The last thing you need at this time is an unpleasant surprise about what is covered or how much you will have to pay for medical services.

Costs for Having a Baby in Canada   The Canadian health care system is very different from the health-care system in the United States. Canadians pay a health-care premium on a monthly basis. Cost varies depending on the province a person lives in. The doctor who delivers your baby is paid by the government. He or she submits his or her bill to the government, not the patient. You can't say that it costs X dollars to have a baby in Canada.

Week *18*

Age of Fetus — 16 Weeks

How Big Is Your Baby?

The crown-to-rump length of your growing baby is 5 to 5.6 inches (12.5 to 14cm) by week 18. Weight of the fetus is about 5.25 ounces (150g).

How Big Are You?

Your uterus can be felt just below your umbilicus. If you put your fingers sideways and measure, it is about 2 finger widths below your umbilicus (about 1 inch below).

Your uterus is the size of a cantaloupe or a little larger. Your weight gain to this point should be 10 to 13 pounds (4.5 to 5.8kg). However, this can vary widely. If you have gained more weight than this, talk to your doctor. You may need to see a nutritionist. You still have quite a bit of your pregnancy ahead of you, and you're going to gain even more weight.

Dieting during pregnancy is *not* a wise idea, but that doesn't mean not watching your caloric intake. You should! It's important for your baby to get proper nutrition from the foods you eat. You must choose your foods for the nutrition they provide for you and your growing baby.

One way of telling how your baby is growing and things are progressing is by your weight gain. Average weight gain during pregnancy is 25 to 35 pounds total. If you gain it all early, you'll gain more than 35 pounds. This can make pregnancy and delivery harder on you, and these extra pounds are hard ones to lose afterward.

How Your Baby Is Growing and Developing

Your baby is continuing to grow and develop, but the very rapid growth rate slows down a little. As you can see, your baby has a very human appearance now.

Development of the Heart and Circulatory System   The development and maturation of blood flow in the fetus begins early. It is a continual process of growth modification and development. Development of the heart and its chambers is an involved process.

At about the third week of fetal development, two tubes come together to form the heart. The heart begins to contract by day 22 of development or about the beginning of the 5th week of gestation. A beating heart can be seen as early as 5 to 6 weeks of pregnancy during an ultrasound examination.

The heart tube divides into bulges. These bulges develop into chambers in the heart, called *ventricles* (left and right) and *atria* (left atrium and right atrium). These divisions occur between weeks 6 and 7.

During week 7, a dividing tissue separating the left and right atria grows. There is an opening between the atria called the *foramen ovale*. This opening lets blood pass from one atrium to the other, allowing it to bypass the lungs. At birth, this opening closes.

The ventricles, the lower chambers of the heart lying below the atria, also develop a partition. The ventricle walls are very muscular. Blood is pumped from the left ventricle to the body and brain, and from the right ventricle to the lungs.

Heart valves develop at the same time as the chambers. These valves fill and empty the heart. Heart sounds and heart murmurs are caused by blood passing through these valves.

Your baby gets oxygen from you. Blood from your baby flows to the placenta through the umbilical cord. In the placenta, oxygen and nutrients are transported from your

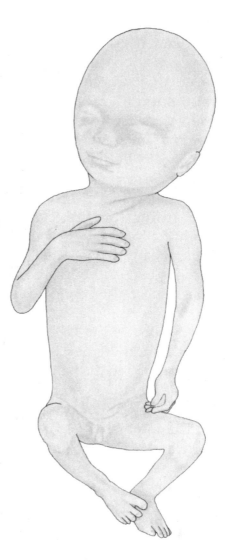

Your baby continues to grow. By this week, it is about 5 inches (12.5cm) from crown to rump. It looks much more human now.

blood to the fetal blood. Although the circulation of your blood and that of your baby come close, there is no direct connection. These circulations are completely separate.

From the placenta, blood returns to your baby through the umbilicus in the umbilical vein that enters the fetus. Some of the blood goes through your baby's liver. Some bypasses the liver and enters the inferior vena cava, a large vein leading to the heart. In the vena cava, the blood mixes with blood returning from the lower limbs, pelvis and abdomen. This blood enters the heart via the right atrium.

From the right atrium (the first chamber of the heart), blood goes through the foramen ovale to the left atrium. At this time, blood is already oxygenated but fetal lungs are unable to provide oxygen, so the lungs are bypassed. After birth, blood goes to the right ventricle, the lungs and the right atrium.

The main flow of blood from the left atrium goes to the left ventricle then through the aorta, a major vessel in the circulation. It is distributed to the head and body.

At birth, the fetus has to go very rapidly from depending entirely on your oxygenation to depending on its own heart and lungs. The foramen ovale closes, and blood goes to the right ventricle, the right atrium and to the lungs for oxygenation. It is truly a miraculous conversion.

At 18 weeks of gestation, some abnormalities of the heart can be detected using ultrasound. This can be helpful in detecting some problems, such as Down's syndrome. A skilled ultrasonographer looks for specific heart defects. If an abnormality is suspected, further ultrasound exams may be used to follow its development as pregnancy progresses.

Changes in You

Does Your Back Ache? Nearly every pregnant woman experiences backache at some time in pregnancy. It may have occurred already or may come later as you get bigger. Some women have severe back pain following excessive exercise,

✧

walking, bending, lifting or standing. It is more common to have mild backache than severe problems.

The growth of the uterus in front of you changes your center of gravity. Your center of gravity is shifted over your lower extremities (legs). There is an increased mobility of your joints. The sacrococcygeal, sacroiliac and pubic joints can all be affected. Changes are believed to be caused by hormonal changes.

A change in mobility of joints may contribute to the change in your posture and may cause discomfort in the lower back. This is particularly true in the latter part of pregnancy.

For some women, care must be taken in getting out of bed or getting up from sitting. In severe instances, some women find it difficult to walk.

Backache can be helped with heat, rest and analgesics, such as acetaminophen (Tylenol®). Special maternity girdles are available that can provide some support. Keeping weight under control and exercising may also help. In a severe case, physical therapy or a consultation with an orthopedic surgeon may be necessary.

Watch your diet and weight gain. Continue exercising within guidelines during pregnancy. Get in the habit of lying on your side when you sleep. During the day (whether you work outside the home or not), find time to get off your feet and lie down for 30 minutes on your side. If you have other children, find ways to get some rest during the day. If they take a nap, get some rest of your own. Start early to do these things; it'll pay off for you as your pregnancy advances.

Nasal Problems   Some women complain of stuffiness of their nose or frequent nosebleeds during pregnancy. Some researchers believe these symptoms occur because of changes in circulation due to hormonal changes during pregnancy. This can cause the mucous membranes of your nose and nasal passageways to swell and bleed more easily.

❖

Don't try different medications to help, such as decongestants and nasal sprays. Many of these are combinations of several medications and may be ill-advised during pregnancy.

It may help to use a humidifier, particularly during the winter months when heating may dry out the air. Some women get relief from increasing their fluid intake and using a gentle lubricant, such as petroleum jelly. As for other relief, you may just have to wait until your baby is born to breathe normally through your nose again.

How Your Actions Affect Your Baby's Development

Some women are very active in fitness activities. They are concerned about their limitations in exercise and sports activities. They want to know what they can do and what they should avoid while pregnant.

The pregnant woman now participates safely in many sports and activities. This is very different from the attitudes 20, 30 and 40 years ago! Bed rest and decreased activity were common then. Today, we believe exercise and sports activity can be very beneficial to you and your growing baby.

However, some caution about sports activity is wise. Your body is heavier, and oxygen demands for you and your baby increase. You may not have the balance you are accustomed to, which can affect your performance. You may tire more easily.

As with any activity, discuss your particular sports activities with your doctor. If you are a high-risk patient or have had several miscarriages, discuss it with your doctor *before* starting a particular activity. Now is *not* the time to train for any sport or to increase activity.

What about specific sports? Below is a discussion of various activities you might be interested in. Aerobic exercise is discussed on page 49.

Swimming Swimming can be very good for you when you are pregnant. It may also make you feel very comfortable.

The support and buoyancy of the water can be very relaxing.

If you swim, you are encouraged to swim throughout pregnancy. If you can't swim, exercising in a swimming pool in the shallow end can be very enjoyable. Classes are offered in many places. Ask at local spas or health clubs.

Bicycling   Now is *not* the time to learn to ride a bike! If you're comfortable riding and have safe places to ride, it can be an exercise you can enjoy with your partner or family.

Your balance will change as your body changes. This can make getting on and off a bicycle difficult. And a fall from a bicycle could injure you or possibly injure your baby.

A stationary bicycle is good for bad weather and for later in pregnancy. Many doctors suggest you ride a stationary bike to avoid the danger of a fall in the last 2 to 3 months of pregnancy.

Walking   Walking is a very desirable exercise during pregnancy. If you are just starting, gradually increase the time and distance you walk. Two miles of walking at a good pace is adequate.

Walking can be a good time for you and your partner to talk. Even when the weather is against you, there are places like enclosed shopping malls where you can walk and get a good workout. As pregnancy progresses, you may need to decrease your speed and distance.

Jogging   Many women continue to jog during pregnancy. Jogging is permitted during pregnancy, but check with your doctor first. If you are a high-risk pregnancy, jogging is not a good idea.

Pregnancy is *not* the time to increase mileage or train for a race. Wear comfortable clothing and shoes with good cushioning. Allow plenty of time to cool down.

During the course of your pregnancy, you'll probably need to slow down and decrease the number of miles run or even change to walking. If you notice pain, contractions, bleeding or other symptoms during or after jogging, call your doctor immediately.

Other Sports Activities   Tennis and golf are safe but may provide little actual exercise. Horseback riding is not advisable during pregnancy. Avoid water skiing while you're pregnant. Bowling is OK, although the amount of exercise you get varies. Be careful in late pregnancy; back strain could occur. Your balance changes, and bowling may be difficult for you.

Talk to your doctor about snow skiing. In the latter part of pregnancy, your balance will change significantly. A fall could be harmful to you and your baby. Most physicians agree that skiing in the second half of pregnancy is not a good idea. Some doctors may allow skiing in early pregnancy, but only if there are no complications with this or previous pregnancies.

Riding snowmobiles and motorcycles is not advisable. Some doctors may allow you to ride if it is not strenuous. But most feel the risk is too great. This is particularly true if you have had problems during this or other pregnancies.

You Should also Know

Bladder Infections   One of the first symptoms you may notice early in pregnancy is frequent urination. This problem will continue during pregnancy and may get you up frequently at night.

It is more common to get urinary-tract infections during pregnancy. Other names for urinary-tract infections are *bladder infections* and *cystitis*. Symptoms of a bladder infection include painful urination (dysuria), particularly at the end of urination, the feeling of urgency to urinate and frequent urination.

Most doctors will test your urine at your first visit. Your doctor will check it for infection if and when bothersome symptoms arise.

✧

You can help avoid infection by not "holding" your urine. Empty your bladder as soon as you feel the need to. Drink plenty of fluid. Cranberry juice helps acidify your urine and may help avoid infections. For some women, it helps to empty the bladder after having intercourse.

See your doctor if you think you have a bladder infection. It should be treated. There are safe antibiotics that can be used during pregnancy for this problem.

If left untreated, urinary-tract infections can get worse. They can even cause pyelonephritis, a serious infection in the kidneys. If you have pyelonephritis, you may have to be hospitalized to treat the infection.

A urinary-tract infection during pregnancy may also be a possible cause of premature labor and low-birth-weight infants. If you think you have an infection, talk to your doctor. If you are diagnosed as having a urinary-tract infection, take the antibiotics prescribed by your doctor.

Week 19

Age of Fetus — 17 Weeks

How Big Is Your Baby?

Crown-to-rump length of the growing fetus is 5.2 to 6 inches (13 to 15cm) by week 19. Your baby weighs about 7 ounces (200g). It's incredible to think your baby will increase its weight more than 15 times between now and delivery.

How Big Are You?

Your uterus can be felt about 0.5 inch (1.3cm) below your umbilicus. The illustration on page 181 gives you a good idea of the relative size of you, your uterus and your developing baby. A side view really shows the change in you!

Total weight gain at this point is between 8 and 14 pounds (3.6 and 6.3kg). Of this weight gain, only about 7 *ounces* (200g) is your baby! The placenta weighs about 6 ounces (170g); the amniotic fluid weighs about 11 ounces (320g). The uterus also weighs 11 ounces (320g). Your breasts have increased in weight by 6.3 ounces (180g) each.

You may feel huge, but you've got a long way to go.

How Your Baby Is Growing and Developing

Your Baby's Nervous System   The beginning of the baby's nervous system (brain and other structures like the spinal cord) is seen as early as week 4 as the neural plate begins to develop. By week 6 of gestation, the main divisions of the central nervous system are established. These divisions consist of the forebrain, midbrain, hindbrain and spinal cord. In week 7, the forebrain divides into the two hemispheres that will become the two hemispheres of the brain, called *cerebral hemispheres.*

Hydrocephalus   Organization and development of the brain continues from this early beginning. Cerebral spinal fluid (CSF), which circulates around the brain and the spinal cord, is made by an area called the *choroid plexus.* CSF must be able to flow without restriction. If openings are blocked and flow of the fluid is restricted for any reason, it can cause *hydrocephalus* (water on the brain).

Hydrocephalus causes enlargement of the head. Enlargement of the fetal head occurs in about 1 in 2000 babies and is responsible for about 12% of all severe fetal malformations found at birth.

Hydrocephalus is often associated with spina bifida and occurs in about 33% of these cases. The amount of fluid that can accumulate is about 15 to 45 ounces (500 to 1500ml) but can be as high as 5.3 quarts (5 liters)! A major concern is the amount of fetal brain tissue compressed by all this fluid.

Because of the increased size of the head, about 35% of these babies enter the birth canal feet first. Many others have heads that are too large for a vaginal delivery.

Diagnosis of this problem is best made by ultrasound examination. Finding this condition is one reason for suggesting an ultrasound at a time in pregnancy when it can be diagnosed. Hydrocephalus can usually be seen on ultrasound by 19 weeks of pregnancy. Occasionally it is found by routine exams and "feeling" your uterus.

Hydrocephalus is a *symptom*; it can have several different causes. Once it is found, a reason for the problem must be sought. Causes include spina bifida, meningomyelocele and omphalocele.

In the past, nothing could be done until after delivery. Today, in some cases, intrauterine therapy—while the fetus

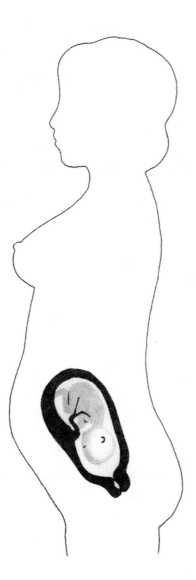

Comparative size of the uterus at 19 weeks of pregnancy (fetal age—17 weeks).
The uterus can be felt just under the umbilicus (bellybutton).

is still in the uterus—can be performed. The cases in which this is helpful are limited but may be important in specific problems.

There are two methods of treating hydrocephalus in utero. In one method, a needle passes through your abdomen into the area of the baby's brain where fluid is collecting. Some fluid is removed to prevent further accumulation of fluid and the resulting pressure on the brain. In another method, a small plastic tube is placed into the area of fluid in the fetal brain. This tube is left in place to continuously drain fluid from the baby's brain.

Hydrocephalus is a high-risk problem. These procedures are very specialized and should be performed *only* by someone experienced in the latest techniques. This requires consultation with a perinatologist who specializes in high-risk pregnancies.

Changes in You

Feeling Dizzy Feeling dizzy during pregnancy is a fairly common symptom. This is often caused by hypotension. It doesn't usually appear until the second trimester but can happen earlier.

There are two common reasons for hypotension (*low blood pressure*) during pregnancy. It can be caused by the enlarging uterus putting pressure on your aorta and vena cava. This is called *supine hypotension* and occurs when you lie down. It can be alleviated or prevented by not sleeping or lying on your back.

The second cause of hypotension is rising rapidly from a sitting, kneeling or squatting position. This is called *postural hypotension*. Your blood pressure drops when you rise rapidly, and blood leaves your brain because of gravity. This is cured by rising slowly from a sitting or lying position.

If you are anemic, it may also cause you to feel faint or tired, or you may fatigue easily. Your hematocrit is checked routinely during pregnancy. Your doctor will advise you of this problem if you suffer from it.

❖

Pregnancy also affects your blood sugar. High blood sugar *(hyperglycemia)* or low blood sugar *(hypoglycemia)* can make you feel dizzy or faint. Many doctors routinely test pregnant women for problems with blood sugar during pregnancy, particularly if they have problems with dizziness. The problem may be avoided or improved by eating a balanced diet, by not skipping meals and by not going a long time without eating. It's a good idea to carry a piece of fruit or several crackers with you for a quick boost in blood sugar when you need it.

How Your Actions Affect Your Baby's Development

Your Allergies May Be Affected During Pregnancy   If you suffer from allergies, you may feel they're getting worse during your pregnancy. Difficulty in breathing is not something you need at this time.

Drink plenty of fluid, especially if the weather is hot. If you have allergy medication, *don't* take it and assume it's safe. Ask your doctor about your medicine, whether it is prescription or non-prescription. Taking some types of allergy medication could cause problems for your baby. Many allergy medicines are combinations of several medicines, including aspirin. This advice applies to nasal sprays as well.

If you know there are foods you are allergic to, stay away from them. This applies to other possible irritants, such as animals or cigarette smoke.

On the other hand, some women notice their allergies get better during pregnancy, and symptoms improve. Certain things they had trouble with before pregnancy are no longer a problem.

You Should also Know

Warning Signs of Pregnancy   Most women have a pregnancy with few problems. But if you do have problems, do you know what to look for? What are some danger signals to watch for during pregnancy? When should you call your doctor?

Below is a list of the most important things to watch for. Call your doctor if you experience *any* of them!

+ Vaginal bleeding.
+ Severe swelling of the face or fingers.
+ Severe abdominal pain.
+ Loss of fluid from the vagina, usually a gushing of fluid, but sometimes a trickle or continual wetness.
+ A big change in the movement of the baby or a lack of fetal movement.
+ High fever (more than 101.6F; 38.7C) or chills.
+ Severe vomiting or an inability to keep anything down.
+ Blurring of vision.
+ Painful urination.
+ A headache that won't go away or a severe headache.
+ An injury or accident injuring you or giving you concern about the well-being of your pregnancy. The most common examples are falls and automobile accidents.

When talking to your doctor, don't be embarrassed to ask questions about anything. Your doctor would rather know about problems while they are small. One way to get to know your doctor is to ask his or her opinion about your concerns.

If problems warrant it, you may be referred to a perinatologist. This is an obstetrician who has spent an additional 2 or more years in specialized training. These specialists have experience caring for women with high-risk pregnancies. They spend most of their time taking care of these women and their babies.

You may not have a high-risk pregnancy at the beginning of your pregnancy. However, if problems develop, you may need to be referred for consultation for a problem with you, such as premature labor, or a problem found with the baby, such as spina bifida. A perinatologist may provide your care during pregnancy. It may be possible for you to return to your regular doctor for your delivery.

✧

If you are seeing a perinatologist, you may have to deliver your baby at a hospital other than the one you had chosen. This is usually because of specialized facilities or the availability of specialized tests for you or your baby.

Electric Blanket Use   There has been controversy about use of electric blankets to keep you warm during pregnancy. There is still much disagreement and discussion about their safety. At this time, no one knows the answer to the question, *"Is it safe to use an electric blanket during pregnancy?"*

Electric blankets produce a low-level electromagnetic field. Some experts question whether these low-level electromagnetic fields can cause cancer or other health problems. The developing fetus may be more sensitive than an adult to these electromagnetic fields. Fetal damage might occur.

Researchers are uncertain about "acceptable levels" of exposure for a pregnant woman, so the safest alternative at this time is not to use an electric blanket during pregnancy. There are many other ways to keep warm, such as down comforters and wool blankets. One of these alternatives is a better choice.

Week 20

Age of Fetus — 18 Weeks

How Big Is Your Baby?

At this point in development, the crown-to-rump length is 5.6 to 6.4 inches (14 to 16cm). Your baby weighs about 9 ounces (260g).

How Big Are You?

Congratulations—you're halfway through your pregnancy! Twenty weeks marks the halfway point. Remember, the entire pregnancy is 40 weeks from the beginning of your last period if you go full term.

Your uterus is probably just about even with your umbilicus. Your doctor has been watching your growth and the enlargement of your uterus. Growth to this point may be irregular but usually becomes more regular after the 20th week.

Measuring the Growth of Your Uterus   The growth of your uterus is often measured to keep track of your baby's growth. Your doctor usually uses his or her fingers and measures by finger breadth. A measuring tape may not be used for a while.

Your doctor needs a point of reference. Some doctors measure from your umbilicus (bellybutton). Many measure from the pubic symphysis. The pubic symphysis is the place where the pubic bones meet in the middle-lower part of

✧

your abdomen. This bony area is just above your urethra (where urine comes out). It is 6 to 10 inches (15.2 to 25.4cm) below the umbilicus, depending on how tall you are. It may be felt 1 or 2 inches (2.5 to 5cm) below your pubic hairline.

Measurements are made from the pubic symphysis to the top of the uterus, which is about even with the umbilicus. After 20 weeks of pregnancy, you should grow about 0.4 inch (1cm) each week. So if you are 8 inches (20cm) at 20 weeks, at your next visit (4 weeks later), you should measure about 9.6 inches (24cm).

If you measure 11.2 inches (28cm) at this point in pregnancy, you may require further evaluation with ultrasound to determine if you are carrying twins or to see if your due date is correct. If you measure 6 inches (15 to 16cm) at this point, it may be a reason for further evaluation with ultrasound. Your due date could be wrong or there may be a concern about intrauterine-growth retardation or some other problem.

Not every doctor measures the same way, and not every woman is the same size. Babies vary in size. If pregnant friends ask, "How much did you measure?" don't get upset if their measurements are different. Measurements are different for different women and may be different for a woman from one pregnancy to another.

If you see a doctor you don't normally see or if you see a new doctor, you'll probably measure differently. This does not indicate a problem or that someone is measuring incorrectly. It's just that everyone measures a little differently.

Having the same person measure you on a regular basis can be very helpful in following the growth of your baby. Within limits, it is a sign of fetal well-being and fetal growth. If growth appears abnormal, it can be a warning sign.

If you're concerned about your size and the growth of your pregnancy, ask your doctor about it. If you have been pregnant before, it can be helpful to compare your growth and weight gain with previous pregnancies.

❖

Your growth is an important part of your pregnancy. If you're not growing fast enough or if you're growing too fast, your doctor can do many things to help you and your growing baby.

How Your Baby Is Growing and Developing

Your Developing Baby's Skin   The skin covering your baby begins growing from two layers. These layers are the *epidermis*, which is on the surface, and the *dermis*, which is the deeper layer.

In the beginning, the embryo is covered by a single layer of cells. By this point in your pregnancy, the epidermis is arranged in four layers. One of these layers contains epidermal ridges. They are responsible for patterns of surfaces on fingertips, palms and soles of the feet. They are genetically determined.

The dermis lies below the epidermis. It forms dermal papillae, which push upward into the epidermis. These projections contain a small blood vessel (capillary) or a nerve. This deeper layer also contains large amounts of fat.

When a baby is born, skin is covered by a white substance that looks like paste. It is called *vernix (vernix caseosa)*. It is first secreted by the glands in the skin at about 20 weeks of pregnancy. Vernix protects your growing baby's skin from amniotic fluid.

Hair appears around 12 to 14 weeks of pregnancy. It grows from the epidermis; the end of the hair (hair papillae) pushes down into the dermis. Hair is first seen on the fetus on the upper lip and eyebrow. It is usually shed around the time of birth and is replaced by thicker hair from new follicles.

Ultrasound Pictures   The illustration on page 191 shows a picture of an ultrasound exam (and an interpretive illustration of the ultrasound) in a pregnant woman at about 20 weeks gestation. An ultrasound exam is often easier to understand

✧

when it is actually being done. The pictures you see are more like motion pictures.

If you look closely at the illustration, it may make sense to you. Read the labels and try to visualize the baby inside the uterus. An ultrasound picture is like looking at a slice of an object. The picture you see is 2-dimensional.

If you have an ultrasound exam and don't see everything or it doesn't make sense, don't feel bad. It is reassuring to see the heart beat and see your baby move.

An ultrasound done at this point in pregnancy is very helpful for confirming or helping to establish your due date. If the ultrasound is done very early or very late (first or last 2 months), the accuracy for dating a pregnancy is not as good. If two or more fetuses are present, they can usually be seen. In many cases, fetal problems can also be seen at this time.

Depending on the quality of the ultrasound equipment and the expertise of the person doing the exam, it may be *possible* to determine the sex of the baby. But the baby must also cooperate. Sex is recognized by seeing the genitals. This is a little early for this kind of determination, and you may not be able to really tell. Even if it looks obvious, don't paint the baby's room blue or start making a pink quilt! Ultrasounds have been known to be wrong about the sex of a baby.

Changes in You

Increased Vaginal Discharge   It is normal to have an increase in vaginal discharge or secretion during pregnancy. This is called *leukorrhea*. This discharge is usually white or yellowish and fairly thick. It is not an infection. It is probably caused by the increased blood flow to the skin and muscles around the vagina. This increase in blood flow brings about a symptom visible to your doctor early in pregnancy called *Chadwick's sign*. It causes a violet or blue coloration of the vagina.

Wall of uterus   Head

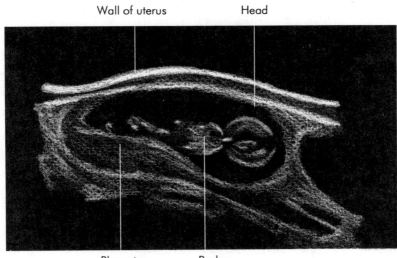

Placenta   Body

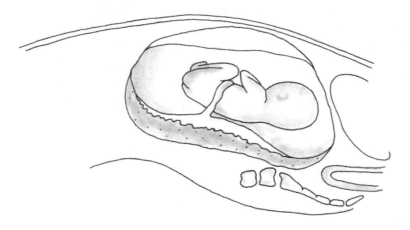

Ultrasound of a baby at 20 weeks gestation (fetal age—18 weeks). The interpretive illustration may help you see more detail.

✧

Don't douche with this type of discharge if you're pregnant or think you might be pregnant. You may have to wear sanitary pads if you have a heavy discharge. Avoid wearing pantyhose and nylon underwear. Wear underwear with a cotton crotch.

Infections can and do occur during pregnancy. The discharge that accompanies these infections is often foul-smelling, has a yellow or green color, and causes irritation or itching around or inside the vagina. If you suffer from any of these symptoms, report it to your doctor. Treatment is often possible. Many creams and antibiotics can be used safely during pregnancy.

Douching During Pregnancy   Most doctors agree you should *not* douche during pregnancy. Bulb-syringe douches are definitely out! Some doctors permit a douche with a bag or can, but keep the level low and avoid high pressure. The nozzle should not penetrate the vagina more than 1 inch (2.5cm).

Using a douche may cause you to bleed or may cause more serious problems, such as an air embolus. An air embolus is caused by air getting into your circulation from the pressure of the douche. It is rare, but it can cause very serious problems for you.

Abdominal Itching   As your uterus has grown and filled your pelvis, your abdominal skin and muscles have stretched. Many women complain that their abdomen itches with stretched skin.

With the stretching of the abdominal skin, the itchiness is a fairly natural consequence. Lotions are acceptable to use to help reduce itching. Try not to scratch and irritate your skin. That can make it worse!

Stretching Abdominal Muscles   Your abdominal muscles are also being stretched and pushed apart as your baby grows. Muscles are attached to the lower portion of your ribs and

✧

run vertically down to your pelvis. They may separate in the midline. These muscles are called the *rectus muscles.* When they separate, it is called a *diastasis recti.*

You will notice the separation most often when you are lying down and you raise your head, tightening abdominal muscles. It will look like there is a bulge in the middle of your abdomen. You might even feel the edge of the muscle on either side of the bulge. It isn't painful and doesn't harm you or your baby.

What you are feeling in the gap between the muscles is the uterus. Movement of the baby may be more easily felt here.

If this is your first baby, you may not notice the separation at all. With each pregnancy, separation may be more noticeable. Exercising can strengthen these muscles, but you may still have the bulge or gap.

Following pregnancy, these muscles fall back together. The separation won't be as noticeable, but it may still be present. A girdle probably won't help the problem.

How Your Actions Affect Your Baby's Development

Will You Get Varicose Veins? Varicose veins, also called *varicosities* or *varices,* occur to some degree is most pregnant women. There appears to be an inherited predisposition to varicose veins that can be made more severe by pregnancy, increased age and from pressure caused by standing for long periods of time.

Varicose veins are blood vessels that fill up with blood. They occur primarily in the legs but can be seen in the area of the birth canal in the vulva. The change in blood flow and the pressure from the uterus make varices worse, and this makes you uncomfortable.

In most instances, varicose veins get worse and become more noticeable and more painful as pregnancy progresses. With increasing weight (especially if you spend a lot of time standing), they will get worse.

✧

Symptoms will vary. For some, it is a blemish or purple-blue spot on the legs with minimal or no discomfort except perhaps in the evening. Some women have bulging veins that require elevation at the end of the day.

Treating Varicose Veins   Many women try wearing support hose. Many types of hose are available; they can be helpful. Wearing clothing that doesn't restrict circulation at the knee or the groin may also help a little. Spending only a little time on your feet and a lot of time lying on your side or elevating your legs can be beneficial. This allows drainage of these veins.

If you have varicose veins in your legs or vulva, stay off your feet as much as possible. Wear flat shoes whenever you can. When you're sitting down, don't cross your legs! This cuts off circulation and can make problems worse. Following these measures may help keep veins from swelling as much.

Following pregnancy, swelling in the veins should go down and not be as severe. But varicose veins probably won't disappear altogether. Surgery that can get rid of these veins is called *vein stripping*. It would be unusual to operate on varicose veins during pregnancy, although it is a treatment to consider when you are not pregnant.

You Should also Know

Hearing Your Baby's Heartbeat with a Stethoscope   It may be possible to hear your baby's heartbeat with a stethoscope at 20 weeks. Before doctors had doppler equipment that allowed them to hear the heartbeat and ultrasound to see the heart beating, the stethoscope helped the listener hear the baby's heartbeat. This usually occurred after quickening for most women.

Listening with a stethoscope gives a different sound than you might be used to hearing at the doctor's office. It isn't a loud sound. If you've never listened through a

✧

stethoscope before, it may be difficult at first. It does get easier as the baby gets larger and sounds are louder.

If you can't hear your baby's heartbeat with a stethoscope, don't worry. It's not always easy for a doctor who does this on a regular basis!

If you hear a swishing or beating sound, you have to differentiate it from your own heartbeat. A baby's heart beats very rapidly, usually 120 to 160 beats every minute. Your heartbeat or pulse rate is slower, in the range of 60 to 80 beats a minute. Don't be afraid to ask your doctor to help you differentiate the sounds.

Lyme Disease   Lyme disease refers to an infection caused by a spirochete carried and transmitted to humans by ticks. There are several stages of the illness. In about 80% of those bitten, there is a skin lesion with a distinctive look, called a *bull's eye*. There may also be flu-like symptoms. After 4 to 6 weeks, there may be signs of heart problems or neurologic problems. Later, arthritis can become a problem.

At the beginning of the illness, blood tests may not diagnose the illness. A blood test done later in the illness can be used.

It is known that spirochetes do cross the placenta. Whether this is dangerous to the fetus is unknown at this time. Researchers are studying the problem.

Treatment for Lyme disease requires long-term antibiotic therapy and sometimes intravenous antibiotic therapy. Many medications used to treat Lyme disease are safe to use during pregnancy.

Avoid exposure to Lyme disease, if possible. Stay out of areas known to have ticks, especially heavily wooded areas. If you can't avoid these areas, wear long-sleeved shirts, long pants, socks and boots or closed shoes. Be sure to check your hair when you come in; ticks often attach themselves there.

Week 21

Age of Fetus —19 Weeks

How Big Is Your Baby?

Your baby is getting larger in this first week of the second half of your pregnancy! It now weighs about 10.5 ounces (300g). Its crown-to-rump length is about 7.2 inches (18cm). It is about the size of a large banana.

How Big Are You?

You can feel your uterus about half an inch (1cm) above your bellybutton. At the doctor's office, your uterus measures almost 8.5 inches (21cm) from the pubic symphysis. Your weight gain should be between 10 and 14 pounds (4.5 and 6.3kg).

By this week, your waistline is definitely gone. Your friends and relatives, and strangers, too, can tell you're pregnant. It would be hard for you to hide your condition!

How Your Baby Is Growing and Developing

The rapid growth rate of your baby has slowed down. However, the fetus is continuing to grow and develop. Different organ systems within the baby are maturing and developing.

The Fetal Digestive System   The fetal digestive system is functioning in a rudimentary way. By the 11th week of your

✧

pregnancy, the small intestine has begun to have movement, which pushes substances through it. The small intestine is capable of passing sugar from inside of the small intestine into the baby's body.

By this point in your pregnancy (at 21 weeks), the fetal digestive system has developed enough to allow the fetus to swallow amniotic fluid. After swallowing amniotic fluid, the fetus can absorb much of the water in it and pass unabsorbed matter as far as the large bowel.

Hydrochloric acid and adult digestive enzymes are present in small amounts in the fetal digestive system. If an infant is born prematurely, there may be uneven amounts or deficiencies of these enzymes, depending on the gestational age of the baby.

Fetal Swallowing   As mentioned above, your baby can swallow before it is born. Swallowing by the baby at different stages of your pregnancy can be observed by ultrasound. We have seen babies swallowing amniotic fluid as early as 21 weeks of pregnancy.

Why does a baby in the womb swallow? Researchers believe swallowing amniotic fluid may help growth and development of the fetal digestive system. It may condition the digestive system to function after birth.

Studies have been done to determine how much fluid a fetus swallows and passes through its digestive system. There is evidence that indicates babies at full-term may swallow large amounts of amniotic fluid, even as much as 17 ounces (500ml) of amniotic fluid in a 24-hour period.

The amniotic fluid swallowed by the fetus contributes only a small amount to the caloric needs of the fetus. But researchers believe it may contribute essential nutrients to the developing baby.

Meconium   During your pregnancy, you may hear the term *meconium* and wonder what it means. It refers to undigested debris from swallowed amniotic fluid in the fetal digestive

❖

system. It is a greenish-black to light-brown substance that your baby will pass from its bowels several days or weeks before delivery, during labor or after birth.

The presence of meconium can be important at the time of delivery. If a baby has had a bowel movement and meconium is in the amniotic fluid, the infant may swallow the fluid before birth or at the time of birth. If meconium is inhaled into the lungs, it may cause pneumonia or pneumonitis. For this reason, if meconium is seen at the time of delivery, an attempt is made to remove it from the baby's mouth and throat with a small suction tube.

Passage of meconium into the amniotic fluid may be caused by distress in the fetus. If meconium is seen during labor, it may be an indication of fetal distress.

Changes in You

Besides your growing uterus, other parts of your body are continuing to change and grow. You may notice swelling in your lower legs, particularly at the end of the day. If you are on your feet a large part of the day, you may notice less swelling if you're able to get off of your feet and rest for a while during the day.

Blood Clots in the Legs   A complication of pregnancy that can be a serious problem is a blood clot in the legs or groin. Symptoms of the problem are swelling of the legs accompanied by leg pain and redness or warmth over the area in the legs.

The problem has many names, including *venous thrombosis, thromboembolic disease, thrombophlebitis* and *lower deep-vein thrombosis*. The problem is not limited to pregnancy, but pregnancy is a time when this condition is more likely to occur. This is due to the changes in your circulation, with slowing of blood flow in the legs because of pressure in the uterus and changes in the blood and its clotting mechanisms.

✧

The most probable cause of blood clots in the legs in pregnancy is decreased blood flow, also called *stasis*. If you have had a previous blood clot—in your legs or any other part of your body—tell your doctor at the beginning of your pregnancy. It's important information, and he or she needs to know it.

Deep-Vein Thrombosis   A distinction is often made between superficial thrombosis and deep-vein thrombosis in the leg. If the blood clot (thrombosis) is in the superficial veins of the leg, it is not as serious. This is usually noted by veins very close to the surface of the skin that can often be felt on the surface. This type of thrombosis does not require hospitalization and is treated with mild pain reliever, such as acetaminophen (Tylenol®), elevation of the leg, support of the leg with an ace bandage or support stockings and occasionally heat. If the condition doesn't improve rapidly, deep-vein thrombosis must be considered.

Deep-vein thrombosis is a more serious problem. It requires serious diagnostic and treatment steps. Signs and symptoms of deep-vein thrombosis in the lower leg can differ greatly, depending on the location of the clot and how bad it is. The onset of the pain with thrombophlebitis can be very rapid and very abrupt, with severe pain and swelling of the leg and thigh. This type of thrombosis involves the deeper veins in the leg.

With deep-vein thrombosis, the leg may occasionally appear pale and cool. But usually a portion of the leg is tender, hot and swollen. Often skin over the area of the veins is red. There may even be streaks of red on the skin over the veins where the blood clots have occurred.

Squeezing the calf or leg may cause extreme pain. It may be extremely painful to walk. If you are lying down and flex your toes up toward your knee and the back of the leg is tender, it is a positive Homans' sign. (This type of pain may also occur with a strained muscle or a bruise.) Check with your doctor if you are concerned.

✧

Diagnostic studies of deep-vein thrombosis may be different for a pregnant woman than a non-pregnant woman. In the non-pregnant woman, an X-ray may be accompanied by an injection into leg veins to look for blood clots. This test is not usually performed on a pregnant woman because of exposure to radiation and dye.

We now have tests that can be done with ultrasound instead of X-ray. This type of test is not available everywhere, but it is available at most major medical centers.

Treatment of deep-vein thrombosis usually consists of hospitalization and heparin (a blood thinner) therapy. Heparin must be given intravenously and cannot be taken as a pill. It thins the blood and allows the clot to be dissolved. At the same time the heparin is administered, the woman is required to stay in bed. The leg may be elevated and heat applied, and mild pain medicine is prescribed.

Recovery, including hospitalization, may be 7 to 10 days. After this time, it is necessary for the woman to continue taking heparin during pregnancy. Following pregnancy, it is necessary to continue taking heparin or another blood thinner. This may continue for several weeks, depending on the severity of the blood clot.

If a woman has a blood clot during pregnancy, it may be necessary for her to use heparin during subsequent pregnancies. If so, heparin can be given by an in-dwelling I.V. catheter or by daily injections the woman administers to herself under her doctor's direction.

Two medications are usually used to treat deep-vein thrombosis. As I've already discussed, heparin is used most often during pregnancy and can be given only by injection. It is safe during pregnancy and is not passed to the fetus. A woman may be required to take extra calcium during pregnancy if she receives heparin.

The other medication used is warfarin, an oral medication. Warfarin (Coumadin®) is *not* given during pregnancy because it crosses the placenta and can be harmful to the baby. Warfarin is usually given to the woman after pregnancy is

✧

over to prevent blood clots. It may be prescribed for a few weeks or a few months, depending on the severity of the blood clot.

If you have had a blood clot in the past for *any* reason, pregnancy-related or not, it's important to see your doctor early in your pregnancy. Be sure to tell him or her about any problems with blood clots at your first prenatal visit.

The greatest danger from deep-vein thrombosis is a pulmonary embolism. With a pulmonary embolism, a piece of the blood clot breaks off and travels from the legs to the lungs. This is an uncommon problem during pregnancy and is reported in only 1 in every 3,000 to 7,000 deliveries. It is a serious complication in pregnancy, but it can often be avoided with proper treatment.

How Your Actions Affect Your Baby's Development

Safety of Ultrasound   On the opposite page is an illustration of an ultrasound exam, accompanied by an interpretive illustration. The ultrasound illustration shows a baby inside a uterus. The mother-to-be has a large cyst in her abdomen. Ultrasound is discussed in depth beginning on page 116.

Many women wonder about the *safety* of ultrasound exams. Most medical researchers agree that ultrasound exams do not pose any kind of significant risk to you or your baby. The possibility of ultrasound having teratogenic effects has been studied many times without evidence the test causes problems. (A teratogen is something that damages a developing tissue.)

Ultrasound has not been shown to cause mutations in a developing fetus. (Mutations are changes in genetic information, usually changes in the chromosome information or DNA.) Chromosomal damage has not been found in studies on the safety of ultrasound.

The safety of ultrasound has been established but will be continually examined through further tests. Information will continue to be collected. But ultrasound is an extremely

Body   Head

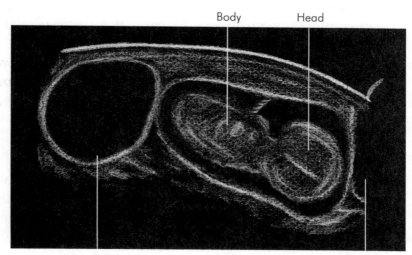

Cyst in abdomen   Mother's bladder

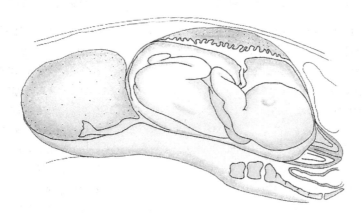

Ultrasound of a baby in utero. There is a cyst in the mother's-to-be abdomen. Look at the interpretive illustration for clarification of the ultrasound image.

✧

helpful tool in diagnosing problems during pregnancy. Knowing the answers to some very difficult questions can be reassuring for the doctor and the pregnant woman.

If your doctor has recommended you have ultrasound performed and you're concerned about it, discuss it with him or her. There may be a very important reason for having an ultrasound exam done that could affect the well-being of your developing baby.

You Should also Know

In the early weeks of pregnancy, your body did not change significantly. Now your body is changing rapidly. Your uterus is beginning to project out in front of you. Should you be making many changes at this point in your pregnancy?

Exercise Everyone has heard stories of women who continued with strenuous exercise or strenuous activities until the day of delivery without problems. Stories are told of Olympic athletes who were pregnant at the time they won medals in the Olympic games. But this kind of training and physical stress is not a good idea for everyone and probably isn't a good idea for you.

You know exercise is important for your well-being and is good for you during your pregnancy. But now is probably *not* the time to be competing or training for competition.

As your uterus is growing and your abdomen is getting larger, you may find your sense of balance is affected even more. You may feel very "clumsy." This isn't the time for contact sports, such as basketball, or sports where you might fall easily, injuring yourself or striking yourself in the abdomen.

It's good for you to continue to exercise. It will help you feel better and may help you control your weight. But be wise about your choices. During the course of your pregnancy, you are going to have to decrease the level of

✧

exercise. This point in pregnancy—21 weeks—may be the time to begin decreasing the amount of exercise you are doing.

Listen to your body! It will tell you when it's time to slow down.

Sexual Relations   Pregnancy can be an important time of growing closer to your partner and in planning your future together. As you get larger, sexual intercourse may become difficult because of discomfort for you. With some imagination and with different positions (ones in which you are not on your back and your partner is not directly on top of you), you can continue to enjoy sexual relations during this part of your pregnancy.

If you feel pressure from your partner—either his concern about the safety of intercourse or requests for frequent sexual relations—discuss it openly with him. Don't be afraid to invite your partner to visit your doctor with you to discuss these things.

If you're having problems with contractions, bleeding or complications, discuss it with your doctor.

Week 22

Age of Fetus — 20 Weeks

How Big Is Your Baby?

Your baby now weighs about 12.25 ounces (350g). The crown-to-rump length at this time is about 7.6 inches (19cm).

How Big Are You?

Your uterus is now about 0.8 inch (2cm) above your belly-button or almost 9 inches (22cm) from the pubic symphysis. At this point, you may feel "comfortably pregnant." Your enlarging abdomen is not too large—it doesn't get in your way very much. You're still able to bend over and to sit comfortably. Walking shouldn't be an effort. Morning sickness has probably passed, and you're feeling pretty good. It's kind of fun being pregnant now!

How Your Baby Is Growing and Developing

Your baby continues to grow. Its body is getting larger every day. As you can tell by looking at the illustration on page 209, your baby's eyelids and even the eyebrows are developed. Fingernails can also be seen.

Liver Function Organ systems in your baby are becoming specialized for their particular functions. The function of the liver in the fetus is different from that of an adult. Enzymes (chemicals) are made in an adult liver that are important in the function of the body. In the fetus, these enzymes are present but in lower amounts than compared to their levels after birth.

An important function of the liver is the breakdown and handling of bilirubin. *Bilirubin* is a breakdown product from blood cells. The life span of a fetal red blood cell is shorter than that of an adult. Because of this, more bilirubin is produced by the fetus than by an adult.

The fetal liver has a limited capacity to convert bilirubin and remove it from the fetal bloodstream. Removal of bilirubin is accomplished through the help of liver enzymes. Bilirubin passes from fetal blood in the placenta to your blood. If a baby is born prematurely, it may have trouble with bilirubin because the liver is too immature to get rid of bilirubin from its bloodstream.

A newborn baby with high bilirubin may exhibit *jaundice*. A baby with jaundice has a yellow tint to the skin and eyes. Jaundice is usually treated with phototherapy. Phototherapy uses light that penetrates the skin and destroys the bilirubin inside the baby.

The main cause of jaundice in a newborn is the transition from bilirubin being handled by the mother's system to the baby handling the bilirubin on its own. Jaundice is more likely to happen in an immature infant when the liver is not ready to take over this function.

Changes in You

Anemia in Pregnancy   Anemia is a common medical problem that occurs during pregnancy. If you suffer from anemia, its treatment is important to you and your baby. If you are anemic, you won't feel well during pregnancy. You'll be fatigued and tire easily. You may also experience dizziness.

There is a fine balance in your body between the production of blood cells that carry oxygen to the rest of your body and destruction of these cells. *Anemia* is the condition in

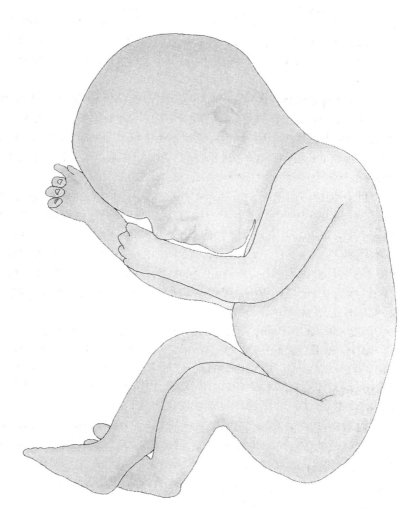

By the 22nd week of pregnancy (fetal age—20 weeks), your baby's eyelids and eyebrows are well developed. Fingernails have grown and now cover the fingertips.

which the number of red blood cells is low. If you have anemia, the quantity of your red blood cells is inadequate. You will have a hematocrit lower than 37; your hemoglobin will be lower than 12.

During pregnancy, the number of red blood cells in your bloodstream increases. The amount of plasma (the liquid part of the blood) also increases but at a higher rate. Your hematocrit is a measure of the percentage of the blood that is red blood cells.

A hematocrit determination is usually done at the first prenatal visit along with other lab work. It may be repeated once or twice during pregnancy. It is done more often if you are anemic.

Because the amount of plasma increases more than the cell part of the blood, the hematocrit may actually go down during pregnancy. This is called *physiologic anemia of pregnancy*. Your hematocrit drops to its lowest values around the middle of pregnancy (20 to 22 weeks). There is often a slight increase in the concentration of hemoglobin to plasma around the end of a normal pregnancy.

Pregnancy is a time of many changes in your blood system. Delivery is a time of blood loss. If you are anemic when you go into labor, you're at higher risk of needing a blood transfusion after your baby is born. Follow your doctor's advice about diet and supplementation if you suffer from anemia.

Iron-Deficiency Anemia One of the more common types of anemia during pregnancy is *iron-deficiency anemia*. During pregnancy, your baby uses some of the iron stores you have in your body. With iron-deficiency anemia, your body is able to make red blood cells, but there is not enough iron to raise your hematocrit or hemoglobin.

Iron is contained in most prenatal vitamins and can be taken as a supplement. If you are unable to take any prenatal vitamins, you may be given an iron supplement. If you take an iron supplement, it is usually given in the form of ferrous sulphate or ferrous gluconate, which is usually 300 to 350mg, taken 2 or 3 times a day. Iron is the most important supplement to take. It is required in almost all pregnancies.

Even with supplemental iron, some women still develop iron-deficiency anemia during pregnancy. Several factors may make a woman more likely to have this condition in pregnancy. These include the following:

+ Failure to take iron or to take a prenatal vitamin containing iron.
+ Bleeding during pregnancy.
+ Multiple fetuses
+ If you have had surgery in the past on your stomach or part of your small bowel, you may be unable to absorb an adequate amount of iron before pregnancy.
+ Antacid use may cause a decrease in absorption of iron, and more iron is lost through the gastrointestinal tract.
+ Poor dietary habits may increase iron-deficiency anemia.

The goal in treating iron-deficiency anemia is to increase the amount of iron the body takes in. Iron is poorly absorbed through the gastrointestinal tract and must be taken on a daily basis. It can be given in the form of an injection, but it's painful and may stain the skin.

The side effects of taking iron supplements include nausea and vomiting, with stomach upset. If this occurs, it may be necessary to decrease the amount of iron you take. Taking iron may also cause constipation.

If you cannot take an oral iron supplement, an increase in dietary iron from foods such as liver or spinach may help prevent anemia.

Sickle-Cell Anemia   For women who are black or dark-skinned, sickle-cell anemia can cause significant anemia during pregnancy. Anemia occurs in these cases because of the inability of the bone marrow, the part of the body that produces red blood cells, to keep up with the destruction of red blood cells in the body.

In sickle-cell anemia the red blood cells that are produced are abnormal. This may cause anemia or severe pain.

You may carry the trait for sickle-cell anemia without having the disease. You could possibly pass either to your infant. If you have sickle-cell anemia or carry the sickle-cell trait, tell your doctor.

The sickle-cell trait is easily detected in you by a blood test. Sickle-cell anemia can be diagnosed in your infant through the use of amniocentesis, discussed on page 157, or chorionic villus sampling, discussed on page 110.

Women with sickle-cell trait have shown an increase in the occurrence of pyelonephritis and bacteria in the urine during pregnancy. These women are also susceptible to sickle-cell anemia during pregnancy.

Women with sickle-cell anemia may have repeated episodes of pain, called *sickle crisis,* throughout their lifetime. This is pain in the abdomen or limbs, caused by the blockage of blood vessels by abnormal red blood cells. Episodes of pain may be severe and may require hospitalization for treatment with fluids and pain medication.

There is a new treatment for the pain of sickle-cell anemia. *Hydroxurea* has been proved effective as the treatment of the disease, but its use carries some risks. Because we do not have research data on long-term effects, pregnant women are advised *not* to use it.

Sickle-cell disease risks to a pregnant mother are those of painful sickle crisis, infections and even congestive heart failure. Risks to the fetus include a high incidence of miscarriage and stillbirth. This is estimated to be as high as 50%.

Thalassemia   Another type of anemia encountered less frequently is called *thalassemia.* This type of anemia occurs most often in Mediterranean populations. It is characterized by genetically determined underproduction of part of the globulin that makes up red blood cells. Anemia results from this underproduction.

If you have a family history of thalassemia or know you have thalassemia, discuss it with your doctor.

How Your Actions Affect Your Baby's Development

Lower-Back Pain   Lower-back pain is a common problem during pregnancy. As mentioned previously, it may be an indication of more serious problems, such as pyelonephritis or a kidney stone. However, almost every pregnant woman experiences back pain at some point in pregnancy. This includes mild to moderate pain and may increase as pregnancy progresses.

It's all right to take acetaminophen (Tylenol®) for back pain. Use heat on the area that is painful. If pain becomes constant or more severe, it's important to talk to your doctor about it.

Driving a Car   One question I am often asked is whether or not it's safe to drive a car during pregnancy. The answer is "Yes." But it may become more uncomfortable for you to get in and out of a car as your pregnancy progresses. It should not interfere with your ability to drive.

As discussed on pages 126-128, it's important for you to use a seat belt and shoulder harness during pregnancy, as well as other times. There is no reason not to drive while you're pregnant if your pregnancy is normal and you feel OK.

Fluid Intake   A woman often wants to know whether she should consume more fluid during pregnancy and how much. Fluid intake during pregnancy is important. You may feel better if you drink more fluid than you normally do.

Many women who suffer with headaches and various other problems during pregnancy find increasing their water intake helps resolve some of their symptoms.

It's best to avoid fluids that contain a lot of calories, such as soda. Drink plain water or water with a little fruit juice added for flavor. You'll find it can be very refreshing and tasty.

As I've already discussed, one of the major changes occurring in your body is the changes in your bloodstream.

Your blood volume increases 50% or more. To keep up with this change in your blood volume, it's important to take in adequate amounts of liquid.

Some women have found it helps to have a glass of water available all day. Decrease your intake in the early evening—you don't want to be up all night going to the bathroom! However, even if you decrease your fluid intake at night, you may find you're going to the bathroom a lot anyway. This is a normal part of pregnancy; there's very little you can do about it.

You Should also Know

Do You Have Hemorrhoids?   Hemorrhoids are a very common problem during and/or following pregnancy. Hemorrhoids are dilated blood vessels around the area of the anus or up inside the anus. They are caused during pregnancy by the increase in blood flow around the area of the uterus and the pelvis because of the weight of the uterus.

Usually hemorrhoids get worse toward the end of pregnancy. They may also get worse with each succeeding pregnancy.

Treatment of hemorrhoids includes avoiding constipation by eating adequate amounts of fiber and drinking lots of fluid. Hemorrhoids may also be avoided through the use of stool softeners. Other measures may include sitz baths or suppository medications, which can be bought without a prescription. Very rarely, hemorrhoids are treated during pregnancy with surgery.

After pregnancy, hemorrhoids usually improve. But they may not go away completely. The methods mentioned above will help in their treatment even when your pregnancy is over.

If you experience a great deal of pain with hemorrhoids, discuss it with your doctor. He or she will know what treatment method is best for you.

Toxic Streptococcus A

A great deal of press has been given to a "new," toxic form of strep A that can cause severe damage to those who suffer from it. Unlike the far less dangerous strep A, this toxic form usually starts in a cut in the skin, not as a sore throat. The strep A bacteria can get in through a very small scratch, then turn red and become swollen, painful and infected *very* quickly. Along with the infected scratch, you also experience flu-like symptoms.

The disease spreads quite rapidly and can soon involve the entire body. There are some warning signs to help you prevent a full-fledged strep-A problem.

✦ **Fever above 102F (38.9C)**   It could be no more serious than flu, but when you have a fever that high, seek medical attention, especially when you are pregnant.

✦ **An inflamed cut**   A cut or scratch that turns red and becomes infected while you have flu-like symptoms may signal strep A infection. Seek medical care immediately.

✦ **Unusually cold extremities**   Coldness and numbness in the feet, legs, hands and arms with the above symptoms.

Preventive treatment   Any time you cut or scratch yourself, clean the affected area with soap and water, alcohol or hydrogen peroxide. All are safe to use during pregnancy. After careful washing, apply triple antibiotic cream or ointment (available over the counter) to the area, and put a light bandage over it, if necessary. Keep the area clean, and reapply antibiotic ointment, as needed.

Week 23

Age of Fetus — 21 Weeks

How Big Is Your Baby?

By this week, your baby weighs almost 1 pound (455g)! Its crown-to-rump length is 8 inches (20cm). Your baby is about the size of a small doll.

How Big Are You?

Your uterus extends about 1.5 inches (3.75cm) above your bellybutton or about 9.2 inches (23cm) from the pubic symphysis. The changes in your abdomen are progressing slowly, but you definitely have a round appearance now. Your weight gain should be between 12 and 15 pounds.

How Your Baby Is Growing and Developing

Your baby is continuing to grow larger. Its body is getting more plump, but its skin is still fairly wrinkled because of a lack of subcutaneous fat. See the illustration on page 219. Lanugo hair on the body occasionally turns darker at this time.

At this point, the face and body of the baby assume more of the appearance of an infant at birth.

Pancreas Function The pancreas is developing in your baby. It is important in hormone production, particularly insulin production. Insulin is necessary for metabolizing sugar.

When the fetus is exposed to high blood-sugar levels, called *hyperglycemia,* the fetal pancreas is able to respond by increasing the plasma- or blood-insulin level. Insulin has been identified in a fetus in its pancreas as early as 9 weeks of pregnancy. Plasma insulin has been detectible as early as 12 weeks of pregnancy.

Insulin levels are found to be high in the blood of babies born to diabetic mothers. That is one reason your doctor may monitor you closely for diabetes.

Changes in You

You will find your growth increases as your uterus continues to enlarge. Friends may tell you you're either too big or too small. They may say they think you must be carrying twins because you're so large. Or they may say you're too small for how far along you think you are. If these things concern you, discuss them with your doctor.

Your doctor will measure you at every visit after this point. He or she is watching for changes in your weight gain and in the size of your uterus. You must remember women and babies are different sizes and grow at different rates. What's important is the continual change and continual growth.

As your baby gets larger, the placenta gets larger. There is also an increase in the amount of amniotic fluid.

Loss of Fluid As your pregnancy grows, your uterus grows larger and gets heavier. It lies directly behind the bladder, in front of the rectum and the sigmoid colon, which is part of the bowel.

The uterus sits on top of the bladder. As it increases in size, it can put a great deal of pressure on your bladder. You may notice times when your underwear is wet or your clothing is damp. You may be uncertain as to whether or not you have lost urine or if you are leaking amniotic fluid. It may be very difficult for you to tell the difference between the two. When your membranes rupture, you usually

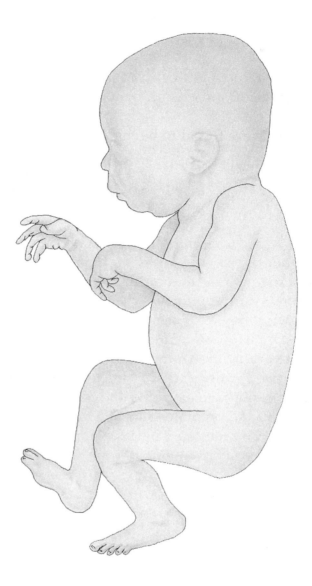

By the 22nd week of pregnancy (fetal age—20 weeks), your baby's eyelids and eyebrows are well developed. Fingernails have grown and now cover the fingertips.

experience a gush of fluid or a continual leaking from inside of the vagina. If you experience this, call your doctor *immediately!*

Loss of amniotic fluid or rupture of your membranes is *very* important. It should not occur at this early point of pregnancy.

Urinary-Tract Infections The chance of a urinary-tract infection increases during pregnancy because of changes in your urinary tract. The uterus sits directly on top of the bladder and on the tubes leading from the kidneys to the bladder, called *ureters.*

Urinary-tract infections may cause you to lose urine more frequently while you're pregnant. A urinary-tract infection is the most common problem involving your bladder or kidneys during pregnancy.

Your doctor may do a urinalysis and culture of the urine at your first prenatal visit. He or she may check the urine on subsequent visits to look for infection.

Symptoms of a urinary-tract infection include frequent urination, burning urination and the feeling as though you need to urinate and nothing will come out. A severe urinary-tract infection can even cause blood to appear in the urine.

If you think you have a bladder infection, it's possible to do a culture of the urine to look for the specific bacteria causing the infection. Call your doctor if you have any problems.

Pyelonephritis A more serious problem resulting from bladder infections is *pyelonephritis* (kidney infection). This type of infection occurs in 1 to 2% of all pregnant women. Most often, the right kidney is affected.

Symptoms include frequent urination, burning urination, the feeling as though you need to urinate and nothing will come out, high fever, chills and back pain. Pyelonephritis may require hospitalization and treatment with intravenous antibiotics.

✧

If you have pyelonephritis or recurrent bladder infections during pregnancy, it may be necessary for you to take antibiotics during your entire pregnancy to prevent recurrent infections.

Kidney Stones   Another problem involving the kidneys and bladder is kidney stones or urinary calculi. They occur about once in every 1,500 pregnancies. Kidney stones cause severe pain in the back or lower abdomen. They may also be associated with blood in the urine.

A kidney stone during pregnancy can usually be treated with pain medication and by drinking lots of fluid. In this way, the stone may be passed without having to be removed surgically or with lithotripsy (an ultrasound treatment).

Emotional Changes Continue   Do you find your mood swings are worse? Are you still crying easily? Do you wonder if you'll ever be in control again?

Don't worry. These emotions are very typical at this point in your pregnancy. Most believe they occur from the hormonal changes that continue during pregnancy.

There is little you can do about these periods of moodiness. If you think your partner or others are suffering from your emotional outbursts, talk about it with them. Explain that these feelings are very common in pregnant women. Ask them to be understanding. Then relax, and try not to get upset about being emotional. It's a very normal part of being pregnant.

How Your Actions Affect Your Baby's Development

Diabetes in Pregnancy   Diabetes was once a very serious problem during pregnancy. It continues to be an important complication of pregnancy. But today most diabetic women may be able to go through pregnancy safely with proper medical care, good nutrition and adherence to their doctor's instructions.

✧

Diabetes is a chronic metabolic disorder characterized by a relative lack or an absolute lack of insulin in the bloodstream. *Insulin* is important in metabolizing sugar and in transporting sugar to the cells. If you do not have insulin, the result is high blood sugar, called *hyperglycemia,* and high sugar content in your urine.

The condition of diabetes can cause several medical problems. These include kidney problems, eye problems and other blood or vascular problems, such as atherosclerosis or myocardial infarction. These can be serious for you and your baby.

Before insulin was available, it was unusual for a diabetic woman to get pregnant. It was likely to be very serious for both the mother and baby. A maternal mortality rate of 25 to 30% and a perinatal mortality rate of 50% or more were common in the early 1900s. With the discovery of insulin and use of various types of monitoring in the fetus, such as ultrasound and fetal heart-rate monitoring, it is uncommon to have a severe problem today. The fetal survival rate is good.

During pregnancy, the fetus continually removes sugar and amino acids from your circulation. Placental hormones, human placental lactogen (HPL), estrogen, progesterone and increases in cortisol also exert an effect on insulin in your bloodstream. The result can be a problem with handling blood sugar.

After a meal, blood sugar is high. If you have problems, insulin levels elevate but are not high enough to respond to the increased amount of blood sugar.

At the beginning of pregnancy, the developing fetus uses up maternal glucose and amino acids. In the second half of pregnancy, placental hormones increase the need for insulin in the mother.

Pregnancy is well known for its tendency to reveal those women who are predisposed to diabetes. Women who have trouble with elevated blood sugars during pregnancy are found to have a higher incidence of diabetes in later life.

❖

Symptoms of diabetes include:

+ An increase in urination.
+ Blurred vision.
+ Weight loss.
+ Dizziness.
+ Increased hunger.

It may be necessary to do blood tests to diagnose diabetes during pregnancy. In some areas, this testing is done routinely on every pregnant woman.

The diagnosis of diabetes is important for the health of both mother and child. Even today, the maternal mortality rate among pregnant diabetic women is about 20 times higher than the general population. Problems with kidneys or eyes or other complications of diabetes can be accelerated by pregnancy. They can become significant problems.

For the baby, the miscarriage rate is suggested to be increased slightly above the normal amount for pregnant women. There can also be an increase of major abnormalities at the time of birth—3 to 6%—double that for a normal delivery. The most common fetal abnormalities seen with maternal diabetes are heart problems, genitourinary problems, such as absence of kidneys, and gastrointestinal problems.

These problems can be avoided by carefully monitoring blood sugar. In most women who have diabetes during pregnancy, treatment consists of altering the diet.

If you have a history of diabetes or know members of your family have had diabetes in the past, tell your doctor. He or she will want to make a decision on what course of action is best for you.

Sodium Intake It's wise to avoid foods that contain a large amount of salt, such as salted nuts, potato chips, pickles and canned and processed foods. *Sodium* is really the culprit. Most salty foods contain large amounts of sodium. Taking in an excess amount of sodium may make you

❖

retain water. This can cause you to swell and bloat more during pregnancy.

For your own benefit, keep your consumption of sodium to under 3g (3000mg) a day. It may help reduce fluid retention.

If you want to watch your sodium intake during pregnancy, read labels. Food labels list the amount of sodium in a serving. Some books contain sodium content of foods that have no labels, such as fast foods. Check them out. You'd be surprised how many grams of sodium a fast-food hamburger contains, not to mention French fries!

Look at the chart of some foods and their sodium content so you can see foods that contain sodium do *not* always taste salty. Read labels, and check other available information before you eat!

Sodium Content of Various Foods		
Food	Serving Size	Sodium Content (mg)
American cheese	1 slice	322
Asparagus	14.5-oz. can	970
Big Mac hamburger	1 regular	963
Chicken a la king	1 cup	760
Cola	8 oz.	16
Cottage cheese	1 cup	580
Dill pickle	1 medium	928
Flounder	3 oz.	201
Gelatin, sweet	3 oz.	270
Ham, baked	3 oz.	770
Honeydew melon	1/2	90
Lima beans	8.5-oz. can	1070
Lobster	1 cup	305
Oatmeal	1 cup	523
Potato chips	20 regular	400
Salt	1 teaspoon	1938

✧

You Should also Know

Are Microwave Ovens Safe?   A common concern many women have is about the safety of being exposed to radiation from a microwave oven. Microwave ovens are very helpful in the preparation of meals for a busy woman and for a working mother. However, we don't know if there is danger to you if you use a microwave oven during pregnancy. More research is required.

Initial research has indicated tissues developing in the body, which would include the human fetus, may be particularly sensitive to the effects of microwaves. A microwave oven heats up tissues from the inside.

Follow the directions provided with your microwave oven. It's probably a good idea not to stand next to or directly in front of the microwave oven while it is in use.

Week 24

Age of Fetus — 22 Weeks

How Big Is Your Baby?

By this week, your baby weighs about 1.2 pounds (530g). Its crown-to-rump length is about 8.4 inches (21cm).

How Big Are You?

Your uterus is now about 1.5 to 2 inches (3.8 to 5.1cm) above the umbilicus. It measures almost 10 inches (24cm) above the pubic symphysis. You are definitely getting bigger and rounder!

How Your Baby Is Growing and Developing

Your baby is filling out. Its face and body look more like that of an infant at the time of birth. Although it weighs a little over 1 pound at this point, it is still small.

The Role of the Amniotic Sac   The baby rests inside the amniotic sac in the amniotic fluid. See the illustration on page 229. The amniotic fluid has several important functions.

+ It provides an environment in which the baby can easily move.
+ It provides a cushion for the fetus against injury.
+ Amniotic fluid regulates temperature for the baby.
+ It provides a way of assessing the health and maturity of the baby.

By about the 12th day after fertilization, there is an early beginning of the amniotic cavity where the fetus will grow and develop during pregnancy.

❖

Amniotic Fluid The amniotic fluid increases rapidly to an average volume of 1.5 ounces (50ml) by 12 weeks pregnancy and to 12 ounces (400ml) at midpregnancy. Following the 24th week of pregnancy, the volume of amniotic fluid increases as your due date approaches. There is a maximum of about 2 pints (1 liter) of fluid at 36 to 38 weeks gestation.

The composition of the amniotic fluid changes during pregnancy. During the first half of pregnancy, amniotic fluid is very similar to maternal plasma (the fluid in blood without blood cells), except it has a much lower protein content. As pregnancy advances, chemicals called *phospholipids* appear in the amniotic fluid. Phospholipids are made in the fetal lungs and come from the baby in the amniotic fluid.

Amniotic fluid also contains old fetal blood cells, lanugo hair and vernix. As pregnancy advances, fetal urine makes an increasingly important contribution to the amount of amniotic fluid.

The fetus swallows amniotic fluid during much of pregnancy. If it is unable to swallow amniotic fluid, you will have a condition of excess amniotic fluid. This condition is called *hydramnios* or *polyhydramnios*. On the other hand, when urination does not occur, such as in the case of absence of the kidneys, the volume of amniotic fluid surrounding the fetus may be very small. This is called *oligohydramnios*.

Amniotic fluid is important in providing the fetus space to move and to allow the fetus to grow. In cases in which there is an inadequate amount of amniotic fluid, such as those mentioned above, the fetus usually showed decreased growth.

Changes in You

An Incompetent Cervix An important problem during pregnancy is an *incompetent cervix*. The term is applied to women who have had a painless dilatation of the cervix, which occurs prematurely. It usually results in delivery of a premature baby.

Uterus

Umbilical cord

Leg

Arm

Head

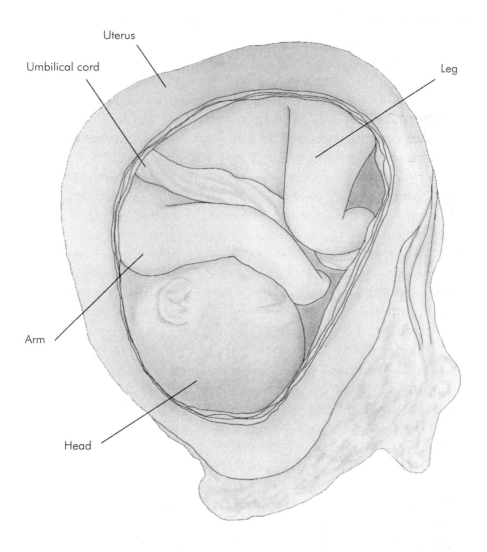

The fetus doesn't appear to have a great deal of room to move in the uterus by the 24th week. As the weeks pass, space gets even tighter!

The dilatation or stretching of the cervix is unnoticed by the woman until the baby is delivering. Often dilatation occurs and membranes rupture without any warning to the pregnant woman. Diagnosis of the problem is usually made *after* one or more deliveries of a premature infant without any pain before delivery.

The cause of cervical incompetence is usually unknown. Some medical researchers believe it occurs because of previous trauma to the cervix, such as with dilatation and curettage (D&C) for an abortion or a spontaneous miscarriage. It may also occur after conization of the cervix or other types of surgery performed on the cervix.

Usually this type of cervical dilatation does not occur before the 16th week of pregnancy. Before this time, the products of conception are not sufficiently large to cause the cervix to dilate and thin out.

Loss of a pregnancy from an incompetent cervix is completely different from a spontaneous abortion. A spontaneous abortion during the first trimester is extremely common. Incompetent cervix is a relatively rare complication this early in pregnancy.

Treatment for an incompetent cervix is usually surgical. The weak cervix is reinforced with a suture that sews the cervix shut. There are two names for this type of suturing. Most commonly used is a *McDonald suture* or a *McDonald cerclage*. The other type, a *Shirodkar*, is done less frequently today.

If this is your first pregnancy, there is no way for you to know about the possibility of an incompetent cervix. If you have had problems in the past or have had premature deliveries and have been told you might have an incompetent cervix, share this important information with your doctor.

How Your Actions Affect Your Baby's Development

Eating Out During Pregnancy   A common concern many pregnant women have is related to eating out. They want to know if they should avoid certain foods or types of food, such as Mexican, Vietnamese, Thai or Greek food. They are concerned that spicy foods could be harmful to their baby or their pregnancy.

It's OK to eat out. However, you may find there are certain foods that agree with you and certain foods that don't agree with you. If you know you don't do well eating Mexican food, it doesn't make a lot of sense to go out and eat Mexican food frequently during your pregnancy.

If you're trying to be careful about the foods you eat, don't eat large meals at a restaurant on a regular basis. It's all right to eat out occasionally; it may give you a break.

The best types of food to eat are usually those you tolerate well at home. Fish, fresh vegetables and salads are usually tolerated best. Restaurants that feature spicy foods or unusual cuisine, such as salty foods, may cause you more difficulty. You may even notice an increase in weight from water retention after visiting one of these restaurants.

During pregnancy avoid restaurants that serve highly salted foods, foods high in sodium or foods loaded with calories and/or fat, such as gravies, fried foods and rich desserts. It's almost impossible to control your calorie intake at specialty restaurants.

Avoid fast food and junk food when you eat out. Don't eat foods you have found difficult to digest during pregnancy.

Overeating and eating before going to bed are major causes of heartburn, which can become extremely severe after eating out. At this point, you may be happier with 5 to 6 smaller meals a day rather than 3 regular or large meals.

You Should also Know

When You're Feeling "Under the Weather" It is possible for you to have diarrhea during pregnancy as well as viral infections, such as the flu. These types of problems can raise many concerns for you.

+ What can you do when you feel ill?
+ What medication or treatment is acceptable?
+ If you're sick, should you take your prenatal vitamins?
+ If you're sick and are unable to eat your usual diet, what should you do?

If you become sick during pregnancy, don't hesitate to call the office. Talk to your doctor and get his or her advice about a plan of action. He or she will be able to advise you about what medications you may be able to take to help you feel better. Even if it's only a cold or the flu, your doctor wants to know you're feeling ill. If any further measures are needed, your doctor will recommend them.

Is there anything you can do to help yourself? There are some things you can do. One of the best things you can do if you have diarrhea or a possible viral infection is to increase your fluid intake. Drink a lot of water, juice and other clear fluids, such as broth. You may find a bland diet without solid food helps you feel a little better.

If you're off your regular diet for a few days, it won't be harmful to you or your baby. It *is* important for you to drink plenty of fluids. This will help correct the diarrhea. Solid foods may be difficult for your gastrointestinal tract to handle. They can make diarrhea more of a problem. Milk products may also make diarrhea worse.

If diarrhea continues beyond 24 hours, call your doctor. Discuss with him or her which medications you can take for your diarrhea during pregnancy. *Don't* take any medication without consulting your doctor first. Usually a viral illness with diarrhea is a short-term problem and won't last more than a few days. It may be necessary to stay home from work or rest in bed until you feel better.

Week 25

Age of Fetus — 23 Weeks

How Big Is Your Baby?

Your baby now weighs about 1.5 pounds (700g). Its crown-to-rump length is about 8.8 inches (22cm). These are average lengths and weights. They can vary a great deal from one baby to another and from one pregnancy to another.

How Big Are You?

Look at the illustration on page 235. By this 25th week of pregnancy, your uterus has grown quite a bit. When you look at a side view, it's obvious you're getting bigger.

The measurement from the pubic symphysis to the top of your uterus is about 10 inches (25cm). If you saw your doctor when you were 20 or 21 weeks pregnant, you have probably grown about 1.5 inches (4cm). At this point, your uterus is about the size of a soccer ball.

The top of the uterus is about halfway between your bellybutton and the lower part of your sternum. (The sternum is the bone between your breasts where the ribs come together in the middle.)

How Your Baby Is Growing and Developing

Survival of a Premature Baby It may be hard to believe, but if your baby were delivered at this time, it would have a chance of surviving. During the past few years, some of the greatest advances in medicine have been in the care of the premature baby. No one wants a baby to deliver this early, but with new treatment methods, such as ventilators, monitors and medication, a baby would have a chance of living if born at this time.

The baby weighs under 2 pounds and is extremely small. Survival is very difficult for an infant delivered this early. The baby would probably have to spend several months in the hospital, with risks of infection and other possible complications.

Is It a Boy? Is It a Girl? One of the most common questions asked of obstetricians is what is the sex of the baby that is being carried. Without tests being performed, such as ultrasound or amniocentesis, a baby's sex cannot be reliably determined. Amniocentesis can reveal the sex of the baby by chromosome study. Ultrasound examination can also be used to determine the sex of the baby, but it may be inaccurate. Don't get your heart set on a particular sex if ultrasound is used.

Sex of a baby is determined by the sperm that reaches and fertilizes the egg. Your baby's sex was determined 23 weeks ago by the sperm that fertilized the egg.

The ratio of boy babies to girl babies is about 106 males to every 100 females. Why this ratio is not 100 males for every 100 females is unknown.

Sometimes a woman will ask her doctor to guess whether or not she is carrying a boy or girl based on the heartbeat. Some believe how fast the baby's heart beats can indicate its sex. A normal heart rate for a baby is from 120 to 160 beats a minute. This is a very fast rate. Your normal pulse rate is probably between 60 and 80. Some people believe a fast heartbeat indicates a girl, and a slower heartbeat indicates a boy. Unfortunately, this is lacking in scientific substance. Don't pressure your doctor to guess based on this method because it will only be a guess.

A more reliable source might be a mother, mother-in-law or someone who can look at you and tell by how you're carrying the baby whether or not it is a boy or girl. Although I

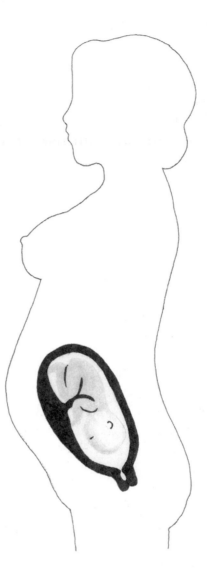

Comparative size of the uterus at 25 weeks of pregnancy (fetal age—23 weeks). The uterus can be felt about 2 inches (5cm) above your umbilicus (bellybutton).

❖

make this statement with my tongue in my cheek, many people believe it's true. Some people claim they have never been wrong about guessing or predicting the sex of a baby before its birth. Again, there is no basis in scientific fact for this.

Without certain tests, your doctor cannot accurately predict the sex of your child. So don't pressure him or her about it. Your doctor is more concerned about your health and well-being and that of your baby. He or she will concentrate on making sure you and your baby, whether it's a boy or girl, are progressing through pregnancy safely and that you both get through pregnancy, labor and delivery in good health.

Changes in You

Your Growing Abdomen   Beginning around week 20 or 21, your doctor began measuring you. You will be measured on every visit after that. You may notice in addition to your uterus growing upward from your umbilicus you are also getting bigger on the sides of your abdomen.

Your doctor does not measure you around your waist or around your sides. Many women carry their pregnancies on their sides or low in their abdomen. This may make you look different than a pregnant friend just by the appearance of the size of your abdomen. Don't be concerned; it's just a variation from one person to another.

Thyroid Disease   Thyroid problems and/or thyroid disease are important in pregnancy. Thyroid hormone is made in the thyroid gland, which is in the front part of your neck right over the area of your trachea. This hormone affects your entire body. It is very important in your metabolism, and it may be important in your ability to get pregnant. Often a woman who is having difficulty getting pregnant will have a thyroid-hormone test done to see if the level of this hormone is normal.

✧

Thyroid-hormone levels may be high or low. High levels of thyroid are called *hyperthyroidism;* low levels of thyroid are called *hypothyroidism.* Women who have a history of miscarriage or premature delivery or who have problems around the time of delivery may have problems with their thyroid-hormone levels.

Symptoms of thyroid disease may be hidden by pregnancy. Or you may experience changes during pregnancy that may cause you and your doctor to believe the thyroid is not functioning properly, such as the thyroid enlarging, changes in your pulse, redness of the palms and warm, moist palms. Because thyroid hormone levels can change during pregnancy *(because* of pregnancy), your doctor must be careful interpreting lab results about this hormone while you're pregnant.

The thyroid is tested primarily by blood tests. These tests measure the amount of thyroid hormone produced. They also measure levels of another hormone, *thyroid stimulating hormone (TSH),* which is made in the base of the brain. Blood tests usually include measurement of these hormones; tests may be called a *thyroid panel.* Another test, an X-ray study of the thyroid, called a *radioactive iodine scan,* should *not* be done during pregnancy.

If your thyroid hormone level is low and you have hypothyroidism, thyroid replacement is given. The medication for thyroid replacement is thyroxin. It is believed to be safe during pregnancy. The level may need to be checked during pregnancy with a blood test to make sure you are receiving enough thyroid hormone.

If you have hyperthyroidism, the medication used for treatment is propylthiouracil. This medication does pass through the placenta to the baby. Your doctor will prescribe the lowest possible amount to reduce risk to your baby. Blood testing during pregnancy is necessary to monitor the amount of medication needed.

Another medication used for hyperthyroidism is iodide. This medication should be *avoided* during pregnancy

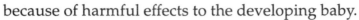

because of harmful effects to the developing baby.

After delivery, it's important to test the baby and watch for signs of thyroid problems related to the medications given to you during pregnancy.

If you have a past history of problems with your thyroid, if you are taking medication or if you have taken medication in the past for your thyroid, tell your doctor. Talk with him or her about the possibility of problems during pregnancy.

How Your Actions Affect Your Baby's Development

Systemic Lupus Erythematosus (SLE) Some women have conditions before pregnancy that require medication for the rest of their lives. They are often concerned about the effects medication may have on their developing babies. One such condition is systemic lupus erythematosus (SLE).

Many young women have this condition today, and they must take steroids to control the problem. They want to know if the medication they take can harm their baby. Should they continue to take steroids during pregnancy?

Lupus is a disease of unknown cause. Women who have lupus have a large number of antibodies in their bloodstream. (Women have lupus much more frequently than men—about 9 women to every man.) The reason these antibodies are directed toward the woman's own tissues is not understood at this time.

Lupus occurs most often in young or middle-aged women. The diagnosis of SLE is made through blood tests. These blood tests look for antibodies in the body. Because antibodies are directed against the woman's own body, they are called *autoantibodies* or *cell antibodies*. The blood tests done for lupus are a lupus antibody test and/or an anti-nuclear antibody test.

Antibodies can be directed to various organs in the body and may actually cause damage to them. The organs that are affected include the joints, skin, kidneys, muscles,

✧

lungs, the brain and the central nervous system. The most common symptom of lupus is joint pain, which is often mistaken for arthritis. Other symptoms or problems include lesions, rashes or sores on the skin, fever, kidney problems and hypertension.

There is no cure for lupus. Systemic lupus erythematosus is generally unaffected by pregnancy. However, spontaneous abortion or miscarriage, premature delivery and complications around the time of delivery are slightly increased in the woman who has lupus. If there was kidney involvement and kidney damage during times of disease activity, you must be on the lookout for kidney problems during pregnancy.

Steroids, short for *corticosteroids*, are generally prescribed for treatment of lupus. The primary medication used is prednisone. It is prescribed on a daily basis. It may be unnecessary to take prednisone every day, but if complications from the lupus occur during pregnancy, it may be necessary to take prednisone daily.

Many studies have been done on the safety of prednisone during pregnancy. It has been found to be safe. If you take prednisone when you become pregnant, *don't* stop taking it. Call your doctor immediately! It's important for you to talk to your doctor early if you have lupus or if you have had treatment for the problem in the past.

Other medications are used when a woman is not pregnant. These include many anti-inflammatory medications, such as aspirin. It is best to avoid anti-inflammatory medications during pregnancy.

You Should also Know

Sugar in Your Urine   A common concern of some women during pregnancy is sugar in the urine. It is common for normal, pregnant, non-diabetic women to have a small amount of sugar in their urine. This occurs because of the changes in the sugar levels and how sugar is handled in the kidneys.

❖

Your kidneys control the amount of sugar in your system. If there is excess sugar, you will lose it through the urine. Sugar in the urine is called *glucosuria*. It is a common occurrence during pregnancy, particularly in the second and third trimesters of pregnancy.

Many doctors test every pregnant woman for diabetes. This is usually done around the end of the second trimester. Testing is particularly important if there is a history of diabetes in your family. The blood tests to diagnose diabetes are called a *fasting blood sugar* and a *glucose-tolerance test (GTT)*.

For a fasting-blood-sugar test, you eat in the evening the night before the test. In the morning, before breakfast, you go to the lab and have the blood test done. A normal result indicates the unlikelihood of diabetes. An abnormal result is a high level of sugar in the blood, which needs further study.

Further study involves a glucose-tolerance test. For a glucose-tolerance test, you again fast overnight. In the morning at the lab, you are given a solution to drink that has a measured amount of sugar in it. It is similar to a bottle of soda pop but doesn't taste as good.

Before drinking the sugar, a fasting-blood-sugar test is done. After you drink the solution, blood is drawn at predetermined intervals. Blood is usually drawn at 30 minutes, 1 hour and 2 hours and sometimes even 3 hours. Drawing the blood at intervals gives an indication of how your body handles sugar.

About 2% of all pregnant women develop a mild form of diabetes called *gestational diabetes* or *pregnancy diabetes*. The chance of this happening increases as a woman gets older. Gestational diabetes usually disappears after the baby is born. During pregnancy, it is usually managed with diet.

Week 26

Age of Fetus — 24 Weeks

How Big Is Your Baby?

Your baby now weighs almost 2 pounds (910g). By this week, its crown-to-rump length is around 9.2 inches (23cm). See the illustration on page 243. Your baby is growing rapidly and beginning to put on weight.

How Big Are You?

The measurement of your uterus is about 2.5 inches (6cm) above your bellybutton or nearly 10.5 inches (26cm) from your pubic symphysis. During this second half of pregnancy, you will grow about 0.4 inch (1cm) each week. If you have been following a nutritious, balanced meal plan, your weight gain is probably between 16 and 22 pounds (7.2 to 9.9kg).

How Your Baby Is Growing and Developing

By now you have heard your baby's heartbeat at several visits. You have probably gotten used to hearing a very fast rate. The normal fetal heartbeat is 120 to 160 beats a minute. Listening to your developing baby's heart beat is very reassuring.

◇

Heart Arrhythmia When listening to your baby's heartbeat during pregnancy, you may be startled to hear a skipped beat. An irregular heartbeat is called an *arrhythmia.* This is best described by regular pulsing or pounding with a skipped beat or a missed heartbeat. Arrhythmias in a fetus are not unusual.

An arrhythmia in your baby's heartbeat is not necessarily a reason for alarm or concern. One possible explanation of an irregular heartbeat is the equipment you are using to listen to the heartbeat may be faulty or may have some other problem transmitting the sound.

When an arrhythmia is detected during pregnancy (and it's confirmed the equipment is working properly), it may be a reason for consultation with an ultrasound specialist or a perinatologist.

Arrhythmias are not usually serious in a fetus before birth; many disappear after the baby is delivered. However, you may feel better consulting with someone to determine whether or not a fetal heart arrhythmia is something to be concerned about.

There are many causes of fetal arrhythmias. An arrhythmia may occur as the heart grows and develops. As the heart matures, the arrhythmia may disappear. It may also occur in the fetus of a pregnant woman who has lupus.

If an arrhythmia is discovered *before* labor and delivery, you may require fetal heart-rate monitoring during labor. This is discussed on page 331.

When an arrhythmia is detected *during* labor, it may be desirable to have a pediatrician present at the time of delivery. He or she will make sure the baby is all right and is treated right away if any problem exists.

Changes in You

You are getting bigger as the uterus, placenta and baby grow larger. Some discomforts, such as back pain, pressure in your pelvis, leg cramps and headaches, may occur more frequently.

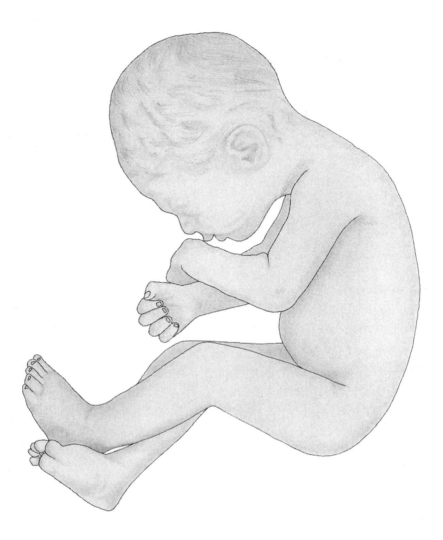

By this week, your baby weighs about 2 pounds (910g). It is now putting on some weight and filling out.

❖

Don't be discouraged. You are approaching the end of the second trimester. Two-thirds of the pregnancy is behind you with only a third remaining.

How Your Actions Affect Your Baby's Development

Seizures A history of seizures—before pregnancy, during a previous pregnancy or during this pregnancy—is information you must share with your doctor. Another term for seizure is *convulsion.*

Seizures can and usually do occur without any warning. The serious nature of a seizure is that it indicates an abnormal condition related to the nervous system, particularly the brain. Seizures may even threaten a person's life. During a seizure, a person often loses body control. The serious nature of this problem during pregnancy is compounded because of the concern about safety of the baby.

Many different types of seizures have been described. Generalized convulsions or seizures involving the entire body are called *grand mal seizures.* A grand mal seizure begins with the sudden loss of consciousness. The person then usually falls to the ground. There are often movements of the arms and legs and sometimes loss of urine or stool at the same time. Following a seizure, the person may be in a state of recovery, called the *post-ictal state,* which may last for several minutes. As the coma passes, there can be mental confusion, headache and drowsiness.

Another type of seizure is a *petit mal seizure.* This type of seizure also comes without warning. It is noted for its short nature and only minimal movement of the arms or legs. It usually consists of a brief loss of consciousness that lasts only a few seconds. Other types of seizures can occur and are not within the realm of this book.

If you have never had a problem with seizures before, a short episode of dizziness or lightheadedness is *not* usually a "seizure." Seizures are usually diagnosed by someone observing the seizure and noting the symptoms previously

❖

mentioned. An electroencephalogram (EEG) may be needed to diagnose a seizure. On page 293, seizures (eclampsia) are discussed.

Medication to Control Seizures   If you take medication for seizure control or prevention, share this important information with your doctor at the beginning of pregnancy. Medication can be taken during pregnancy for seizure control, however some medications are safer than others.

For example, Dilantin® can cause birth defects in a baby, which include facial problems, microcephaly (a small head) and developmental delay. Other medications are used during pregnancy for seizure prevention. One of the more common is phenobarbital.

Seizures, either during pregnancy or at any other time, can be a serious problem. They require serious discussion with your doctor and increased monitoring during pregnancy. If you have any questions or concerns about a history of possible seizures, it's important to notify your doctor of the problem and discuss it with him or her, preferably before the pregnancy.

You Should also Know

Feeling Your Baby Move   The movement of your baby is usually a very reassuring thing and one that pregnant women enjoy. Unfortunately, it is one your partner can enjoy only by feeling your abdomen as the baby moves.

Women often ask about how often the baby should move. They want to know if they should be concerned if the baby moves too much or doesn't move enough.

These are hard questions to answer because your sensation is different from that of another woman's. And the movement of each baby may be different. It is usually more assuring to have a baby that moves frequently. But it isn't unusual for a baby to have quiet times when there is not as much activity.

✧

If you've had a busy day and have been on the go, you may not have noticed the baby move because you've been active and busy. It may help to lie on your side and notice whether the baby is moving or if it is still. Many women report their baby is much more active at night. This may keep you awake, making it hard to sleep.

There is reassurance that comes from movement of the baby. If your baby is quiet and not as active as what seems normal or what you have expected, discuss it with your doctor. You can always visit your doctor to hear the baby's heartbeat if it hasn't been moving in its usual pattern.

In most instances, there is nothing to worry about. But you can be reassured by being able to hear the baby's heartbeat if you are concerned.

Pain Under Your Ribs   Some women complain of pain up under their ribs and in their lower abdomen when their baby moves. Is this normal?

This type of pain isn't an unusual problem, but it may cause enough pain to concern you. The movement of the baby by now has increased to a point where you will probably feel it every day. These movements are getting stronger and harder.

At the same time, your uterus is getting larger and putting more pressure on all your organs. Your growing, expanding pregnancy presses on the small bowel, bladder and rectum.

There is little or nothing you can do about the pain or pressure you feel from the baby's movement. The best thing to do is to lie on your side and rest. This will help take the pressure off the area that is hurting you. If you're feeling pressure up under your right ribs, lie on your left side.

If the pressure is more than pressure and it really *is* pain, don't ignore it. This is something you need to discuss with your doctor. In most cases, it isn't a serious problem. Reassurance can often be found by discussing it with your physician.

✧

If you're feeling a great deal of pressure now and feel like you're large, lie on your side. Getting into the habit of lying on your side and resting to relieve this pressure may be very helpful.

Don't Use Retin-A® During Pregnancy   Many women are waiting until they're older to have their first baby. In fact, more women over the age of 35 are having a first baby than ever before! This increase in age of a mother-to-be raises questions and concerns that wouldn't have applied a few years ago.

One of these concerns is the use of Retin-A (retinoic acid isotretinoin), not to be confused with Accutane. Retin-A is a substance in cream or lotion form that is used by many women to help them get rid of fine skin wrinkles on the face. The medicine was originally used by dermatologists to treat people with acne. After it was used for a while, doctors began noticing some of the wrinkles on their patients' faces were also disappearing! When word of this spread, many women in their mid- to late-30s began asking their doctor for a prescription.

What course of action should you follow if you are now using Retin-A? Unfortunately, the medication is too new for us to know whether or not it's safe to use during pregnancy. But we do know any type of medication you use—whether taken internally, inhaled, injected or used topically (spread on the skin)—gets into your bloodstream. And any substance in your bloodstream can be passed to your baby. Some medications a mother-to-be uses become concentrated in the baby. Your body can handle it, but your baby's can't. If some substances build up in the baby, they can have significant effects on development of the fetus.

I recommend you avoid using Retin-A during your pregnancy. In the future, we may know more about its effects on a growing baby. However, at this time, data isn't available. If you don't know if a substance is safe, it's best to avoid using it for the sake of your baby.

Steroid Creams and Ointments   Conditions may arise during pregnancy requiring treatment with creams or ointments. This might include steroid preparations.

Consult your doctor. Any medication used on the skin can be absorbed into the body and passed on to the baby.

Caution: Do *not* use any medication, cream or ointment that you used before pregnancy without consulting your doctor first.

Week 27

Age of Fetus — 25 Weeks

How Big Is Your Baby?

This week marks the beginning of your third trimester. In addition to weight and crown-to-rump length, I'm adding total length of your baby's body from head to toe. This will give you an even better idea of how big your baby is during this last third of your pregnancy.

Your baby now weighs a little over 2 pounds (1000g). Crown-to-rump length of your growing baby is about 9.6 inches (24cm) by this week. Total length is 15.3 inches (34cm). See the illustration on page 251.

How Big Are You?

Your uterus is about 2.8 inches (7cm) above your umbilicus. If measured from the pubic symphysis, it measures over 10.5 inches (27cm) from the pubic symphysis to the top of the uterus.

How Your Baby Is Growing and Developing

Eye Development   The developing eyes first appear around day 22 of development in the embryo (about 5 weeks gestation). In the beginning, eyes first look like a pair of shallow grooves on each side of the developing brain. These grooves continue to develop and eventually turn into pockets called *optical vesicles*. The ectoderm gives rise to the lens of each eye. (Ectoderm is discussed on page 55.)

Early in development, the eyes are on the side of the head. They move toward the middle of the face between 7 and 10 weeks of gestation.

At about 8 weeks gestation, blood vessels form that lead to the eye. During the 9th week of gestation, the pupil forms, which is the round opening in the eye.

By the 8th or 9th week of gestation, the neurological (nerve) connections from the eyes to the brain begin to form. This nerve is called the *optic nerve.*

Eyelids that cover the eyes are fused or connected together around 11 to 12 weeks. They remain fused until about 27 to 28 weeks of pregnancy, when they open.

The retina, which is at the back of the eye, is important in the reception of light images. It develops its normal layers by about the 27th week of gestation. These layers are important in receiving light and light information and transmitting it to the brain for interpretation.

Congenital Cataracts   One congenital problem (a problem that is present at birth) that may occur with the eyes is a *congenital cataract.* Most people believe cataracts only happen in old age, but that's a misconception. They can appear in a newborn baby!

With a cataract, the lens that is the part of the eye that focuses light onto the back of the eye is not transparent or clear. It is opaque or cloudy. Although this problem is usually caused by a genetic predisposition, it has been found in children born to mothers who had German measles (rubella) around the 6th or 7th week of pregnancy.

Microphthalmia   Another abnormal congenital condition of the eye is *microphthalmia.* With this condition, the overall size of the eye is too small. The eyeball may be reduced to two-thirds of its normal size. This abnormality often occurs with other abnormalities of the eyes. It frequently results from infections from inside the uterus, such as cytomegalovirus (CMV) or toxoplasmosis.

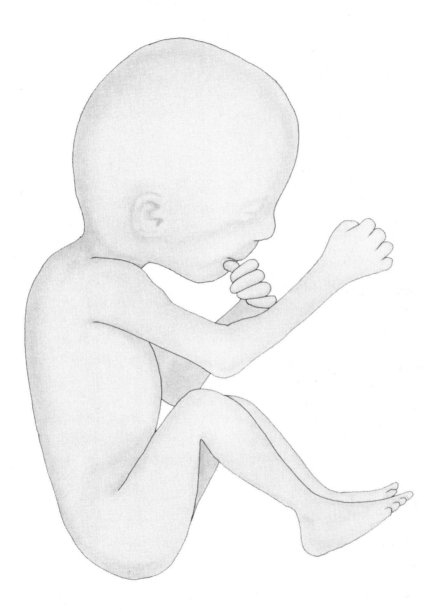

Around this time, your baby's eyelids open. Your baby begins opening and closing its eyes.

✧

Changes in You

Your breasts have probably gone through changes as your pregnancy has progressed. Your breasts were probably very tender or sore early in pregnancy. This discomfort may have continued as they have increased in size.

Discovering a Breast Lump   Discovering a breast lump at any time is important, whether during pregnancy or any other time. It's important for you to learn at an early age how to do a breast exam on yourself and to perform this on a regular basis (usually after every menstrual period). Most breast lumps are found by women examining themselves. This is the case with 9 out of 10 breast lumps.

Have your doctor perform regular exams at regular intervals, usually when you have your annual Pap smear. If you have an exam every year and are lump-free, it will help assure you no lumps are present before beginning pregnancy.

Finding a breast lump may be delayed during pregnancy because of changes in your breasts. It may be more difficult to feel a lump. Enlargement of your breasts during pregnancy and nursing tends to hide lumps or masses in the tissue of the breast.

Usually a breast exam is done at some point during pregnancy. Your doctor may do this at your first prenatal visit. If your breasts are very tender, this exam may be postponed until later in pregnancy.

Tests for Breast Lumps   The routine test for breast lumps is examination by yourself or your doctor. Other tests include X-ray examination, called a *mammogram,* and ultrasound examination of the breast. Other methods, such as thermography, which evaluates heat given off from the breast, are still in the developmental stage.

If a lump is found, it may be necessary to have an ultrasound exam performed on the breast, or a mammogram may be done. Because a mammogram utilizes X-rays, your

✧

pregnancy must be protected during the procedure, usually by shielding your abdomen with a lead apron.

It has not been shown that pregnancy accelerates the course or growth of a breast cancer. But we do know it is difficult to find a breast lump because of the changes in your breasts.

Treatment for Breast Lumps During Pregnancy   Often a lump in the breast can be drained or aspirated. In this procedure, a needle is used to drain the lump or cyst. Fluid removed from the cyst is sent to the lab for evaluation. This is to ensure there are no abnormalities, such as abnormal cells, in the fluid.

If the fluid is clear, it's a good sign. Bloody fluid is of more concern and must be studied microscopically in the laboratory.

If a lump or cyst cannot be drained by a needle, a biopsy of the cyst or lump may be necessary.

Treatment of breast cancer during pregnancy is not significantly different from treatment for non-pregnant women. Complications of the treatment of breast lumps or breast cancer during pregnancy include the need for medication, such as anesthesia for a biopsy. In more-serious cancers, the need for radiation therapy and chemotherapy, which should be avoided during pregnancy, may cause problems for you and your baby.

How Your Actions Affect Your Baby's Development

Falling and Injuries from Falls   A fall is the most frequent cause of minor injury during pregnancy. Fortunately, a fall is usually without serious injury to the fetus or to the mother. The uterus is well protected in the abdomen inside the bony pelvis because the uterus lies within the pelvis, especially during the first trimester. And the fetus is protected against injury by the cushion of amniotic fluid surrounding it. Your uterus and abdominal wall also offer some protection.

Signs to Watch for   Some signs and symptoms can alert you to a problem after a fall. Signs that indicate more-serious problems after a fall include:

+ Bleeding.
+ A gush of fluid from the vagina, indicating rupture of membranes.
+ Severe abdominal pain.

Movement of the baby after a fall may be reassuring, but watch for the above warning signs.

Placental abruption, discussed on pages 308-312, is one of the most serious things that can occur with a fall or injury. With placental abruption, the placenta separates from the uterus prematurely. Another important type of injury is a broken bone or some injury that immobilizes you.

If You Fall   If you fall, contact your doctor. He or she may want to check you out. There may be reassurance for you in being monitored and having the baby's heartbeat checked.

Minor injuries to the abdomen are treated in the usual fashion, as though you were not pregnant. However, avoid X-rays if at all possible.

Ultrasound evaluation may be important following an injury from a fall. This is judged on an individual basis, depending on the severity of your symptoms and the severity of your injury.

Remember your balance and mobility are changing as you get larger during pregnancy. Be careful about falling, particularly during the winter when parking lots and sidewalks may be wet or icy. Many pregnant women also fall on stairs. Service stations often have slick surfaces with oily spills that can cause falls.

Slow down a little as you get larger and your pregnancy progresses. You may not be able to jump up and get around as quickly as you are used to. With the change in your balance, plus any dizziness you may experience, it's important to be vigilant. You want to avoid any falls or possible injury to you or your baby.

✧

You Should also Know

Prenatal Classes   Even though you're just beginning the third trimester of your pregnancy, it isn't too early to think about and register for prenatal classes. It's a good idea to get signed up for classes so you can take them *before* you get to the end of your pregnancy. By doing this, it'll give you time to practice what you learn. And you won't be just beginning your classes when you deliver!

During pregnancy, you have probably been learning what's going to happen at the time of delivery by talking with your doctor and by asking questions. You have also learned what lies ahead from reading materials given to you by your doctor and by other books or pamphlets you have read. Childbirth classes offer you another way to learn about this important end to pregnancy. They are another way for you to prepare for labor and delivery.

Classes are usually held for small groups of pregnant women and their partners or labor coachs. This provides an opportunity to learn from the information you are presented. It also provides an opportunity for you to interact with other couples and ask questions. You'll discover other women are concerned about many of the same things, such as labor and delivery. It's good to know you aren't the only one who is worried or anxious about what lies ahead.

Childbirth classes are offered in various settings. Most hospitals that deliver babies offer prenatal classes at the hospital. They are often taught by the labor and delivery nurses or by a midwife. Other types of classes have different degrees of involvement. This means the time commitment or depth of subject covered will be different for different classes that may be available.

Ask your doctor or your doctor's nurse about which classes they recommend. They will know which type of class would be best for you.

Classes are intended to inform you and your partner or labor coach about what to expect, what happens at the hospital and what happens during labor and delivery. Some couples find these classes are a good opportunity to get the partner more involved and make him feel more comfortable with the pregnancy. This may make him more of an active part and a bigger help to you at the time of labor and delivery, as well as during your pregnancy.

Prenatal classes are not necessarily just for couples. Often classes are offered for the single mother or for a pregnant woman whose partner cannot or will not come to prenatal classes.

Besides answering many questions about what to expect during pregnancy, labor and delivery, you may find a prenatal class also raises many questions. By meeting on a regular basis, usually once a week for 4 to 6 weeks, you can learn about things that are of concern to you. Classes often cover a wide range of subjects, including:

+ Will you need an episiotomy?
+ Do you need an enema?
+ When is a fetal monitor necessary?
+ What's going to happen to you when you reach the hospital?
+ Is an epidural or some other type of anesthesia for you?

These are important questions. Discuss them with your doctor if they are not answered during the course of your prenatal classes.

Prenatal classes are not suggested only for first-time pregnant women. If you have a new partner, if it has been a few years since you've had a baby, if you have questions in your mind or if you would like a review of what to expect, a prenatal class can benefit you.

These classes can be a real help for you and your partner. A great deal of information is presented. They may help make the worry and concern about labor and delivery less of a problem for you. And they will help you enjoy the birth of your baby even more.

✧

Home Uterine Monitoring   Home uterine monitoring is used to identify women with premature labor so labor can be stopped to prevent the delivery of a premature baby. Conditions associated with premature delivery include a previous preterm delivery, infections, premature rupture of membranes, pregnancy-induced hypertension and multiple fetuses, such as twins or triplets. Diseases related to premature delivery are a major cause of infant mortality.

Home uterine monitoring combines recording uterine contractions and telephone contact with the healthcare provider on a daily basis. A recording of uterine contractions is transmitted from the woman's home, via telephone, to a center where the contractions can be evaluated. With the use of personal computers, your doctor may be able to view the recordings at his or her own home.

Cost for home monitoring varies but runs between $80 and $100 a day; some insurance companies cover the monitoring. The cost of home monitoring can often be justified if prevention of a premature delivery saves many thousands of dollars in care of a premature baby. Sometimes these costs can run higher than $100,000!

Not everyone agrees that use of home monitoring is beneficial or cost-effective. It is difficult to identify all patients who need this type of monitoring. Need for home uterine monitoring should be considered on an individual basis. It is an option to discuss with your physician if you have experienced preterm labor in the past or have other risk factors for preterm labor.

Week 28

Age of Fetus — 26 Weeks

How Big Is Your Baby?

Your baby weighs about 2.4 pounds (1100g). Its crown-to-rump length is close to 10 inches (25cm). Total length is 15.75 inches (35cm).

How Big Are You?

Your uterus is now well above your umbilicus. Sometimes this growth seems gradual. At other times, it may seem like changes happen very rapidly, as if overnight.

Your uterus is about 3.2 inches (8cm) above your belly-button. If you measure from the pubic symphysis, it is about 11 inches (28cm) from the pubic symphysis to the top of the uterus.

Your weight gain by this time should be between 17 and 24 pounds (7.7 and 10.8kg).

How Your Baby Is Growing and Developing

Until this time, the surface of the developing fetal brain has appeared smooth. At around 28 weeks of pregnancy, the brain forms characteristic grooves and indentations on the surface called the *gyri* and *sulci*. At this time, the amount of brain tissue also increases.

Your baby's eyebrows and eyelashes may be present. Hair on the baby's head is growing longer.

✧

The baby's body is becoming plumper and rounder. It's beginning to fill out a little. This is because of increased fat underneath the skin. Before this time, the fetus has a thin appearance.

Your baby now weighs about 2.4 pounds (1100g). This is an amazing growth compared to just 11 weeks ago when the fetus weighed only about *3.5 ounces (100g)* (at 17 weeks of pregnancy). Your baby has increased its weight 10 times in 11 weeks! In the last 4 weeks, from the 24th week of your pregnancy, its weight has doubled. Your baby is growing rapidly!

Changes in You

The Placenta   The placenta *(afterbirth)* is a very important part of your pregnancy. It plays a very critical role in the growth, development and survival of the fetus. The illustration shows the fetus attached to the umbilical cord, which attaches to the placenta.

Two important cell layers are involved in the development of the placenta and the amniotic sac. These layers are called the *amnion* and the *chorion*. Development and function of the cell layers is complicated, and their description is beyond the scope of this book. However, the amnion is the layer around the amniotic fluid in which the fetus floats.

The placenta begins to form with *trophoblastic cells.* Trophoblastic cells can grow right through the walls of maternal blood vessels and establish contact with your bloodstream. The circulation of the fetus is separate from your circulation. These cells grow into the blood vessels *without* making a vascular connection or opening between the blood vessels. But the blood flow of the fetus in the placenta is very close to your blood flow in the placenta.

We have looked closely at the weight gain of your baby in this book. The placenta is *also* growing and getting larger at a very rapid rate. At 10 weeks gestation, the placenta weighed about 0.7 ounce (20g). Ten weeks later, at 20 weeks gestation, it is almost 6 ounces (170g). In another 10 weeks,

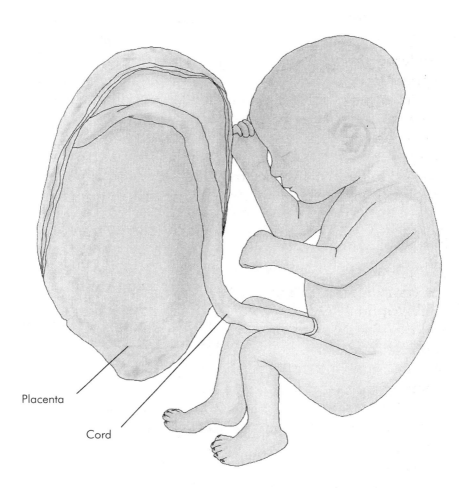

Placenta

Cord

*The placenta, shown here with the baby, carries oxygen and nutrients to the
growing baby. It is a very important part of pregnancy.*

the placenta will have increased to 15 ounces (430g). At full
term, 40 weeks, it will weigh almost 1.5 pounds (650g)!

Connections between the blood vessels of the fetus and
the developing placenta occur as early as the 2nd or 3rd
week of development. During the 3rd week of gestation, the
villi (projections) at the base of the placenta become firmly
attached to the underlying layer of the uterus.

The villi are important during pregnancy. The space
around the villi becomes honeycombed with maternal blood

❖

vessels. The villi absorb nutrients and oxygen from the maternal blood. The nutrients and oxygen are transported to the growing fetus through the umbilical vein in the umbilical cord. Waste products from the fetus are brought through the umbilical arteries to the intervillus space. This is how the fetus gets rid of waste products.

What Does the Placenta Do?   The placenta is involved in respiration (the transport of oxygen and carbon dioxide to and from the fetus). It is also involved in nutrition and excretion of waste products from the fetus.

In addition to these functions, the placenta has a very important hormone role. One hormone it produces is human chorionic gonadotropin (HCG), discussed on pages 68-69. This hormone is found in your bloodstream in measurable amounts within 10 days after fertilization. The presence of HCG in sufficient amounts is the basis of a positive pregnancy test. The placenta also begins making estrogen and progesterone by the 7th or 8th week of pregnancy.

What Does the Placenta Look Like?   At full-term, a normal placenta is flat and has a cake-like, round or oval appearance. It is about 6 to 8 inches (15 to 20cm) in diameter and 0.8 to 1.2 inches (2 to 3cm) thick at its thickest part. The weight is about 17.5 to 24 ounces (500 to 650g) or about one-sixth the weight of the fetus.

Placentas vary widely in size and in shape. A placenta that is too large *(placentamegaly)* can be found when a woman is infected with syphilis or when a baby has erythroblastosis (Rh-sensitization of the baby). Sometimes it occurs without any obvious explanation. A small placenta may be found in normal pregnancies. But it also may be found with intrauterine growth retardation.

The part of the placenta that attaches to the wall of the uterus has a beefy or spongy appearance. The fetal side of the placenta, the side closest to the fetus inside the amniotic sac, is smooth. It is covered with the amniotic and chorionic membranes.

✧

The placenta is a red or reddish-brown color. Around the time of birth, the placenta may have areas of white on it. These are calcium deposits or a type of tissue called *fibrin.*

In most pregnancies, only one placenta is present. Occasionally in a single pregnancy (not a twin pregnancy), a placenta may have two sections or lobes. These lobes are connected by blood vessels that run to the umbilical cord that attach to the fetus.

In multiple pregnancies, there may be more than one placenta. Or there may be just one placenta with more than one umbilical cord coming from it. Usually with twins, there are two amniotic sacs, with two umbilical cords running to the fetuses.

The umbilical cord, which is the attachment from the placenta to the fetus, contains two umbilical arteries and one umbilical vein. It is 12 to 40 inches (30 to 100cm) long. The umbilical cord is usually white and contains large blood vessels.

There can be problems involving the placenta during pregnancy. These include placental abruption, see pages 308-312, and placenta previa, see page 326. After delivery, placental problems include a retained placenta. See page 360.

How Your Actions Affect Your Baby's Development

Dealing with Asthma   *Asthma* is a respiratory illness found fairly often in pregnant women. It is a disease of the breathing tubes. Asthma is characterized by an increased responsiveness or sensitivity to stimulation of the trachea and the bronchi, which make up an important part of your ability to breathe.

Problems with asthma are manifested by difficulty breathing, shortness of breath, coughing and wheezing. (Wheezing is a noise like a whistling or a hissing made as air moves through narrowed airways.)

Asthma is an episodic problem with acute worsening of symptoms interspersed with symptom-free periods. It affects about 2% of the population in the United States and Canada. It is equally common in other countries.

It may occur at any age, but about 50% of all cases occur before age 10. Another 33% of the cases occur by age 40. Pregnancy does not seem to cause any consistent, predictable problem with asthma. Some pregnant women appear to get better during pregnancy, while others remain about the same. A few get worse.

Treating Asthma Attacks   Most pregnant women with asthma can have a safe pregnancy, labor and delivery. If a woman has severe asthma attacks when she isn't pregnant, it is likely she will continue to have severe asthma attacks during pregnancy.

In general, the treatment plan used before pregnancy will probably continue to be helpful. This includes medications prescribed for asthma before or during pregnancy.

During your pregnancy, your oxygen consumption increases by about 25%. Your fetus does not tolerate low oxygen levels very well. That's why treatment of asthma is very important while you're pregnant.

Asthma medication, such as terbutaline, and steroids, such as hydrocortisone or methylprednisolone, can be used during pregnancy. Another common medication for asthma, aminophylline or theophyline, may also be used.

Many women have found they can help themselves with their asthma during pregnancy fairly easily. Maintaining good hydration with more-than-adequate or excess fluid intake seems to help some women.

You Should also Know

Additional Testing   Twenty-eight weeks of gestation is a time when many doctors initiate or repeat certain blood tests or procedures. This is a time when glucose-tolerance testing may be done.

✧

RhoGAM™ Injections RhoGAM injections and Rh-sensitivity are discussed in detail beginning on page 156. Week 28 is the point in your pregnancy when RhoGAM is given to protect you from becoming sensitized if you are Rh-negative.

How Is the Baby Lying? It is very common at this time in pregnancy to ask your doctor which way the baby is lying. Is the baby headfirst? Is it bottom-first (breech)? Is the baby lying sideways?

This is a common concern. At this point in pregnancy, it's difficult and usually impossible to tell just by feeling your abdomen how the baby is lying and whether or not it is coming bottom first, feet first or head first. The baby may change position during pregnancy and may continue to change its position for another month.

It doesn't hurt to try to feel the abdomen to see where the head is and where the abdomen is. But this will be easier in another 3 to 4 weeks when the head is harder. It's easier to feel then, and your doctor may be able to determine how the baby is lying (called *presentation of the fetus*). Then your doctor will know a little better which part of the baby is coming first into the birth canal or pelvis.

Week 29

Age of Fetus — 27 Weeks

How Big Is Your Baby?

By this time, your baby weighs about 2.7 pounds (1250g). Crown-to-rump length is 10.4 inches (26cm). Its total length is 16.7 inches (37cm).

How Big Are You?

Measuring from your bellybutton, your uterus is about 3.5 to 4 inches (7.6 to 10.2cm) above it. Your uterus is close to 11.5 inches (29cm) above the pubic symphysis. If you saw your doctor 4 weeks ago, around the 25th week of your pregnancy, you probably measured about 10 inches (25cm) at that time. You've grown about 1.5 inches (4cm) in 4 weeks.

Your weight gain by this week should be between 19 and 25 pounds (8.55 and 11.25kg).

How Your Baby Is Growing and Developing

Fetal Growth   The change in the size of the fetus during pregnancy has been noted in every chapter. I use *average* weights to give you an idea of about how large your baby is at a particular time. However, these are only averages; babies do vary greatly in size and weight.

At 10 weeks of gestation, the embryo weighs less than an ounce (5g)! At 20 weeks of pregnancy, it weighs 10.5 ounces

✧

(300g). At 30 weeks, it weighs 3.3 pounds (1500g). At 40 weeks of pregnancy, it will weigh 7.5 pounds (3400g).

Notice that from 10 to 20 weeks the fetus increases in weight *60 times!* From 20 weeks to 30 weeks, it increases 5 times. From 30 weeks to 40 weeks, the fetus more than doubles its weight.

Because of this rapid growth during pregnancy, infants who are born prematurely may be very small. Growth is so rapid during pregnancy that even a few weeks have a dramatic effect on the size of your baby. The baby continues to grow after 36 weeks of gestation but at a slower rate.

Three interesting factors have been identified with regards to the birth weight of your baby.

+ Boys weigh more than girls.
+ Birth weight of an infant increases with the increasing number of pregnancies or babies you deliver.
+ White babies at term weigh more than black babies at term.

These are general statements and don't apply to everyone. But they appear to apply in most cases. The average baby's birth weight at full term is 7 to 7.5 pounds (3280g to 3400g).

Is Your Baby Mature at Birth?   A fetus born between the 38th and 42nd weeks of pregnancy is called a *term baby* or *full-term infant*. Before the 38th week, the term *preterm* can be applied to the fetus. At 42 weeks of pregnancy, and after this time, *post-term* is the appropriate term. *Post-dates* is a newer term that some doctors use; it has less specificity and its definition is not as clear as *post-term*.

When a baby is born before the end of pregnancy, many people use the terms *premature* and *preterm* interchangeably. There is a difference. An infant that is 32 weeks gestational age but has mature pulmonary or lung function at the time of birth is more appropriately called a

✧

preterm infant rather than a *premature infant*. The term *premature* best describes an infant that has immature lungs at the time of birth.

Premature Babies   *Premature birth* increases the risk of physical or mental impairment in the baby. It also increases the risk of fetal death. Babies born prematurely usually weigh less than 5.5 pounds (2500g).

The illustration on page 271 shows a premature baby with several monitors attached to it. These monitor the baby's heart rate. Many other monitors can be used, such as I.V.s, tubes and masks that provide oxygen. They help the baby breathe and monitor the infant's ability to breathe adequately.

In 1950, the neonatal death rate (covering the time of delivery and the first 30 days after delivery) was about 20 per 1000 live births. Today, the rate is less than 10 per 1000 live births. This decrease is due largely to the fact that more preterm infants now survive.

The decreasing mortality rate applies primarily to infants delivered during the third trimester (27+ weeks of gestation) who weigh at least 2.2 pounds (1000g) and are without malformations. When gestational age and birth weight are below these levels, mortality increases.

Part of this improvement in survival statistics comes from better methods of caring for premature babies. Today, infants born as early as 25 weeks of pregnancy can survive. However, the long-term survival and quality of life, such as mental retardation and developmental problems, remain to be seen as these children grow older.

What is the survival rate for premature babies? The most recent information indicates for infants that weighed 1.1 pound (500g) to 1.5 pounds (700g) the survival rate is about 43%. For babies weighing between 1.5 pounds and 2.2 pounds (1000g), the survival rate is about 72%. These rates vary from hospital to hospital.

The average hospital stay for these premature babies ranges from 125 days for infants who weighed between 1.3

and 1.5 pounds (600 and 700g) to 76 days for babies in the 2- to 2.2-pound (900 to 1000g) birth-weight range.

An important consideration is the frequency of severe handicaps premature babies suffer. In the lower birth-weight range, most of the babies that survived were handicapped. The other group of babies suffered severe handicaps, but statistics were much lower.

The total cost of hospital care during this period ranges from thousands to hundreds of thousands of dollars. Survival rates, the rates of survival with serious problems and hospital costs are all on the increase.

It's best for the baby to remain in the uterus as long as possible to grow and develop fully. Occasionally it is best for the baby to be delivered, such as when the fetus is not receiving adequate nutrition, but this is a highly unusual occurrence.

Causes of Premature Labor In most cases, the cause of premature labor is unknown. Causes we do understand include:

+ A uterus with an abnormal shape, such as a division.
+ A large uterus, from multiple fetuses.
+ The occurrence of polyhydramnios or hydramnios.
+ An abnormal placenta, such as placental abruption or placenta previa.
+ Premature rupture of membranes.
+ An incompetent cervix.
+ Abnormalities of the fetus.
+ Fetal death.
+ Retained IUD.
+ Abortion performed late in pregnancy (with previous pregnancies).
+ Serious maternal illness.
+ Incorrect estimate of gestational age.

Diagnosing the cause of premature labor and delivery may be difficult. An attempt is always made to determine

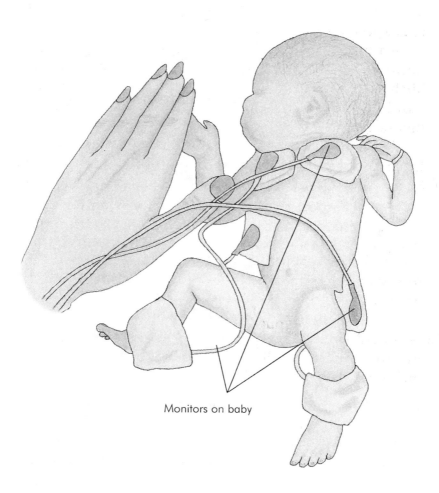

Monitors on baby

Premature baby (born at 29 weeks of pregnancy) shown with fetal monitors attached to it. Note size of adult hand in comparison.

what causes preterm labor *before* active labor begins. In this way, treatment may be more effective.

Some difficult questions that must be answered when premature labor begins include:

+ Is it better for the infant to be inside the uterus or to be delivered?
+ Are the dates of the pregnancy correct?
+ Is this really labor?

Knowing when your pregnancy began and when you are due is important. Visiting your physician for prenatal appointments and as directed may help deal with problems before they become severe.

Retarded Fetal Growth   Intrauterine-growth retardation (IUGR) refers to a fetus that does not grow as fast as it should while in the uterus. A baby suffering from IUGR has a higher risk of serious problems, such as fetal death. IUGR is discussed in depth beginning on page 287.

The word *retardation* may cause a mother-to-be some concern. Retardation in this sense doesn't apply to the development or function of the baby's brain. It doesn't mean the baby will be *mentally* retarded. It means the growth and size of the fetus are inappropriately small; *growth* and *size* are considered to be retarded.

Changes in You

Treatment of Premature Labor   To continue our discussion of premature labor, what can you do about it? There are several methods of treating premature labor.

The treatment most often used for premature labor is *bed rest.* You are advised to stay in bed and lie on your side. Either side is OK—whichever side is most comfortable is preferable. Bed rest is often very successful in stopping contractions and premature labor. It may mean you can't go to work or continue many activities, but it's worth it if you can avoid premature delivery of your baby.

Magnesium sulfate is often used to treat pre-eclampsia. See pages 291-293 for information on pre-eclampsia. It helps avoid seizures. We have known for quite awhile that magnesium sulfate can also be used to help stop labor. This medication is most often given through an I.V.; it requires hospitalization. However, it can occasionally be given as an oral preparation, without hospitalization. It requires frequent monitoring by your doctor.

More commonly used to suppress labor are beta-adrenergic agents, also called *tocolytic agents*. At this time, only ritodrine (Yutopar®) is approved by the Food and Drug Administration (FDA) to treat premature labor. Beta-adrenergics relax the uterus and decrease contractions. The main part of the uterus is muscle, which is active in pushing the baby out through the cervix during labor.

Ritodrine is given in three different forms. It can be given intravenously, as an intramuscular injection and as a pill. It is usually given intravenously to begin with. This requires a hospital stay of 1 to 2 days or more.

When premature contractions stop, you can be switched to oral medications. These pills are taken every 2 to 4 hours. Ritodrine is approved for use in pregnancies over 20 weeks and under 36 weeks gestation. In some cases, medication is first used without an I.V. This is done most often in women with a history of premature labor or for a woman with multiple pregnancies, such as twins, triplets or more.

Side effects related to the use of ritodrine may be very uncomfortable. In the mother, these include tachycardia (rapid heartbeat), hypotension, the feeling of apprehension or fear, chest tightness or actual chest pain, changes in the electrocardiogram and pulmonary edema (fluid in the lungs).

The use of ritodrine can cause maternal metabolic problems, including increased blood sugar, low blood potassium and even acidosis of the blood, similar to that occurring with a diabetic reaction. Less-serious complications include headaches, vomiting, shaking, fever and even hallucinations.

Similar problems probably occur in the fetus. Low blood-sugar levels have been seen in babies after birth if the mother took ritodrine before delivery. Tachycardia is also commonly seen in these babies.

Terbutaline is frequently used for the same reason as ritodrine. Although it has been shown to be an effective medication, it has not been approved for this use by the FDA. Terbutaline side effects are similar to those of ritodrine.

Other medications, such as salbutamol, fenoterol and isoxuprine, have been used in the past to stop early labor. These agents are not commonly used at this time.

Sedatives or narcotics may be used in early attempts to stop labor. This may consist of an injection of morphine or meperidine (Demerol®). This is not a long-term solution but may be effective in initially stopping labor.

Two medications for stopping premature labor that I'll mention for historical reasons only include alcohol (ethanol) and progesterone. Neither has been shown to be effective through scientific studies. At this time, neither is used.

Benefits of Stopping Premature Labor   The benefits of stopping premature labor include reducing the risks of fetal problems and problems related to premature delivery. If you experience premature labor, it's important to see your doctor frequently. Your doctor will probably monitor your pregnancy with ultrasound and/or non-stress tests.

In some cases, labor cannot be stopped, and the baby will be delivered.

How Your Actions Affect Your Baby's Development

Most of this discussion about Week 29 has been devoted to the premature infant and treatment of premature labor. If you are diagnosed as having premature labor and your doctor prescribes bed rest and medications to stop it, follow his or her advice!

If you're concerned about instructions given by your doctor, discuss them with him or her. If you're told not to work or you're advised to reduce your activities and you ignore the advice, you're taking chances with your well-being and your unborn baby's. It isn't worth taking chances.

Don't be afraid to ask for another opinion or the opinion of a perinatologist if you experience premature labor.

You Should also Know

Chlamydia Infections You may have heard about or read about an infection called *chlamydia*. It has received a great deal of attention. Chlamydia is a common sexually transmitted disease (STD). It's estimated about 3 to 5 million people are infected every year. It may be difficult to determine if you have a chlamydial infection; it can be symptomless.

Between 20 and 40% of all sexually active women have probably been exposed to chlamydia at some time. Chlamydia infection can cause serious problems if left untreated, but these problems can be avoided with treatment.

Infection is caused by *chlamydia trachomatis*. This germ invades certain types of healthy cells. Infection may be passed through sexual activity, including oral sex.

Chlamydia is most likely to occur in young people who have more than one sexual partner. It may also occur in women who have other sexually transmitted diseases. Some doctors believe chlamydia occurs more commonly in women who take oral contraceptives. Barrier methods of contraception, such as diaphragms and condoms used with spermicides, may offer protection from chlamydial infections.

One of the most important complications of chlamydia is pelvic inflammatory disease (PID). This is a severe infection of the upper genital organs involving the uterus, the Fallopian tubes and even the ovaries. It can result from an untreated infection that spreads throughout the pelvic area. Chlamydia is one of the main causes of PID.

✧

If the infection is prolonged or recurrent, the reproductive organs, Fallopian tubes and uterus may be damaged. This may require surgery to repair them. If tubes are damaged, scar tissue can increase the risk of ectopic or tubal pregnancy.

Chlamydia in Pregnancy During pregnancy, a mother-to-be can pass a chlamydial infection to her baby as it comes through the birth canal and vagina. The baby will have a 20 to 50% chance of getting chlamydia. This may result in an eye infection, however, it is easily treated. More-serious complications include pneumonia, which may require hospitalization of the baby.

Testing for Chlamydia Chlamydia can be detected by a culture. However, more than 50% of those infected with chlamydia have no symptoms. Symptoms that may appear include burning or itching in the genital area, discharge from the vagina, painful or frequent urination, and/or pain in the pelvic area. Men may also experience symptoms.

New tests are available that are faster than cultures used in the past. They are called *rapid diagnostic tests*. They can be done in the office and can provide a result very quickly, possibly even before you go home.

Chlamydia is usually treated with tetracycline. However, tetracycline should *not* be given to a pregnant woman. During pregnancy, erythromycin may be the drug of choice. After treatment, your doctor may want to do another culture to make sure the infection is gone.

If you're concerned about a possible chlamydial infection, discuss it with your doctor.

Week 30

Age of Fetus — 28 Weeks

How Big Is Your Baby?

At this point in your pregnancy, your baby weighs about 3 pounds (1360g). Its crown-to-rump length is a little over 10.8 inches (27cm). Total length is 17 inches (38cm).

How Big Are You?

Measuring from your bellybutton, your uterus is about 4 inches (10cm) above it. From the pubic symphysis, the top of your uterus measures about 12 inches (30cm).

It may be hard to believe you still have 10 weeks to go! You may feel like you're running out of room to grow. However, your fetus, placenta and uterus, along with the amniotic fluid, will continue to get larger.

The average weight gain during pregnancy is 25 to 35 pounds (11.4 to 15.9kg). About half of this weight is concentrated in the growth of the uterus, the baby, the placenta and the amniotic fluid. This growth is mostly in the front of your abdomen and in your pelvis, where it is very noticeable to you. You may experience an increasing degree of discomfort in your pelvis and abdomen as pregnancy progresses.

How Your Baby Is Growing and Developing

Umbilical-Cord Knots   The illustration with this week shows

✧

umbilical cord? You may wonder how a knot like this can occur. We do not believe the knot grows this way.

A baby is usually quite active during pregnancy. We believe these knots occur as the baby moves around in early pregnancy. A loop forms in the umbilical cord; the baby moves through the loop, and a knot forms. Your actions do *not* cause or prevent this kind of complication.

Knots in the umbilical cord, sometimes called a *true knot in the cord,* do not occur often. The flow of blood through the umbilical cord supplies your baby with nutrients and oxygen from you. If a knot tightens through movement of the baby or during labor and delivery, it could deprive the baby of needed oxygen or nutrients. This could be very dangerous to the baby.

Your Baby's Movements Before Birth   Movement of the baby, called *quickening,* is one of the more precious parts of pregnancy. Before you feel the baby move, you probably had a positive pregnancy test and heard the baby's heartbeat at your doctor's office.

Feeling life inside you can be the beginning of your bonding with your baby. Many women feel they begin to relate to the baby and its personality before delivery through feeling the baby's movements. Share with your partner by having him feel your abdomen when the baby moves and describe the sensation to him.

Movement of your baby can vary in intensity from a faint flutter, sometimes described as a feeling of a butterfly or a gas bubble in early pregnancy, to brisk motions or even painful episodes as your baby gets larger.

Changes in You

Pregnancy is a happy time for most women. It is filled with anticipation and excitement. Very occasionally, however, serious problems can occur. Cancer in pregnancy is one serious complication that very rarely occurs.

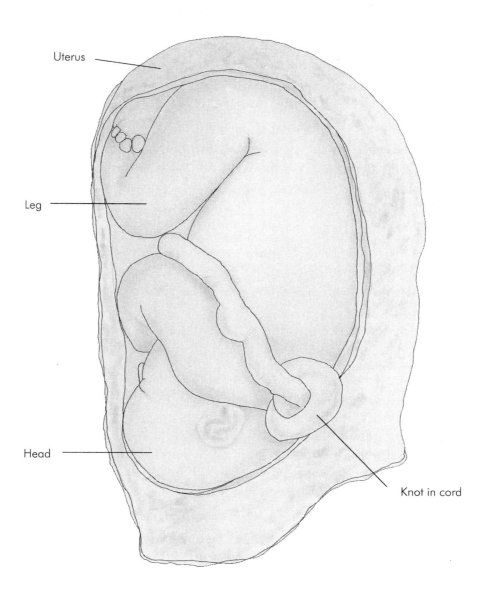

Uterus

Leg

Head

Knot in cord

This fetus has a knot in its umbilical cord.

This discussion on cancer in pregnancy is included *not* to scare you, but to provide you with information. It is not a pleasant subject to discuss, especially at this time. However, I believe every woman should have this information available. Its inclusion in this book is twofold:

+ To increase your awareness of this serious problem.
+ To provide you with a resource to help you formulate questions for a dialogue with your healthcare provider if you wish to discuss it.

Cancer in Pregnancy   The occurrence of cancer at any time is very stressful. When cancer occurs during pregnancy, it can add even more stress. The doctor must consider how to treat the cancer, but he or she is also concerned about the pregnancy.

The resolution of many issues depends on when the cancer is discovered. A woman has many concerns if this occurs. These include:

+ Will the pregnancy have to be terminated so the cancer can be treated?
+ Will medications used for treatment harm the baby?
+ Will the malignancy or therapy to treat the malignancy affect the fetus or be passed to the fetus?
+ Should therapy be delayed until after delivery or after termination of the pregnancy by abortion?

Fortunately, many cancers in women occur after the reproductive years. This lowers the likelihood of cancer during pregnancy. Cancer during pregnancy is a rare occurrence and is seen very occasionally by physicians who care for pregnant women. It must be handled and treated on an individual basis.

Some Cancers Found During Pregnancy   The most common cancers found during pregnancy include breast tumors, leukemia and lymphomas, melanomas, gynecologic cancers

⟡

(cancer of the female organs, such as the cervix, uterus and ovaries) and bone tumors. These cancers are listed in the order in which they occur most often.

Some studies indicate cancer of the breast is the most common cancer to be discovered during pregnancy. Gynecologic cancer is the second most common cancer.

The tremendous changes affecting your body during pregnancy have led several researchers to suggest there may be several influences on the possibility of discovering a cancer during pregnancy.

✦ Many believe some cancers may increase in frequency during pregnancy. These cancers arise from tissues or organs that are influenced by the increased hormone levels during pregnancy. This includes various forms of cancer, such as cancer of the breast which is known to be sensitive to the influence of estrogen.
✦ Anatomical and physiological changes of pregnancy (growth of the abdomen and changes in the breast) can make it difficult to find or diagnose an early cancer.
✦ Increased blood flow, with accompanying changes in the lymphatic system, may contribute to the transfer of a cancer to other parts of the body.

These three beliefs about cancer during pregnancy appear to have some validity but vary widely depending on the cancer and the organ involved.

Pelvic Malignancies Malignancies of the vulva, the tissue surrounding the opening to the vagina, have been reported during pregnancy. But only a few cases have occurred.

Cancer of the vagina is found mainly in women over the age of 50. Diagnosis of this type of cancer during pregnancy is rare.

Cancer of the cervix has been found in pregnant women. There is a difference of opinion about this cancer. Some believe cancer of the cervix prevents a woman from getting pregnant. Others believe pregnancy can prevent cancer of the cervix. Some doctors have reported that pregnancy makes cancer of the cervix grow faster. Others believe pregnancy actually can make cancer of the cervix grow more slowly.

Cervical cancer is believed to occur about once in every 10,000 pregnancies. However, about 1% of the women who have cancer of the cervix are pregnant when the cancer is diagnosed. Cancer of the cervix is curable, particularly if it is found and treated in its early stages.

Uterine cancer, sometimes called *endometrial cancer,* is extremely rare during pregnancy. Cancer of the Fallopian tube is also extremely rare during pregnancy. It occurs most often in women between 50 and 55.

Ovarian cancer is a relatively uncommon complication of pregnancy. It may be difficult to diagnose or treat during pregnancy because the uterus is growing and changing. It is not unusual to have a cyst on the ovary during pregnancy. Both of these factors may make it difficult to diagnose cancer of the ovary during pregnancy.

Cancer of the bladder has been reported in pregnancy, but it is an unusual occurrence. Cancer of the colon or rectum (the large bowel) is also a rare complication of pregnancy. Its incidence is estimated to be approximately 1 in every 100,000 pregnancies. Neither bladder cancer nor bowel cancer appear to be significantly influenced by pregnancy itself.

Breast Cancer Cancer of the breast in pregnancy is a serious problem for a mother and her baby. Breast cancer is rare in women younger than 35. Fortunately, it is not a common complication of pregnancy.

One problem with cancer of the breast is that during pregnancy it may be harder to find this cancer because of changes in the breasts, such as tenderness, increased size and even lumpiness. Of all women who have breast cancer, about 2% are pregnant at the time of diagnosis. Most evidence indicates pregnancy does *not* increase the rate of growth or spread of a breast cancer.

✧

Treatment of breast cancer during pregnancy varies; it must be individualized. Cancer of the breast may require surgery, chemotherapy or radiation. A combination of all these treatments may be used. There is no clear evidence that pregnancy can adversely affect the course of breast cancer, but many researchers are suspicious that this is the case.

Breast-feeding by a woman with breast cancer is a difficult situation to resolve. Most doctors recommend a woman not breast-feed if she has breast cancer.

Other Cancers in Pregnancy   Hodgkin's disease (a form of cancer) very commonly effects young people. It is now being cured and controlled for long periods of time with radiation and chemotherapy. The disease occurs in about 1 of every 6000 deliveries. Pregnancy does not appear to have a harmful effect on the course of Hodgkin's disease. An abortion is not usually recommended when a woman discovers she has Hodgkin's disease during pregnancy.

The lymph system, also called the *lymphatic system,* is affected by Hodgkin's disease. This includes lymph nodes found in close location to blood vessels. Treatment must be individualized.

Other diseases, called *lymphoma* or *lymphosarcoma,* may be discovered. A lymphoma is a cancer of the lymphatic system; this system helps remove abnormal cells and infection from the body; it lies close to blood vessels. Fortunately, lymphomas occur most often in men between 50 and 60 years of age.

Leukemia (cancer of the blood or blood cells) is another concern. Pregnant women who have leukemia have demonstrated an increased chance of premature labor. They may also experience an increase in bleeding after pregnancy, called *postpartum hemorrhage.* Leukemia is usually treated with chemotherapy or radiation therapy.

Melanoma is another type of cancer that may occur during pregnancy. A *melanoma* is a cancer derived from skin cells that produce melanin (pigment). A *malignant melanoma* spreads through the body; pregnancy may cause symptoms or problems to worsen. A melanoma can spread to the placenta and to the fetus.

Almost 50% of all tumors that spread to the placenta and 90% of all tumors that spread to the fetus from the mother are melanomas. For this reason, some experts recommend a woman should avoid pregnancy for at least 3 years after surgical removal of a melanoma. The highest risk of return or relapse of the melanoma is during this 3-year period.

Bone tumors are rare during pregnancy. However, two types of benign (non-cancerous) bone tumors can affect pregnancy and delivery. These cancers, which are called *endochondromas* and *benign exostosis*, can involve the pelvis. Tumors may interfere with labor. The possibility of having a Cesarean delivery is more likely with these tumors.

Cancer of the thyroid occurs most often in women between 30 and 34 years old. It is usually indicated by enlargement of the thyroid gland. The thyroid gland may enlarge normally during pregnancy, which can make diagnosis of this problem more difficult.

Thyroid cancer associated with pregnancy is rare. It can be diagnosed by blood tests. It is treated with surgery, radiation and possibly chemotherapy. A pregnant woman should *not* receive radioisotope scans.

Some cases of a cancer spreading from the pregnant woman to the placenta or fetus have been reported. Most were melanomas, breast cancer, leukemia or lymphoma. The number of cases is small and should not concern the normal pregnant woman. If you have any type of cancer during pregnancy and are concerned about its spread to the placenta or baby, discuss it with your doctor.

How Your Actions Affect Your Baby's Development

Treating Pelvic Cancer in Pregnancy   Many chemotherapeutic agents (drugs used to treat cancer) are teratogenic in animals *and* humans, especially when received early in pregnancy. A teratogen causes abnormal fetal development. Both the mother-to-be and fetus are at risk. Chemotherapeutic drugs can cause abortion, fetal death, malformations and growth retardation. The pregnant woman may experience side effects. Long-term effects of these medications on the fetus are unknown.

Radiation therapy raises concern about effects on a developing fetus. Radiation is often used to treat early or developing cancers. The developing embryo is probably most affected by radiation at an early stage.

You Should also Know

Bathing During Pregnancy A common question pregnant women have concerns the safety of bathing toward the end of pregnancy. There is no easy answer. Most doctors believe it's safe to bathe during pregnancy. Their only precaution might be to avoid slipping and falling as you get in or out of the bathtub. Most will not tell you to avoid a bath while you're pregnant. If you think your water has broken, avoid bathing.

Women also want to know if they are in the bathtub and their water breaks, how will they know it's happened? When your water breaks, it is usually a gush of water followed by leakage. If your water breaks while you're in the tub, you may not notice the initial gush of fluid. However, you'll probably notice the slow leakage of fluid that can last for quite awhile.

Rupture of Membranes The membranes around the baby that contain the amniotic fluid are called the *bag of waters.* They usually do not break until just before labor begins, when labor begins or during labor. But that isn't always the case.

If you think your water has broken or begun to leak, stop what you're doing. Call your doctor immediately!

✧

Once your water breaks, certain precautions need to be taken. The membranes of pregnancy help protect your baby from infection. When your water breaks and you leak fluid, your risk of getting an infection increases. An infection could be harmful to your baby.

Week 31

Age of Fetus — 29 Weeks

How Big Is Your Baby?

Your baby is continuing to grow. It weighs about 3.5 pounds (1600g). The crown-to-rump length is 11.2 inches (28cm). Its total length is 18 inches (40cm).

How Big Are You?

Measuring from the pubic symphysis, it is now a little more than 12 inches (31cm). From your bellybutton, it is about 4.4 inches (11cm).

At 12 weeks gestation, the uterus was just filling up the pelvis. As you can see in the illustration on page 289, by this week the uterus fills a large part of your abdomen.

Your weight gain by this time should be between 21 and 27 pounds (9.45 and 12.15kg).

How Your Baby Is Growing and Developing

Intrauterine-Growth Retardation (IUGR) Intrauterine-growth retardation (IUGR) indicates a newborn infant is small for gestational age. By definition, birth weight is below the 10th percentile for the baby's gestational age. This means 9 out of 10 babies of normal growth are larger. This baby falls into the lowest 10%.

When gestational age is appropriate—meaning dates are correct and the pregnancy is as far along as expected—and weight falls below the 10th percentile, there is reason for concern. Risk of fetal death increases significantly.

✧

Causes of IUGR   What causes intrauterine-growth retardation? Below are some conditions that increase the chance of intrauterine-growth retardation or a small fetus.

Maternal anemia may be a cause for IUGR. Anemia is discussed in depth on pages 208-212. However, maternal anemia as a cause of intrauterine-growth retardation is not accepted as a reason by all.

Smoking tobacco and other tobacco uses impair growth of the fetus. The more cigarettes smoked, the greater the impairment.

Poor weight gain in the mother-to-be can also cause problems in the fetus. If a woman is average size or smaller and doesn't gain enough weight, it may result in a growth-retarded baby. As I've stated many times, do *not* attempt to restrict normal weight gain during pregnancy. Research indicates when calories are restricted to under 1500 calories a day for an extended time, IUGR may result.

Vascular disease—problems with the blood flow, particularly pre-eclampsia—may cause IUGR. A more common problem is high blood pressure (hypertension), which can have a marked effect on fetal growth and fetal-growth retardation.

Kidney disease can cause retardation of fetal growth. Long-term hypoxia is another cause. Women who live at high altitudes are more likely to have babies that weigh less than women who live at low altitudes.

Alcoholism can cause intrauterine-growth retardation. Drug use and abuse can also cause IUGR. Multiple fetuses, such as twins or triplets, may cause a decrease in fetal growth. Infections in the fetus, such as cytomegalovirus, rubella or other long-term infections, may cause a decrease in fetal growth.

Abnormalities of the umbilical cord or placenta may cause decreased growth because of decreased nutrition to the fetus inside the uterus. History of an earlier delivery of a growth-retarded infant indicate it might happen again in subsequent pregnancies.

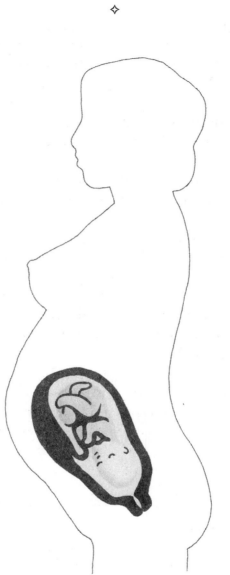

Comparative size of the uterus at 31 weeks of pregnancy (fetal age—29 weeks). The uterus can be felt about 4.4 inches (11cm) above the bellybutton.

✧

Another reason for a small baby, unrelated to IUGR is that a woman who is small might have a small baby.

Prolonged pregnancy can lead to an undernourished, smaller baby. A malformed or abnormal fetus may also experience decreased growth. This is especially true when chromosomal abnormalities are present.

Diagnosing and Treating Intrauterine-Growth Retardation
Diagnosing IUGR can be difficult. One reason your doctor measures you at each visit is to see if your uterus is growing.

Intrauterine-growth retardation can be diagnosed by ultrasound. Ultrasound may also be used to assure the baby is healthy and no malformations exist that must be taken care of at birth. A problem is usually found by measuring the uterus over a period of time and finding no change. If you measured 10.8 inches (27cm) at 27 weeks gestation and at 31 weeks you measure only 11 inches (28cm), your doctor might become concerned about IUGR and order an ultrasound examination.

Diagnosis of this type of problem is an important reason to see your doctor regularly and to keep your appointments. You may not like being weighed at every appointment, especially as your weight increases, but it helps your doctor see your pregnancy is growing and the baby is getting bigger.

When IUGR is diagnosed, avoid anything that can make it worse. Stop smoking. Improve your nutrition. Stop using drugs and alcohol.

Another treatment is bed rest. Resting allows the baby to receive the best blood flow—the best chance it has to improve growth. If IUGR is caused by maternal disease, attempts may be made to improve the mother's general health.

An infant with intrauterine-growth retardation is at risk of dying before delivery. To avoid this, it may require delivering the baby before it is full term. Infants with IUGR may not tolerate labor well; the possibility of a C-section increases because of fetal distress. The baby may be safer outside the uterus than inside where there is some problem. Growth-retarded infants have a 400 to 800% higher rate of death and injury than infants in the normal-weight range.

Changes in You

What Is Pre-Eclampsia During Pregnancy?   Pre-eclampsia is development of hypertension, protein in the urine and swelling, along with changes in reflexes. *Eclampsia* refers to seizures or convulsions in a woman with pre-eclampsia. They are not caused by a previous history of epilepsy or a seizure disorder.

The term *pre-eclampsia*, also called *toxemia* and *toxemia of pregnancy*, is commonly used to describe a variety of conditions that occur during pregnancy or shortly after delivery. For our discussion, I will use the term *pre-eclampsia* to simplify matters.

Pre-eclampsia problems are characterized by a collection of symptoms, including:

✦ Swelling (edema).
✦ Protein in the urine (proteinuria).
✦ Hypertension (high blood pressure).
✦ A change in reflexes (hyperreflexia).

Other non-specific, important symptoms with pre-eclampsia include pain under the ribs on the right side, headache, seeing spots and/or changes in vision. These are all warning signs. Report them to your doctor immediately, particularly if you've had problems with your blood pressure during pregnancy!

Most pregnant women have *some* swelling during pregnancy. Swelling in the legs doesn't mean you have pre-eclampsia. You must have some of the other symptoms of pre-eclampsia as well. It is also possible to have hypertension during pregnancy without having pre-eclampsia.

❖

What Causes Pre-Eclampsia? No one knows the exact cause of pre-eclampsia or eclampsia. However, the serious nature of seizures to both the mother and fetus are known.

Pre-eclampsia occurs most often in a woman during her first pregnancy. Women over 30 years old who are having their first baby are at an increased risk of having high blood pressure and pre-eclampsia.

Treating Pre-Eclampsia The goal in treating pre-eclampsia is the avoidance of eclampsia (avoidance of seizures). Part of this entails keeping a close watch on you throughout pregnancy.

Your blood pressure is taken at every prenatal visit. This is an important part of your visit to the doctor. Weight gain can be another sign of pre-eclampsia or worsening pre-eclampsia. This is one reason you're weighed at every prenatal visit. The change in your weight with pre-eclampsia is caused by an increase in water retention. Edema, increased blood pressure and protein in the urine are symptoms of pre-eclampsia. Other symptoms may also be less-exact warnings. If you notice *any* symptoms, call your doctor's office. He or she will probably want to see you.

Treatment of pre-eclampsia begins with bed rest at home. You may not be able to work or spend much time on your feet. Lie on your side not on your back. This type of treatment allows for the most efficient functioning of your kidneys and blood flow to the uterus.

Drink lots of water. Avoid salt, salty foods and foods that contain sodium, which may make you retain fluid. Diuretics are not prescribed to treat pre-eclampsia. These medications were used in the past, but they are not used today and are not recommended.

If you can't rest at home in bed or symptoms do not improve, it may be necessary to admit you to the hospital or to deliver your baby. The cure for pre-eclampsia is delivery. However, if your baby is premature, it may be a problem. It is most desirable to have the baby mature enough for delivery.

✧

If symptoms do not improve or if they get worse, it may become important to deliver the baby for three reasons. These are:

+ For your well-being.
+ To avoid seizures in you.
+ For the well-being of the baby.

During labor, pre-eclampsia may be treated with magnesium sulfate. It is given in an I.V. to prevent seizures during and after delivery. High blood pressure may be treated with anti-hypertensive medication.

If you think you've had a seizure, call your doctor immediately! Diagnosis may be difficult. It may be helpful to have someone who observed the possible seizure describe it to your doctor. Eclampsia (seizure) is treated with medications similar to those prescribed for seizure disorders, see page 245.

Pregnancy-Induced Hypertension   Pre-eclampsia and toxemia of pregnancy have more recently been called *pregnancy-induced hypertension.* This type of high blood pressure (hypertension) occurs only during pregnancy.

A blood pressure reading has two numbers. The first is the *systolic pressure.* The second is the *diastolic pressure.* For an average person, 120/70 (120ml of Hg/70ml of Hg) is normal.

With hypertension of pregnancy, there is an increase in the systolic pressure (the first number) to higher than 140ml of mercury or a rise of 30ml of mercury over your beginning blood pressure. A diastolic reading of 90 or a rise of 15ml of mercury also indicates a problem. An example is a woman whose blood pressure at the beginning of pregnancy is 100/60. Later in pregnancy, it is 130/90. This indicates she is developing hypertension of pregnancy or pre-eclampsia.

Keeping a watch on your blood pressure is another reason you should keep *all* your prenatal appointments. Your doctor will be able to determine if your blood pressure is rising to a serious level.

❖

How Your Actions Affect Your Baby's Development

Bed Rest and Reducing Your Activities   During pregnancy, especially as the end of pregnancy approaches, your doctor may recommend bed rest or a decrease in activities for many reasons. This is a good recommendation to follow.

Don't ignore this advice. If you ignore it, you're risking the health and well-being of your baby.

Sleeping Positions   Resting on a regular basis and lying on your side when you sleep have already been discussed. See page 159. Now is when it will pay off for you. You may notice you begin to retain water if you don't lie on your side when sleeping or resting. Lying on your side could help you feel better very quickly.

Visiting Your Doctor   It's *important* to keep appointments with your doctor. They may seem boring, or it may seem to you that you don't do much at these visits. You may believe this when everything is normal and going well.

But problems do occur. Your doctor is watching for signs that tell him or her you might have a problem, such as changes in your blood pressure, changes in your weight or inadequate growth of the baby. If these problems are not discovered early, there may be serious consequences for you and your baby at the end of pregnancy.

You Should also Know

You Can Affect the Blood Flow to Your Legs and Arms   Blood flow to your extremities, particularly your legs and feet, can be affected by the clothing you wear and by the way you sit.

Wearing tight-fitting clothing that restricts your blood flow can produce a problem in blood return from your extremities. Clothing that is very tight at the waist, knees, ankles, shoulders, elbows or wrists can cause problems.

❖

You may notice, especially as you near the end of pregnancy, that when you take your shoes off you may not be able to get them back on if you leave them off for a while. This is related to swelling.

You may also notice an indentation in your legs if you wear nylon stockings that are tight at the knee or if you wear tight socks. It may look like you still have clothing on!

Crossing your legs, either at the knee or at the ankle, restricts the blood flow to your legs. To improve circulation, don't cross your legs!

Wearing rings and watches can also cause problems. Sometimes rings become so tight on a pregnant woman's fingers that they must be cut off by a jeweler. You might not want to wear your rings if swelling occurs. I've known some pregnant women who purchased inexpensive rings in larger sizes to wear during pregnancy!

Does Every Woman Need an Enema? Many women want to know if their doctor performs routine procedures at the time of delivery. One procedure that may be done is an *enema.*

In the past, many doctors and many hospitals gave enemas routinely, without giving you much choice in the matter. There are benefits to having an enema early in labor. It decreases the amount of contamination by bowel movement or feces at the time of delivery and during labor. It may also help after delivery if you have an episiotomy. You may be happy not to have a bowel movement for a while and may be more comfortable.

Ask your doctor about whether or not an enema is routine or considered helpful. Tell him or her you'd like to know about the benefits of an enema and the reason for giving an enema in early labor. It isn't required by all doctors or all hospitals. It may be a decision you can help make.

Week 32

Age of Fetus — 30 Weeks

How Big Is Your Baby?

By this week, your baby weighs almost 4 pounds (1800g). Crown-to-rump length is over 11.6 inches (29cm). Total length is 18.9 inches (42cm).

How Big Are You?

Measurement to the top of the uterus from the pubic symphysis is about 12.8 inches (32cm). Measuring from your bellybutton, the top of the uterus now measures almost 5 inches (12cm).

How Your Baby Is Growing and Developing

Twins? Triplets? More?   When talking about pregnancies of more than one baby, in most cases we refer to twins. The chance of a twin pregnancy is more likely than pregnancy with triplets, quadruplets, quintuplets or more!

The possibility of problems rises, and there is an increase in injury and death of the fetuses when more than one baby is present during pregnancy. Possible problems include:

+ Increased miscarriage.
+ Fetal death or mortality.
+ Fetal malformations.
+ Low birth weight or growth retardation.

✧

+ Pre-eclampsia.
+ Maternal anemia.
+ Problems with the placenta, including placental abruption and placenta previa.
+ Maternal bleeding or hemorrhage.
+ Problems with the umbilical cord, including entwinement or tangling of the umbilical cords with the babies.
+ Hydramnios or polyhydramnios.
+ Labor complicated by abnormal fetal presentation, such as breech or transverse.
+ Premature labor.

Twin fetuses most commonly result from the fertilization of two separate eggs. They are called *dizygotic twins* or *fraternal twins*. With fraternal twins, you can have a boy and a girl.

About 33% of the time, twins come from a single egg that divides into two similar structures. Each has the potential of developing into a separate individual. These twins are called *monozygotic twins* or *identical twins*. These two babies will almost always be the same sex. Identical twins are *not* always identical. It is possible for fraternal twins to appear more alike than monozygotic twins!

Either or both processes may be involved when more than two fetuses are formed. For example, quadruplets may result from fertilization of one, two, three or four eggs.

When one egg is involved in the formation of twins, the time of the division of the egg determines whether or not identical twins result. Division of the fertilized egg occurs between the first few days and about day 8. In this book, I refer to it as the third week of pregnancy.

If division of the egg happens after 8 days, the result can be twins that are connected, called *conjoined twins*. (The term used to be *Siamese twins*, but that term has been replaced by *conjoined twins*.) Conjoined twins are a very serious complication of pregnancy. These babies may share important internal organs, such as the heart, lungs or liver. Fortunately this is a rare occurrence.

Frequency of Twin Births The frequency of twins depends on the type of twins developing. Twins from one egg occur about once in every 250 births around the world. This type of twin formation appears to be uninfluenced by age, race, heredity, number of pregnancies or medications taken for infertility (fertility drugs).

The incidence of fraternal twins *is* influenced by race, heredity, maternal age, the number of previous pregnancies and the use of fertility drugs.

The frequency of twin or multiple fetuses varies significantly in different races. Twins occur in 1 out of every 100 pregnancies in white women compared to 1 out of every 79 pregnancies in black women. Certain areas of Africa have an incredibly high frequency of twins. In some places, twins occur once in every 20 births!

The occurrence of twins among Orientals is less common: about 1 in every 150 births. Different twin birth rates among different races appears to be in the frequency of *fraternal* twins.

Heredity also plays a part in the occurrence of twins. The side of the family that is most important is the mother's side of the family rather than the father's. In one study in which the woman was a fraternal twin, the chance of her giving birth to a set of twins was about 1 in 58 births. Women who were not a twin but whose partners were a fraternal twin gave birth to twins at a rate of about 1 set for every 126 pregnancies. Increased maternal age and higher numbers of deliveries are factors that increase the chance of twins occurring.

The occurrence of twins is probably more common than we know. Early ultrasound exams often reveal two sacs or two pregnancies. Later ultrasounds of the same woman may show one sac or one pregnancy has disappeared, while the other pregnancy continues to grow and develop normally. Some researchers believe ultrasound should not be done in the first 8 to 10 weeks of pregnancy. Parents who are informed of twins at this point may be very distraught to learn later that one of the babies will not be born.

❖

Triplets occur once in every 8,000 deliveries. Many doctors never deliver or participate in the delivery of triplets in their medical careers.

Some families are more blessed than others. In one case I know of, a woman had three single births. Her fourth pregnancy was twins, and her fifth pregnancy was triplets! She and her husband decided on another pregnancy—they were surprised (and probably very relieved) when the sixth pregnancy resulted in only one baby.

Fertility Medication, In-Vitro Fertilization and Multiple Pregnancies   We have known for a long time that fertility drugs increase the chance of multiple pregnancies. Several different medications are used to treat infertility; each has a different possibility for increasing the chance of two or more fetuses developing. One of the more common medications is clomiphene (Clomid®); it increases the chance of multiple fetuses somewhat less than other medications. But there is still an increased chance of twins.

The occurrence of twins is more common in pregnancies that result from in-vitro fertilization. This may be due to the frequent use of fertility medications to increase the chance of a pregnancy occurring with in-vitro fertilization. The percentage of male fetuses decreases as the number of fetuses per pregnancy increases. This means more females are born in these pregnancies.

Discovering You're Carrying More than One Baby   Diagnosis of twins was more difficult before ultrasound was available. The illustration on the next page shows an ultrasound of twins. You can see parts of both fetuses.

It is uncommon to discover twin pregnancies just by hearing two heartbeats. Many people believe when only one heartbeat is heard, there could be no possibility of twins. This may not be the case. Two very rapid heartbeats may have a similar or almost-identical rate. That would make it difficult to tell there are two babies.

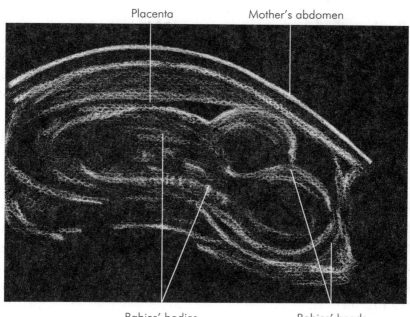

Placenta   Mother's abdomen

Babies' bodies   Babies' heads

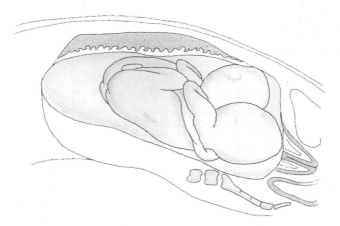

Ultrasound of twins shows two babies in the uterus. If you look closely, you can see the two heads. The interpretive illustration shows how the babies are lying.

✧

A family history of twins provides only a small clue to the possibility of a twin pregnancy. The use of fertility medications, such as Clomid, is a better indication of this possibility.

Measuring and examining your abdomen during pregnancy is important. Usually a twin pregnancy is noted during the second trimester because you are too big and growth seems to be too fast. When your uterus appears too large for the gestational age, there are many possibilities. These include:

+ More than one fetus.
+ A distended bladder.
+ Inaccurate menstrual history.
+ Too much amniotic fluid.
+ Uterine myomas or fibroids (benign tumors or lumps of the uterus).
+ An enlarged ovary, such as with an ovarian cyst.
+ A baby that is large for a specific reason, such as maternal diabetes.

Ultrasound examination is the best method to determine if you are carrying more than one baby. Diagnosis could also be made by X-ray after 16 to 18 weeks of pregnancy, when fetal skeletons are visible. However, this method is used very infrequently today.

Do Multiple Pregnancies Have More Problems? Spontaneous miscarriage is more likely to occur with multiple fetuses. Occasionally one fetus will die during the pregnancy, and the pregnancy will continue with the living fetus. There may or may not be any evidence of this twin pregnancy at delivery. It depends on how early the pregnancy was lost. If the pregnancy developed to the point where there was a fetus and then it was compressed by the other pregnancy, there may be a silhouette called a *fetus papyraceous* on the placental membranes.

❖

The possibility of fetal death also increases with delivery of more than one baby. Some centers have reported a loss as high as 10% or more for multiple pregnancies.

One of the biggest problems with multiple pregnancies is premature delivery. As the number of fetuses *increases*, the length of gestation and the birth weight *decreases*. The average pregnancy for twins is about 37 weeks. For triplets it is about 35 weeks. For every week a baby remains in the uterus, its birth weight increases, along with the maturity of its organs and systems.

Major malformations in multiple pregnancies are almost double those of single pregnancies. The incidence of minor malformation is also twice as high, compared to single pregnancies. Malformations are more common among identical twins than fraternal twins.

Women with multiple fetuses must realize there can be problems with premature delivery and decreased fetal weight. To reduce death and injury in multiple pregnancies, follow your doctor's instructions exactly! He or she is concerned about your health and the health of your babies.

One of the main goals in dealing with multiple fetuses is to continue the pregnancy as long as possible and avoid premature delivery. This may best be accomplished by bed rest. You may not be able to carry on with regular activities during your entire pregnancy. There are risks to your unborn babies and the possibility of premature delivery. If your doctor recommends bed rest, follow his or her instructions.

Every day and every week you're able to keep the babies inside you are days or weeks you won't have to visit them in an intensive-care nursery while they grow, develop and finish their maturing.

Maternal requirements for calories, protein, minerals, vitamins and essential fatty acids also increase with a multiple-fetus pregnancy. If you have a multiple pregnancy, your energy consumption increases by about 300 calories a day more than a normal pregnancy.

❖

Weight gain is of critical importance with a multiple pregnancy. You will gain more than the normal 25 to 30 pounds, depending on the number of fetuses present. Supplementation with iron is essential. Pregnancy with one baby decreases your hematocrit. Pregnancy with multiple fetuses decreases the hematocrit even more, making iron supplementation even more critical.

Some researchers believe use of tocolytic agents, such as ritodrine, is critical in preventing premature delivery. See pages 273-274. These agents are used to relax the uterus to keep you from going into premature labor. It is the only drug approved by the FDA for this use.

Delivering More than One Baby   The method of delivering multiple fetuses is controversial. How they are born often depends on how the babies are lying in your uterus. Possible complications of labor and delivery, in addition to prematurity, include:

+ Abnormal presentations (breech or transverse).
+ Prolapse of the umbilical cord (the umbilical cord comes out ahead of the babies).
+ Placental abruption.
+ Fetal distress, such as that caused by a knot in the umbilical cord.
+ Bleeding after delivery.

These problems occur much more often with multiple fetuses. Because there is higher risk during labor and delivery, precautions are taken before delivery and during labor. These include the need for an I.V., the presence of an anesthesiologist and your doctor, and the availability and possible presence of pediatricians or other medical personnel to take care of the babies.

With twins, all possible combinations of fetal positions can occur. Both babies may come head first, called *vertex*. They may come breech, meaning bottom or feet first. They may come sideways or oblique, meaning at an angle that is neither breech nor vertex. Or they may come in any combination of the above.

Some doctors believe delivery of two or more babies requires a C-section. This is not believed by all. When both twins are head first, a vaginal delivery may be attempted and can be accomplished safely. It may be possible for one baby to deliver normally. The second one could require a C-section if it turns, the cord comes out ahead of the baby or the baby is distressed following delivery of the first fetus.

After delivery of two or more fetuses, strict attention must be paid to maternal bleeding because of the rapid change in size of the uterus. It is greatly overdistended with more than one baby. Bleeding requires an I.V. of medication, usually oxytocin (Pitocin®). It is given to make the uterus contract and stop bleeding so the mother doesn't lose too much blood. A large blood loss could produce anemia and necessitate a blood transfusion or long-term treatment with iron supplementation.

If you are told you are carrying twins, you and your partner may be in shock when you learn you have more than one baby growing inside you! This is a normal reaction. The realization of the joy of two babies at once may eventually help offset the fear and responsibility.

If you are expecting two or more babies, you will need to visit your doctor more often. You will need to plan carefully for delivery and care of the babies after you go home.

Changes in You

Until this week, your visits to the doctor have probably been on a monthly basis, unless you've had complications or problems. At week 32, most doctors begin seeing a pregnant woman every 2 weeks. This will continue until you reach your last month of pregnancy; at that time, you'll probably switch to weekly visits.

It's important to keep your appointments and see your doctor on a regular basis. In this way, he or she will be able to discover and deal with any problems or complications.

By now you probably know your doctor fairly well and feel comfortable talking about your concerns. Asking questions and finding out about things is a good opportunity for you to get to know your doctor. Now is a good time to ask questions and discuss concerns or problems. If there are complications or problems later in pregnancy or at delivery, you'll be able to communicate with your doctor and know what is going on. You'll feel comfortable with the care you're receiving.

Your doctor may plan on talking to you about many things in the weeks to come, but you can't always assume this. You may be taking prenatal classes and hearing different things about labor and delivery, such as stories about enemas, I.V.s and complications. Don't be afraid to ask your doctor any questions you have. Most doctors and nurses are receptive to your queries. They want you to discuss things you're concerned about instead of worrying about them unnecessarily.

How Your Actions Affect Your Baby's Development

Taking Prenatal Vitamins Sometimes late in pregnancy a pregnant woman stops taking her prenatal vitamins because she gets tired of taking them or she decides they're not necessary. This is a mistake!

The vitamins and iron in prenatal vitamins are essential to your well-being and the well-being of your baby. If you're anemic at the time of delivery, a low blood count could impact on you and your baby. Your chance of needing a blood transfusion could be higher. Blood transfusion is avoided whenever possible at delivery.

You Should also Know

Postpartum Bleeding and Hemorrhage It's not unusual to lose blood during labor and delivery. A heavy postpartum hemorrhage can be very significant. *Postpartum hemorrhage* is a loss of blood in excess of 17 ounces (500ml) in the first 24 hours after your baby's birth.

It is desirable to avoid excessive blood loss at the time of labor and delivery. Hemorrhaging after delivery is the cause of about 25% of all maternal deaths from obstetric bleeding.

There can be many reasons for postpartum hemorrhage. The most common causes of immediate postpartum hemorrhage are a uterus that will not contract, called *uterine atony*, and lacerations or tearing of the vagina or cervix during the birth process.

Other causes include trauma to the female genital tract, such as a large or bleeding episiotomy, or a rupture, hole or tear in the uterus. Failure of blood vessels inside the uterus (where the placenta was attached) to compress to stop bleeding may result in problems with blood loss. This may occur when the uterus fails to contract because of very rapid labor, a long labor, history of several previous deliveries, a uterine infection, an overdistended uterus (with multiple fetuses) or with certain agents used for general anesthesia.

Heavy bleeding may also result from retained placental tissue. In this situation, most of the placenta delivers, but part of it remains inside the uterus. Retained placental tissue may cause bleeding immediately, or bleeding may occur weeks or even months later.

Problems with blood clotting or coagulation can cause hemorrhaging. This may be related to pregnancy, or it may be a congenital medical problem that has been present for your entire life.

Bleeding following delivery requires constant attention from your doctor and the nurses caring for you.

Week 33

Age of Fetus — 31 Weeks

How Big Is Your Baby?

Your baby is continuing to grow; it weighs about 4.4 pounds (2000g) by this week. Its crown-to-rump length is about 12 inches (30cm). Its total length is 19.4 inches (43cm).

How Big Are You?

Measuring from the pubic symphysis, the top of the uterus is now about 13.2 inches (33cm). The measurement from your bellybutton to the top of your uterus is about 5.2 inches (13cm). Your weight gain should be between 22 and 28 pounds (9.9 and 12.6kg).

How Your Baby Is Growing and Developing

Placental Abruption   The illustration on page 311 shows the uterus with the fetus inside and placental abruption. *Placental abruption* is the separation of the placenta from the wall of the uterus. Normally, the placenta does not separate from the uterus until after the baby is delivered. When separation occurs before delivery, it can be very serious for the baby. It can even cause fetal death.

The frequency of abruption of the placenta is estimated to be about 1 in every 80 deliveries. We do not have a more-exact statistic because time of separation varies, altering the risk to the fetus. If the placenta separates at the time of delivery and the infant is delivered without incident, it is not as significant as a placenta separating during pregnancy, which causes a serious problem, such as blood loss or death of the fetus.

The cause of placental abruption is unknown. Certain conditions may increase the chance of it occurring. Factors include:

+ Trauma to the mother, such as from a car accident.
+ A short umbilical cord.
+ Very sudden change in the size of the uterus (from delivery or rupture of membranes).
+ Hypertension.
+ Dietary deficiency.
+ An abnormality of the uterus, such as a band of tissue in the uterus (called a *uterine septum*), where the placenta cannot attach properly.

Separation of the placenta may occur with partial or total separation from the uterine wall. The situation is most severe when the placenta totally separates from the uterine wall. The fetus relies entirely on circulation from the placenta. With separation, it receives no blood supply from the umbilical cord, which is attached to the placenta.

Studies indicate that deficiency of folic acid can play a role in causing placental abruption. But not everyone agrees with this theory. Others have suggested maternal smoking and alcohol consumption may make the mother more likely to have placental abruption.

A woman who has had placental abruption in the past is at increased risk of having it occur again. Rate of recurrence has been estimated to be as high as 1 in 10 pregnancies. This can make a pregnancy following placental abruption a high-risk pregnancy.

With placental abruption, the placenta may continue to be partially attached to the uterus, or it may separate completely. Bleeding actually occurs between the placenta and the uterus. It may be obvious bleeding from the vagina, which is usually associated with pain in the abdomen. Or there may be no bleeding at all, if blood is contained behind the placenta inside the uterus. The illustration here shows bleeding behind the placenta with complete separation. There is no apparent bleeding from the cervix and vagina.

Signs and Symptoms of Placental Abruption   Signs and symptoms of placental abruption can vary quite a bit. There may be heavy bleeding from the vagina. Or you may experience no bleeding at all. Other symptoms can include death of the fetus, signaled by a lack of fetal movement. Lower-back pain, tenderness of the uterus or abdomen and contractions or tightening of the uterus are other signs to look for.

Ultrasound may be helpful in diagnosing this problem, although it does not always provide an exact diagnosis. This is particularly true if the placenta is located on the back surface of the uterus where it cannot be seen easily on ultrasound examination.

Serious maternal problems may occur with separation of the placenta, such as shock. Shock can occur because of rapid loss of large quantities of blood. Another problem that can occur is intravascular coagulation, sometimes called *DIC* (*disseminated intravascular coagulation*). In this instance, a large blood clot is present. Factors in the blood that make the blood clot may be used up. This can make bleeding a problem because clotting factors are not available.

Of the various signs and symptoms associated with placental abruption, vaginal bleeding occurs in about 75% of all cases. Tenderness of the uterus occurs about 60% of the time. Fetal distress or problems with the fetal heart rate occur in 60% of the cases. Tightening or contraction of the uterus occurs about 34% of the time. Premature labor occurs in about 20% of the cases, and fetal death occurs about 15% of the time.

Can Placental Abruption Be Treated?   Treatment of placental abruption varies, based on the ability to diagnose the problem and the status of the mother and baby. With very heavy bleeding, delivery of the baby may be necessary to control bleeding and save the lives of the infant and mother.

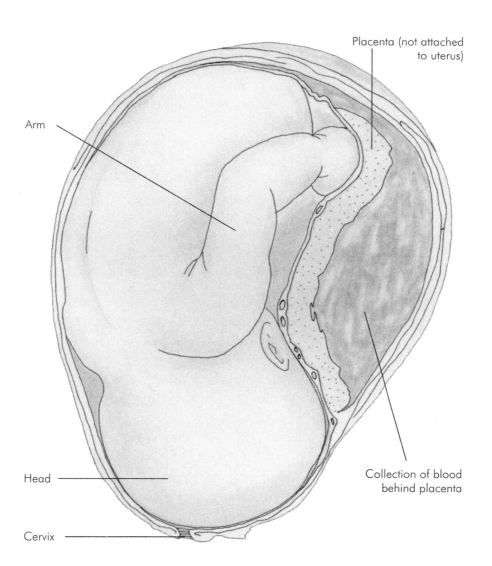

Placenta (not attached to uterus)

Arm

Head

Cervix

Collection of blood behind placenta

This illustration of placental abruption shows the placenta has separated from the wall of the uterus.

When bleeding occurs at a slower rate, the problem may be treated with a more-conservative approach. This depends on whether the fetus is in distress, if it is alive and if it appears to be in immediate danger.

Ultrasound may be used to try to identify placental abruption. However, if no blood clot is seen on ultrasound, it doesn't completely eliminate the possibility of placental abruption.

If it is necessary to deliver the baby rapidly, it may require a C-section. The mother may receive a blood transfusion if blood loss is excessive. If the fetus dies, a normal vaginal delivery may be preferred to avoid bleeding that can accompany a Cesarean section. Each case must be handled on an individual basis.

Placental abruption is one of the most serious problems related to the second and third trimesters of pregnancy. If you have any symptoms, call your doctor immediately!

Changes in You

How Will You Know Your Membranes Have Ruptured?   When your bag of waters breaks, it isn't usually just one gush of water, with no further leakage. There often is a gush of amniotic fluid. However, it is usually followed by a leaking of small amounts of fluid. Women describe it as a constant wetness or water running down their leg when they stand. This continual leakage of water is a good clue your water has broken and you're leaking amniotic fluid.

Amniotic fluid is usually clear. Occasionally it may have a bloody appearance or it may be yellow or green.

It isn't uncommon to have an increased vaginal discharge or to lose urine in small amounts as your baby puts pressure on your bladder. But there are ways for your doctor to tell if your water has broken. Two tests can be done on the amniotic fluid.

One is a *nitrazine test*. When amniotic fluid is placed on a small strip of paper, it changes the color of the paper. This test is based on the acidity or pH of the amniotic fluid. However, blood can also change the color of nitrazine paper, even if your water hasn't broken.

Another test that may be done is a *ferning test*. Amniotic fluid or fluid from the back of the vagina is taken with a swab and placed on a slide for examination under a microscope.

Dried amniotic fluid has the appearance of a fern or branches of a pine tree. Ferning is often more helpful in diagnosing ruptured membranes than looking at color changes on nitrazine paper.

What Do You Do When Your Water Breaks? Your membranes may rupture at any point in pregnancy. Don't assume it will only happen around the time of labor.

If you think your water has broken, notify your doctor. Avoid sexual intercourse at this time. Intercourse increases the possibility of introducing an infection into your uterus and thus to your baby.

How Your Actions Affect Your Baby's Development

Your Weight Gain You are continuing to gain weight as your pregnancy progresses. You may be gaining weight faster than at any other time during pregnancy. This is because your baby is going through a period of growth. It may be gaining as much as 8 ounces (224g) every week!

Don't stop eating or start skipping meals because you're concerned about these pounds. Both you and your baby need the calories and nutrition you receive from your eating.

Eat the right foods for you. Heartburn may be more of a problem now because your growing baby may not allow much room for your stomach. You may find eating several small meals, rather than three large meals, makes you feel more comfortable. Follow the guidelines on pages 82-85, and listen to your doctor's advice.

You Should also Know

Will Your Doctor Perform an Episiotomy? A concern you may have before delivery is whether or not you will need an episiotomy. An *episiotomy* is an incision made from the vagina toward the rectum during delivery to avoid undue tearing as the baby's head passes through. It may be a cut directly in the midline toward the rectum, or it may be a cut to the side, called a *mediolateral episiotomy.*

There is little you can do about whether or not you will need an episiotomy. Some people practice, teach and believe in stretching the birth canal during labor and at the time of delivery to try to avoid an episiotomy. It may work for some, but it doesn't work for every woman. Others suggest an episiotomy to avoid stretching the vagina, bladder and rectum. In some cultures, all deliveries are by C-section. This is done so the vagina is not stretched during delivery. Stretching the vagina can change sensations experienced during sexual intercourse.

The reason for an episiotomy usually becomes clear at delivery when the baby's head is in the vagina. The episiotomy substitutes a controlled, straight, clean cut for a tear or rip that could go in many directions. This may include tearing or ripping into the bladder, into large blood vessels or into the rectum. It's easier to repair a surgical incision that your doctor makes. And an episiotomy heals better than a tear that may be ragged.

Ask your doctor if he or she thinks you may need an episiotomy. Discuss why an episiotomy is necessary. Find out whether it might be a cut in the middle or to the side of the vagina. You might also ask if there is anything you can do to prepare for the possibility of an episiotomy, such as an enema or stretching the vagina.

If forceps are used for delivery, an episiotomy may be done before forceps are placed on the baby's head.

Different doctors have a preference for a midline episiotomy as compared to a mediolateral episiotomy. Don't be afraid to discuss this with your doctor before delivery.

Description of an episiotomy also includes a description of the depth of the incision.

+ A *first-degree episiotomy* cuts only the skin.
+ A *second-degree episiotomy* cuts the skin and underlying tissue, called *fascia*.
+ A *third-degree episiotomy* cuts the skin, underlying tissue and rectal sphincter, which is the muscle that goes around the anus.

✦ A *fourth-degree episiotomy* goes through these three layers and through the rectal mucosa.

Layers are closed separately with absorbable sutures that do not require removal after they heal.

After delivery of your baby, the most painful part of the entire birth experience might be the episiotomy. It may continue to cause some discomfort as it heals. Don't be afraid to ask for medication to ease any pain. There are many safe medications you can take, even if you are breast-feeding your baby, including acetaminophen (Tylenol®). Tylenol with codeine® or other medication may also be prescribed for the pain.

Delivery of the Placenta   In most instances, the placenta is delivered within 30 minutes after the birth of your baby. It is a routine part of the delivery of your baby. However, complications can arise if the placenta adheres to the lining of the uterus.

With a *retained placenta*, the placenta does not deliver spontaneously. See page 360 for further information. An exam may be performed and the placenta removed under local or general anesthesia. The type of anesthesia used depends on how difficult it is to remove the placenta. See page 370 for further information on pain relief during labor and delivery.

Complications may require a D&C. Portions of the placenta are scraped from the lining of the uterus. If the placenta cannot be separated from the uterus, it may be necessary to perform a hysterectomy and remove the entire uterus along with the placenta to prevent serious, heavy bleeding.

A retained placenta is very unusual. However, it is impossible to predict these types of complications ahead of time. Problems may occur more often in women who have had a previous retained placenta, Cesarean delivery or a D&C for miscarriage or heavy bleeding.

Week 34

Age of Fetus — 32 Weeks

How Big Is Your Baby?

Your baby weighs almost 5 pounds (2275g) by this 34th week of your pregnancy. Its crown-to-rump length is about 12.8 inches (32cm). Total length is 19.8 inches (44cm).

How Big Are You?

Measuring up from your bellybutton, it is about 5.6 inches (14cm) to the top of your uterus. From the pubic symphysis you will measure about 13.6 inches (34cm).

It's not important whether or not your measurements match any of your friends' at similar points in their pregnancies. What's important is you're growing appropriately and your uterus grows and gets larger at an appropriate rate. These are signs of normal growth of your baby inside your uterus.

How Your Baby Is Growing and Developing

Testing Your Baby Before Birth? An ideal test done before delivery would determine if the fetus is healthy. It would be able to detect major fetal malformations or fetal stress, which could indicate an impending problem.

Ultrasound accomplishes some of these goals by allowing observation of the fetus inside the uterus along with evaluation of the brain, heart and other organs of the fetal body. Along with ultrasound examinations, monitoring an infant has been done in the form of a non-stress test or a contraction-stress test to indicate fetal well-being or problems. This is described on page 331.

Biophysical Profile   A comprehensive test, called a *biophysical profile,* is used to examine the fetus even further while it is still in the uterus. The test helps determine fetal health. It is done when there is concern about fetal well-being. It may also be done when a pregnancy goes past the expected due date.

A biophysical profile uses a particular scoring system. Five areas are identified and given a score between 0 and 2. The five areas of evaluation include:

✦ Fetal breathing movements.
✦ Gross body movements.
✦ Fetal tone.
✦ Reactive fetal heart rate.
✦ Amount of amniotic fluid.

During the test, fetal "breathing" is evaluated. This is movement or expansion of the baby's chest inside the uterus. It is observed with the use of ultrasound, and a score is given. The score is based on the amount of fetal breathing that occurs. A normal score is 2; abnormal is 0.

Movement of the baby's body is noted. A score of 2 indicates normal body movements. A score of 0 is applied when there are few or no body movements during the allotted time period.

Fetal tone is evaluated by movement of the arms and/or legs of the baby. A normal score is 2; an abnormal score is 0. Fetal movement and tone are also observed with ultrasound.

Fetal heart-rate monitoring is done with external monitors. It evaluates changes in the fetal heart rate that are associated with movement of the baby. A normal score is 2; an abnormal score is 0. The amount of change and number of changes in the fetal heart rate differ, depending on who is doing the test and their definition of normal.

Amniotic-fluid volume is evaluated by using ultrasound. This requires experience in ultrasound examination. A normal pregnancy or normal infant has adequate fluid around

✧

the baby (score 2). An abnormal test indicates no amniotic fluid or decreased amniotic fluid around the baby (score 0).

A score of 1 in any of the tests is a middle score. From these five scores, a total score is obtained by adding the values from all tests. Evaluation may vary depending on the sophistication of the equipment used and the expertise of the person doing the test. The higher the score, the better the baby's condition. With a lower score, there may be concern about the well-being of the fetus.

If the score is low, a recommendation may be made to deliver immediately. If the score is reassuring, the test may be repeated at weekly or twice-weekly intervals. If test results fall between these two values, it may be necessary to repeat the test the following day. This depends on the circumstances of your pregnancy and the findings of the biophysical profile. Your doctor will evaluate all of this information before making any decision.

A biophysical profile may be valuable in evaluating an infant with IUGR, pregnancy of a diabetic mother, a pregnancy in which the baby doesn't move very much, high-risk pregnancies or overdue pregnancies. Because ultrasound is an important part of a biophysical profile, it may be useful in finding major congenital problems and evaluating the well-being of the infant inside the uterus.

Changes in You

How Much Does Your Baby Weigh? By this time, you have probably asked your doctor several times how big your baby is and how much your baby will weigh when it's born. Next to asking about the sex of a baby, these are two of the most frequently asked questions.

Estimating the weight of the baby is extremely difficult. Many doctors will guess and give a range of 1 to 2 pounds in either direction. It's very difficult to determine how much a baby, placenta and amniotic fluid will weigh. Some of my estimates have been really off! It's not uncommon to guess an infant will weigh 8 pounds only to find it is a 6-pound, 8-ounce baby!

As you can see in the illustration, you're getting larger. The baby is growing, the placenta is growing and the amount of fluid around the baby is increasing. All these factors make estimating fetal weight more difficult.

Using Ultrasound to Estimate Fetal Weight Ultrasound can be used to estimate fetal weight, but errors in weight estimates can and do occur. The accuracy of predicting fetal weight using ultrasound is improving and can be valuable.

Several measurements are used in a formula to estimate the weight of a baby. These include diameter of the baby's head, circumference of the baby's head, circumference of the baby's abdomen, length of the femur of the baby's leg and, in some instances, other fetal measurements.

This testing is the method of choice to estimate fetal weight. But even with ultrasound, estimates may vary as much as 0.5 pound (225g) in either direction.

Will Your Baby Fit Through the Birth Canal? Even with an estimation of fetal weight, whether by your doctor or ultra-sound, your doctor can't tell if the baby is too big for you or whether you'll need a C-section.

Usually, it's necessary for you to have labor to be able to see how the baby fits into your pelvis and whether or not there is room for it to pass through the birth canal.

Doctors can't always tell if a baby will fit or not fit through the birth canal before labor begins. In some women who appear to be average or better-than-average size, a 6- or 6.5-pound (2.7 to 2.9kg) baby won't fit through the pelvis. Experience has also shown women who may appear to be petite are sometimes able to deliver 7.5-pound (3.4kg) or larger babies without much difficulty.

The best test or method of evaluating whether your baby will deliver through your pelvis is labor.

✧

How Your Actions Affect Your Baby's Development

The end of your pregnancy begins with labor. One of the end results of labor is the birth of your baby.

Some women are concerned (or hope!) that their actions can cause labor to begin. The old wives' tales about going for a ride over a bumpy road or taking a long walk to start labor aren't true. We do know intercourse and stimulation of the nipples may cause labor to start in some cases, but this isn't true for every woman.

You don't need to fear that going about your daily activities (unless your doctor has advised bed rest) will cause labor to start before your baby is ready to be born.

What Is Labor? It's important to know what to expect when labor occurs and what you should do when it begins. What causes labor? Why does it happen?

At this time, we don't have a good answer to this question. The factors that cause labor to begin are unknown. There are many theories; one is that hormones made by the mother and fetus trigger labor. It could be that a hormone produced by the fetus makes the uterus contract.

Labor is defined as the dilatation (stretching, expanding) of the cervix. This occurs because the uterus, which is a muscle, tightens to squeeze out the contents (the baby). As it pushes the baby out, the cervix stretches. It may be possible to feel tightening, contractions or cramps, but in the purest sense of the definition, it isn't labor until there is a change in the cervix.

Three Stages of Labor Labor is divided into three stages. The *first stage of labor* begins with uterine contractions of great enough intensity, duration and frequency to cause thinning (effacement) and dilatation of the cervix. The first stage of labor ends when the cervix is fully dilated (usually 10cm) and sufficiently open to allow the baby's head to come through it.

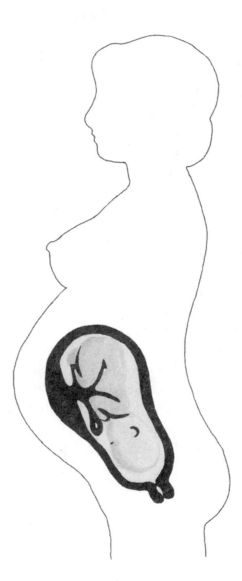

Comparative size of the uterus at 34 weeks of pregnancy (fetal age—32 weeks). The uterus can be felt about 5.6 inches (14cm) above your bellybutton.

✧

The *second stage of labor* begins when the cervix is completely dilated at 10cm. This stage ends with the delivery of the baby.

The *third stage of labor* begins after delivery of the baby. It ends with delivery of the placenta and the membranes that have surrounded the fetus.

Some doctors have even described a *fourth stage of labor*, referring to a time period after delivery of the placenta while the uterus continues to contract. Contraction of the uterus is important in controlling bleeding that can occur after delivery of the baby and the placenta.

False Labor and Braxton-Hicks Contractions   *False labor* often occurs before true labor begins. False labor contractions can be very painful and may appear to be real labor to you.

In most instances, false-labor contractions are irregular. They are usually of short duration (less than 45 seconds). The discomfort of the contraction may occur in various parts of your body, such as the groin, lower abdomen or back. With true labor, uterine contractions produce pain that starts at the top of the uterus and radiates over the entire uterus, through the lower back into the pelvis.

False labor is usually seen in late pregnancy. It seems to occur more often in women who have been pregnant and delivered more babies. It usually stops as quickly as it begins. There doesn't appear to be any danger to your baby.

Braxton-Hicks contractions during pregnancy are painless, non-rhythmical contractions you may be able to feel when you place your hand on your abdomen. These contractions often begin early in pregnancy. Contractions are felt at irregular intervals. They may increase in number and strength when the uterus is massaged. Like false labor, they are *not* positive signs of true labor.

What Is a Bloody Show?   Often following a vaginal examination or with the beginning of early labor and early contractions, you may bleed a small amount of blood. This is called

✧

a *bloody show;* it can occur as the cervix stretches and dilates. It shouldn't be a large amount of blood. If it causes concern or appears to be a large amount of blood, call your doctor immediately.

Along with a bloody show, you may pass mucus, sometimes called a *mucus plug,* at the beginning of labor. This is different from your bag of waters breaking or ruptured membranes. Passing this mucus plug doesn't necessarily mean you'll have your baby soon or even that you'll go into labor in the next few hours. It causes no danger to you or your baby.

How Long Will Labor Last?   Length of labor varies from woman to woman and from pregnancy to pregnancy. It also depends on how many pregnancies or deliveries you've had before.

The length of the first and second stages of labor, from the beginning of cervical dilatation to delivery of the baby, can last 14 to 15 hours or more in a first pregnancy. Women have had faster labors than this, but don't count on it.

A woman who has already had one or two children will probably have a shorter labor, but don't count on that either! The average time for labor is usually decreased by a few hours for a second or third delivery.

Everyone's heard of women who barely make it to the hospital or had labor lasting only 1 hour. For every one of those patients, there are many women who have labored 18, 20, 24 hours or more.

It's almost impossible to predict the amount of time that will be required for your labor. You may ask your doctor about it, but his or her answer is only a guess.

Timing Contractions   Most women are instructed in prenatal classes or by their health-care provider about how to time contractions during labor.

To time *how long* a contraction lasts, you begin timing when the contraction starts and end timing when the contraction lets up and goes away.

✧

It's important to know *how often* contractions occur. There is much confusion about this. There are two methods. With the first, the interval between contractions is noted by the time period when a contraction *starts* to the time when another contraction *starts*. This method is the most common one used and the most reliable.

With the second method, the interval between contractions is noted by the time period from when a contraction *ends* to the time when the next contraction *starts*. Ask your doctor which method he or she prefers.

It's helpful for you and your partner or labor coach to time your contractions before calling your doctor or the hospital. Your doctor will probably want to know how often contractions occur and how long each contraction lasts. With this information, your doctor can make the decision of whether it's time for you to go to the hospital or if you should remain at home longer.

You Should also Know

Will My Baby Drop? Often a few weeks before labor begins or at the beginning of labor, you may notice a gradual or rapid change in your abdomen. When examined by your doctor, measurement from your umbilicus or the pubic symphysis to the top of the uterus may be *smaller* than what you noticed on a previous visit. This phenomenon occurs as the head of the baby enters the birth canal. It can also be a part of the decrease in amniotic fluid that may occur without rupture of membranes or loss of fluid. This change is often called *lightening*.

Don't be concerned if you don't notice lightening or a drop of the fetus. This doesn't always occur with every woman or with every pregnancy. It's very common for your baby to drop during labor or on the day labor begins.

With lightening, you may experience benefits and problems. One benefit may be an increase in room in your upper abdomen. This gives you more room to breathe because

✧

there's more room for your lungs to expand and move. However, with the descent of the baby, you may notice more pressure in your pelvis, bladder and rectum, which can make you more uncomfortable.

In some instances, your doctor may examine you and tell you your baby is "not in the pelvis" or "it is high up." He or she is saying the baby has not yet descended into the birth canal. However, this can change very quickly. When your baby "drops," it begins its descent into the birth canal.

If your doctor says your baby is "floating" or "ballotable," it means the part of the baby felt in the birth canal is high. But the baby is not engaged (fixed) in the birth canal at this point. The baby may even bounce or move away from your doctor's fingers when you are examined.

Some Uncomfortable Feelings You May Experience A common complaint many women have is the feeling the baby is going to "fall out." This feeling is related to the pressure of the baby because it has moved lower in the birth canal. Some women describe the feeling as an increase in pressure.

If you're concerned or worried about it, consult your doctor. It may be a reason to perform a pelvic exam to see how low the baby's head is. In almost all cases, the baby will not be coming out. But at a lower position than what you're used to, it will apply more pressure than you noticed during recent weeks.

Another feeling associated with this increased pressure of the baby may occur around this week. Some pregnant women have described it as "pins and needles." This feeling is tingling, pressure or numbness in the pelvis or pelvic region from the pressure of the baby. It is a common symptom and shouldn't concern you.

These feelings may not be relieved until delivery occurs. You can lie on your side to help decrease pressure in your pelvis and on the nerves, vessels and arteries in the pelvic area.

If the problem is severe, talk to your doctor about it. Don't try to move the baby or push the baby out of the way. It could be dangerous for both of you.

Week 35

Age of Fetus — 33 Weeks

How Big Is Your Baby?

Your baby now weighs over 5.5 pounds (2550g). Crown-to-rump length by this week of pregnancy is about 13.2 inches (33cm). Its total length is 20.25 inches (45cm).

How Big Are You?

Measuring from the umbilicus, it is now about 6 inches (15cm) from your bellybutton to the top of the uterus. Measuring from the pubic symphysis, the distance is about 14 inches (35cm).

By this week, your weight gain should be between 24 and 29 pounds (10.8 and 13kg).

How Your Baby Is Growing and Developing

What Is Placenta Previa?   With *placenta previa*, the placenta lies close to the cervix or it covers the cervix. The illustration on page 329 shows placenta previa.

There are usually four different degrees of placenta previa. These include:

+ *Total placenta previa*. The placenta covers the entire opening to the cervix. (The opening of the cervix is called the *cervical os.)*
+ *Partial placenta previa*. The placenta partially covers the cervical os.

✧

+ *Marginal placenta previa.* The edge of the placenta is at the edge or margin of the opening of the cervix.
+ *Low-lying placenta.* The placenta is low in the uterine segment; the edge of the placenta does not actually reach the cervical os but is very close to it.

If an ultrasound examination is performed early in pregnancy (before the first 20 weeks), the placenta may appear to be low in the uterus. Its normal position is in the middle or upper part of the uterus. However, the placenta may not remain low. If an ultrasound is done later, very often the placenta is much higher in the uterus.

Placenta previa is serious because of the chance of heavy bleeding. Bleeding may occur during pregnancy or during labor. This problem is not a frequent occurrence; it happens about once in every 170 pregnancies.

The cause of placenta previa is not completely known. Risk factors for an increased chance of placenta previa include previous Cesarean delivery, many pregnancies and increased maternal age.

Signs and Symptoms of Placenta Previa   The most characteristic symptom in placenta previa is painless bleeding without any contractions of the uterus. This doesn't usually occur until close to the end of your second trimester or later when the cervix thins out, stretches and tears the placenta loose. Some researchers believe many spontaneous miscarriages occur because location of the placenta is low, meaning placenta previa.

Bleeding with placenta previa may occur without warning and may be extremely heavy. It occurs when the cervix begins to dilate and open with early labor, and blood escapes.

The placenta does not usually attach near the opening of the uterus. When it does, the placenta may be abnormally adherent or stuck to the wall of the uterus. The chance of placenta accreta, placenta increta or placenta percreta are more common. See page 361 for further information. These placental attachments may cause excessive bleeding after delivery.

Placenta previa should be suspected when a woman experiences vaginal bleeding during the latter half of pregnancy. The problem cannot be diagnosed with a physical exam. A pelvic examination may cause heavier bleeding. It is usually necessary to use ultrasound to identify placenta previa. Using ultrasound to locate the placenta can be very accurate, particularly in the second half of pregnancy as the uterus and placenta get bigger.

If you know you have placenta previa, your doctor may tell you not to have a pelvic exam. This is important to remember and to explain if you see another doctor or when you go to the hospital.

With placenta previa, the baby is more likely to be in a breech position. For this reason, and also to control bleeding, a Cesarean delivery is almost always performed. An advantage of Cesarean delivery is the ability to deliver the baby and then remove the placenta so the uterus can contract. Bleeding can be kept to a minimum.

Changes in You

Emotional Changes in Late Pregnancy   As you reach the last trimester and come closer to delivery, you and your partner may become more anxious about the events that will occur. You may even experience an increase in mood swings, which seems to occur for no reason. Many women and their partners report an increase in irritability, which can place a significant pressure or strain on their relationship.

You may be concerned about insignificant or unimportant things. Concern about the health and well-being of the baby may also increase during the last weeks of your pregnancy. This can include concern about whether or not you will be able to tolerate labor and how you will get through delivery. You may be concerned about whether or not you'll be a good mother or be able to raise a baby properly.

✧

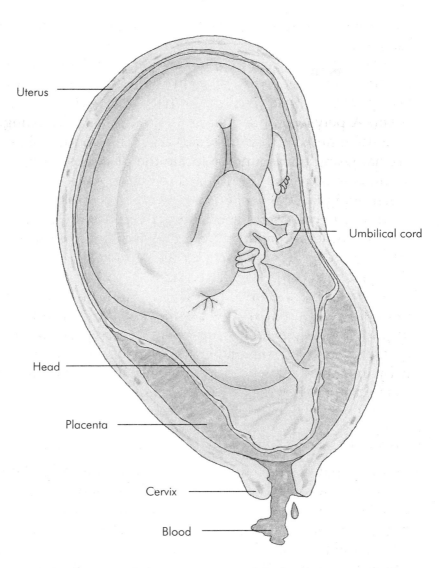

Uterus

Umbilical cord

Head

Placenta

Cervix

Blood

In this illustration of placenta previa, note how the placenta completely covers the cervical opening to the uterus.

And while all of these emotions are raging through you, you'll notice you're getting bigger and aren't able to do things you used to do. You may feel more uncomfortable, and you may not be sleeping well. All this can work together to make your emotions swing wildly from highs to lows.

✧

How Can You Deal with These Changes? Changes are normal; don't feel like the "Lone Ranger." Other pregnant women and their partners have the same concerns.

Talk with your partner about your concerns. Keep him involved in how you feel and what's going on. You may be surprised to learn about the concerns your partner has about you and the baby and about his role during labor and delivery. By talking about these things, it may make it easier for your partner to understand the changes in you—mood swings, crying spells and other uncommon occurrences.

Talk to your doctor about any emotional problems. Reassurance that what you're going through is normal may make you feel a little better. Take advantage of prenatal classes and information available about pregnancy and delivery.

Be aware of the emotional changes that can occur, and be ready for them. Ask your partner, the nurse in the doctor's office and your doctor to help you understand what is normal, and not normal, and what can be done about your emotional swings.

Pregnancy happens only a few times in your life. Enjoy it while you can. Just don't lose sight of the miracle happening to you and your partner!

How Your Actions Affect Your Baby's Development

Can Your Baby Get Tangled in the Cord? Some women are told by friends they shouldn't raise their arms over their head or reach high to get things because it can cause the cord to wrap around the baby's neck. There doesn't seem to be *any* substance to this theory, and it has never been proved.

Some babies get tangled in their umbilical cord and can get the cord tied in a knot or wrapped around their neck. There is nothing *you* can do during pregnancy to prevent this from happening.

It isn't necessarily a problem during labor. It only becomes a problem if the cord is stretched tight around the neck or in a knot. Also see page 277.

✧

Will Working at a Computer Terminal Hurt Your Baby? Some people have expressed concern about a pregnant woman working in front of a computer screen (at a computer terminal). At this time, no reports or studies have come to the conclusion that a woman working at a computer terminal can harm her baby in any way.

If you work at a computer terminal (or at a typewriter), the only things you probably have to be concerned about are the way you sit and how long you sit. Sit in a chair that offers good support for your back and legs. Don't slouch or cross your legs while sitting down. And be sure to get up and walk around at least once every 15 minutes—you need to keep good circulation in your legs.

You Should also Know

Fetal Monitoring Before Labor Begins The biophysical profile, as discussed on page 317, is a method of evaluating the well-being of your baby inside your uterus. Part of the biophysical profile is fetal monitoring, commonly called a *non-stress test*.

A non-stress test is performed in your doctor's office or in labor and delivery. While you are lying down, a fetal monitor is attached to your abdomen. When your baby moves, a signal is recorded on the monitor paper along with a recording of the baby's heartbeat.

Movement of the fetus usually results in an increase in the fetal heart rate that can be seen on the monitor. Specific criteria are used to evaluate how well a baby is tolerating life inside the uterus. Your doctor will decide whether further action is necessary.

Getting Ready for the Birth Many pregnant women and their partners are concerned they won't know when it's time to call the doctor or when to go to the hospital. Talk to your doctor about it at one of your visits so you know what to watch for. Prenatal classes teach you the signs of labor and when you should call your doctor or go to the hospital.

Know what the signs of *labor contractions* are. They are usually regular. They increase in duration and strength and have a regular rhythm to them. Time them so you know how frequently they occur and how long they last. See page 323. How soon you go to the hospital depends in part on your contractions.

Sometimes labor is preceded by *rupture of your membranes*. This is usually a gush of water often followed by a continual leaking from the vagina. This is discussed in more depth beginning on page 312.

During the last few weeks of pregnancy, it's a good idea to have a suitcase packed and ready to go. When labor begins, you'll have the things ready that you want to have with you in the hospital.

If possible, tour the hospital facilities a few weeks ahead of your scheduled due date. Find out where to go and the best way to get there.

Talk with your partner about the best ways to reach him if you think you've gone into labor. It might be a good idea to have him check with you periodically. It is quite common for the partner to wear a pager if he is often away from a phone, especially during the last few months of the pregnancy.

Find out from your doctor what he or she wants you to do if you think you're in labor. Is it better to call the office? Should you go directly to the hospital? Should you call the answering service?

By knowing what to do, and when, you'll be able to relax a little and not worry about the beginning of labor and delivery.

Week 36

Age of Fetus — 34 Weeks

How Big Is Your Baby?

By this week, your baby weighs about 6 pounds (2750g). Its crown-to-rump length is over 13.5 inches (34cm). Total length is 20.7 inches (46cm).

How Big Are You?

Measuring from the pubic symphysis, it's about 14.5 inches (36cm) to the top of your uterus. If you measure from your bellybutton, it's over 5.5 inches (14cm) to the top of your uterus.

You may feel like you've run out of room! Your uterus has grown bigger in the past few weeks as the baby has grown inside of it. Now the uterus is probably up under your ribs. You may feel as if you have no more room to grow.

How Your Baby Is Growing and Developing

What Is a Cesarean Delivery?   Most women plan on a normal vaginal birth. However, the possibility of a Cesarean delivery is always there. With a Cesarean delivery, the baby is delivered through an incision made in the mother's abdominal wall and uterus. The illustration on page 335 shows a Cesarean delivery. Common names for this type of surgery are *C-section*, *Cesarean section* and *Cesarean delivery*. C-sections are done for many reasons, as discussed on the next page.

✧

+ The most common reason is a *previous Cesarean delivery.* Many women who have had C-sections are able to have a vaginal delivery with later pregnancies. It depends on the reason for the previous Cesarean deliveries. Discuss it with your doctor, especially if you've had a C-section and would like to deliver vaginally this time.
+ Repeat C-sections were done *to avoid rupture of the uterus.* There is a risk that the area of repair could stretch and pull apart during subsequent labor and delivery. This could be serious for the baby and mother. However, if pregnancy and labor are closely monitored, a woman may be able to have a normal vaginal delivery.
+ Your baby may be too big to fit through the birth canal. This is called *cephalo-pelvic disproportion (CPD).* CPD not only occurs with a large baby; the problem indicates that proportionately, the baby is too large to fit through your birth canal. CPD can be suspected during pregnancy but usually requires labor contractions before it can be determined.
+ *Fetal distress* is another reason for a Cesarean. Fetal monitors are used during labor to watch the fetal heartbeat and its response to labor. If the heartbeat indicates the baby is having trouble with labor contractions, it may be necessary to perform a C-section for the baby's well-being.
+ *Compression of the umbilical cord* may necessitate a C-section. This may occur when the cord comes into the vagina ahead of the baby's head, called a *prolapsed umbilical cord,* or if the baby presses on part of the cord. This is dangerous because a compressed umbilical cord can cut off the blood supply to the baby.
+ Another reason for a C-section is a *breech position,* which means the baby's feet or buttocks deliver first. Delivering the shoulders and the head after the baby's body may cause damage to the baby's head or neck, especially with a first baby.

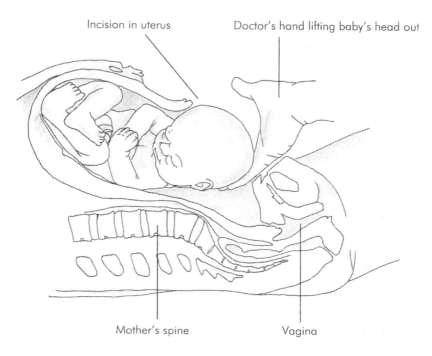

Delivery of a baby by Cesarean section.

◆ *Placental abruption* may necessitate a Cesarean delivery. If the placenta separates from the uterus before delivery, the baby loses its supply of oxygen and nutrients. This is usually diagnosed when a woman has heavy vaginal bleeding.

◆ *Placenta previa* may also be a cause for a C-section. If the placenta blocks the birth canal, delivery of the baby is impossible. If you have placenta previa, you will probably deliver your baby by C-section.

Rising Rate of Cesarean Deliveries In 1965, only 4% of all deliveries were by C-section. Today, in the U.S., 24% of all deliveries are Cesarean deliveries. In some areas it is even a higher percentage. This increase can be related to more stringent monitoring during labor and safer operative procedures for C-sections. Another reason for more Cesarean deliveries is bigger babies. With bigger babies, more women find a C-section is the only way they can deliver.

Researchers believe this increase in the size of babies is due to pregnant women eating a better diet and not smoking during pregnancy.

The rising rate may also be related to the pressure on doctors to deliver a baby safely while at the same time not performing a C-section on every woman. In addition, skyrocketing malpractice rates and fear of litigation are factors that affect the rate of Cesarean deliveries. (Malpractice insurance rates exceed over $100,000 a year for obstetricians in some areas of the U. S.) So as you can see, there isn't any single reason we can point to as to why the Cesarean-delivery rate has increased to almost 25% of all deliveries.

How Is a C-Section Performed? When a C-section is done, you may be awake. An anesthesiologist usually gives you an epidural or spinal anesthetic. Types of anesthesia are discussed beginning on page 370. If you're awake for the procedure, you may be able to see your baby immediately after delivery!

With a C-section, an incision is made through the skin of the abdominal wall down to the uterus. The wall of the uterus is cut. Then the amniotic sac containing the baby and placenta is cut. The baby is removed through the incision in the uterus and abdomen.

After the baby is delivered, the placenta is removed. The uterus is closed in layers with sutures that absorb and do not have to be removed. The remainder of the abdomen is sewn together with absorbable sutures.

Most Cesarean deliveries done today are called *low-cervical Cesareans* or *low-transverse Cesareans*. This means the incision is made low in the uterus.

In the past, a Cesarean was often done with a *classical incision*. The uterus was cut down the midline. This type of incision doesn't heal as well as a low-cervical. It is more likely to break during a subsequent pregnancy because the incision was in the muscular part of the uterus. With contractions (as with a vaginal birth after Cesarean—VBAC), it's more likely to pull apart. This can cause heavy bleeding and injury to the baby. If you have had a classical Cesarean section in the past, you *must* have a C-section every time you have a baby.

A *T-incision* is another type of C-section incision. This incision goes across and up the uterus in the shape of an inverted T. It provides more room to get the baby out. If you have had this type of incision, you will need to have a Cesarean delivery with all subsequent pregnancies because it's more likely to rupture.

Advantages and Disadvantages of Having a C-Section There are advantages to having a C-section. The most important *advantage* is delivery of a healthy infant. The baby you are carrying may be too large to fit through your pelvis. The only safe method of delivery might be a C-section. Usually a woman needs to experience labor before her doctor will know whether the baby will fit or not. It may be impossible to predict ahead of time.

The *disadvantage* of a Cesarean section is that this type of delivery is a major operation and carries with it the risks of major surgery. Risks include infection, bleeding, shock through blood loss, the possibility of blood clots and injury to other organs, such as the bladder or rectum. You will probably stay in the hospital an extra couple of days.

Recovery at home from a Cesarean section takes longer than recovery from a regular delivery. The normal time for *full* recovery is usually 4 to 6 weeks.

In most areas, an obstetrician performs a C-section. In small communities, C-sections may be performed by a general surgeon or a general practitioner.

Will You Need a Cesarean? It would be nice to know you're going to need a C-section before delivery so you wouldn't have to go through labor. Unfortunately, it isn't that easy. Usually it's necessary to await the contractions of labor to see if your baby is stressed by them. It's also necessary to wait to see if the baby will fit through your birth canal.

✧

If you deliver by C-section, don't feel as though you have failed in any way. The goal in pregnancy, labor and delivery is a healthy baby and a healthy mother. In many situations, the only way to achieve this goal is with a Cesarean delivery.

Changes in You

You only have 4 to 5 weeks to go until your due date. It's very easy to get anxious for your baby to be delivered. Everyone has known a friend or relative who has had their baby a little early and everything was OK.

You have been pregnant for about 36 weeks, and you are probably tired of it. But don't begin to ask your doctor to induce labor at this point.

You may have gained 25 to 30 pounds (11.25 to 13.5kg), and you still have a month to go. It isn't unusual for your weight to stay the same at each of your weekly visits after this point.

The maximum amount of amniotic fluid surrounds the baby now. In the weeks to come, the baby continues to grow. However, some amniotic fluid is reabsorbed by your body, which decreases the amount of fluid around the baby and the amount of room for the baby to be able to move. You may notice a difference in sensation of the baby's movements. In some women, it feels as if the baby is not moving as much as it had been.

How Your Actions Affect Your Baby's Development

Vaginal Birth After Cesarean? In this case, discussion of how your actions affect your baby is focused on making a decision about delivery. Should you attempt a vaginal delivery after having had a previous C-section? Vaginal birth after Cesarean (VBAC) is becoming more common. The main goals in delivery are a healthy baby and your good health. The method of delivery is not as important as the well-being of you and your baby!

❖

Before you and your doctor make any final decision, you need to weigh the risks and benefits to you and your baby with both types of delivery. In some cases, you won't have any choice in the matter. In other cases, you and your doctor may decide to let you labor for a while to see if you can deliver vaginally. You need to be as well-informed as you can be to make this decision. Only then will you be able to know how your actions can affect your baby.

Some women like having a repeat Cesarean section. They request it because they don't want to go through labor only to end up with a Cesarean delivery anyway. And if they have children at home already, it's easier to plan the delivery and hospital stay if they have a C-section.

Advantages and Risks of VBAC   Advantages to a vaginal delivery include a decreased risk of injury from a major surgery. Because Cesarean birth is major surgery, it involves risks associated with any surgery. Recovery after a vaginal delivery is shorter. You can be up and about in the hospital and at home in a much shorter amount of time.

The type of incision previously performed on the uterus can dictate whether or not labor can be attempted. With a classical incision that goes high up on the uterus, labor is not permitted.

Other factors to consider in deciding about the possibility of a C-section include whether you are small and the baby is large. This combination makes it less likely for you to have a safe delivery.

Multiple fetuses, such as two or more babies, may make vaginal delivery difficult or impossible without extreme danger to the babies. Medical complications, such as high blood pressure or diabetes, may require a repeat Cesarean section.

If you're going to attempt a vaginal delivery after a Cesarean section, discuss it with your doctor in advance so plans can be made. During labor, you will probably be monitored more closely with fetal monitors. I.V.s may need to be in place in case a Cesarean section needs to be done.

✧

It's important to consider the benefits *and* risks in deciding whether to attempt a vaginal delivery after a previous Cesarean section. It should be discussed at length with your doctor and your partner throughout your pregnancy. Don't be afraid to ask your doctor his or her opinion as to your chances of a successful vaginal delivery. He or she knows your health and pregnancy history.

You Should also Know

Your Baby's Apgar Score   After a baby is born, it is examined and evaluated at 1 minute and 5 minutes after delivery. The system of evaluation is called the *Apgar Score*. This scoring system is a method of evaluating the overall well-being of the newborn infant.

In general, the higher the score, the better the condition of the infant. Areas scored include:

+ Heart rate of the baby.
+ Respiratory effort of the baby.
+ Baby's muscle tone.
+ Reflex irritability.
+ Color of the baby.

Each of these areas is scored with a 0, 1 or 2; 2 points is the highest score for each category. The top total score is 10.

If the heart rate is absent, a score of 0 is given. If it is slow, less than 100 beats per minute (bpm), a score of 1 is given. If it's over 100 bpm, a score of 2 is given.

Respiratory effort indicates the newborn's attempts at breathing. If the baby is not breathing, the score is 0. If breathing is slow and irregular, the score is 1. If the baby is crying and breathing well, the score is 2.

Muscle tone evaluates how the baby moves. If arms and legs are limp and flaccid, the score is 0. If there is some movement and some bending of the arms and legs, the score is 1. If the baby is active and moving, the score is 2.

✧

Reflex irritability is scored 0 if there is no response to stimulus, such as rubbing of the baby's back or arms. A score of 1 is given if there is a small movement or a grimace when the baby is stimulated. A score of 2 is given if the baby cries vigorously.

The baby's color is rated 0 if the baby is blue or pale. A score of 1 is given if the baby's body is pink and arms and legs are blue. A score of 2 is given if the baby is completely pink.

A perfect score of 10 is unusual. Most babies receive scores of 7, 8 or 9 in a normal, healthy delivery.

A baby with a low 1-minute Apgar Score may need resuscitation. This means a pediatrician or nurse must help stimulate the baby to breathe and to recover from the delivery.

In most cases, the 5-minute Apgar is higher than the 1-minute score as the baby becomes more active and more accustomed to being outside the uterus.

Week 37

Age of Fetus — 35 Weeks

How Big Is Your Baby?

Your baby weighs almost 6.5 pounds (2950g). Crown-to-rump length is 14 inches (35cm). Its total length is 21 inches (47cm).

How Big Are You?

Your uterus may stay the same size as measured in the last week or two. Measuring from the pubic symphysis, the top of the uterus is 14.8 inches (37cm). From the umbilicus, it is 6.4 to 6.8 inches (16 to 17cm) in length. Your weight gain by this time should be about as high as it will go at 25 to 30 pounds (11.2 to 13.5kg).

How Your Baby Is Growing and Developing

Is My Baby's Head Down in the Pelvis?   Your baby is continuing to grow and gain weight even during these last few weeks of pregnancy. As the illustration on page 345 shows, the baby's head is usually directed down into the pelvis around this time. However, in about 3% of all pregnancies, the baby's bottom or legs come into the pelvis first. Called a *breech position*, this is discussed on page 357-360.

Maturation of Your Baby's Lungs and Respiratory System
A very important part of your baby's development is maturation of the lungs and respiratory system. When a baby is

born prematurely, a common problem is development of respiratory distress syndrome in the newborn fetus. This problem has also been called *hyaline membrane disease*. In this situation, lungs are not completely mature. The baby is unable to breathe on its own without assistance. Oxygen and possibly even a machine, such as a ventilator, are necessary to breathe for it.

In the early 1970s, methods were developed to evaluate the maturity of fetal lungs through amniocentesis. This allowed a doctor to determine if a baby would be able to breathe on its own, without assistance from a machine. The test is called an *LS-ratio*. It measures the ratio of lecithin to sphingomyelin. Results provide an index of fetal-lung maturation.

Different labs have different values for an LS-ratio, but there is a level at which lungs are mature. The test does not usually indicate a baby is mature until at least 34 weeks of pregnancy. At that time, the amount of lecithin in the amniotic fluid increases, and the amount of sphingomyelin decreases. The ratio indicates whether the baby's lungs are mature.

Another test that is done to evaluate the maturity of the fetal lung is the *phosphatidyl glycerol (PG)*. This test is either positive or negative. If phosphatidyl glycerol is present in the amniotic fluid, there is considerable assurance that respiratory distress will *not* develop in the infant.

Specific cells in the lungs, called *type-2 pneumonocytes*, produce chemicals that are essential for respiration immediately after birth. An important part of a newborn baby's breathing is determined by a chemical called *surfactant*. A baby born prematurely may not have surfactant in its lungs. In a revolutionary treatment started in 1989, surfactant is introduced *directly* into the lungs of the newborn to prevent respiratory-distress syndrome. The chemical is immediately available for use by the baby.

Many of the premature babies that receive surfactant do not have to be put on respirators—they can breathe on their own!

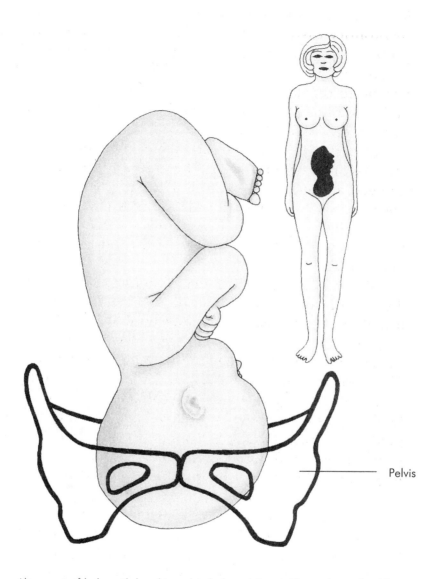

Pelvis

Alignment of baby with head in pelvis before delivery. This is the preferable presentation position.

✧

Changes in You

Pelvic Exam in Late Pregnancy   At this point in your pregnancy, your doctor may do a pelvic exam or one may have been done already. When a pelvic exam is done at this time, many factors are being evaluated. One of the first things observed is whether or not you are leaking amniotic fluid. If you think you are, it's important to tell your doctor.

During a pelvic exam, the cervix is also examined. Its softness or firmness and the amount of thinning are evaluated. During labor, the cervix usually becomes softer and thins out, called *effacement*.

Before labor begins, the cervix is thick. It might be called *0% effaced*. When you're in active labor, the cervix thins out. When it is half-thinned, it is *50% effaced*. Before delivery, the cervix is *100% effaced* or *completely effaced*.

The dilatation (amount of opening) of the cervix is also important. This is usually measured in centimeters; the goal is to be a 10! The cervix is fully dilated when the diameter of the cervical opening measures 10cm, and the cervix is completely opened. Before labor begins, the cervix may be closed. Or it may be open a small amount, such as 1cm (0.4 inch). The goal of labor is the stretching and opening of the cervix so the baby fits through it and can then pass out of the uterus.

Also evaluated at this time during a pelvic exam is the presenting part. This describes whether the baby's head or bottom or legs are coming first. Shape of your pelvic bones is also noted.

The station is also determined. *Station* describes the degree of descent of the presenting part of the baby into the birth canal. If your doctor tells you the baby's head is at a -2 station, the head is higher up inside you than if it is at a +2 station. Zero is at your spine, which is a bony landmark in the pelvis.

When thinking about the station of the presenting part of the baby, think of the birth canal as a tube going from the

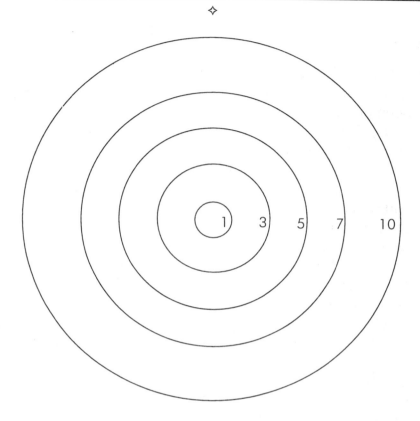

Cervical dilatation in centimeters.

pelvic bone down through the pelvis and out the vagina. This is the area that the baby travels through from the uterus. It is possible during labor for you to dilate but not have the baby move down through the pelvis. A reason for doing a C-section is a situation in which you dilate to a certain degree, but the baby's head doesn't come down through the pelvis far enough. In other words, the baby's head doesn't fit.

What Can Your Doctor Tell from a Pelvic Exam? When you have an exam by your doctor, he or she may describe your situation in medical terms. You might hear you are "2cm,

✧

50% and a -2 station." This means the cervix is open 2cm (about 1 inch), it is halfway thinned out (50% effaced) and the presenting part is at a -2 station.

It's helpful to remember this information when your doctor checks you. When you go to the hospital and are checked there by a nurse or if your doctor isn't there, this information can be helpful. You can tell the medical personnel in labor and delivery what your dilatation and effacement were so they can know if your situation has changed or not.

How Your Actions Affect Your Baby's Development

Choosing Your Baby's Doctor   At this point in your pregnancy, it's time to choose a doctor for your baby. You might choose a *pediatrician*—a doctor who specializes in treating children. Or you might choose a *family practitioner*. If the doctor you are seeing during pregnancy is a family practitioner, and you want him or her to care for your baby, you probably don't need to consider this at all.

It's good to meet the doctor before the birth of your baby. Many pediatricians welcome it. This gives you the opportunity to discuss matters that are important to you with this new care giver. You might want to talk to him or her about a circumcision for your baby if it's a boy. You may want to ask questions about breast-feeding, exams, inoculations and vaccinations, emergencies and other things that concern you. It's also good to find out whether a particular doctor shares your views on child rearing.

One way to find a doctor for your baby is to ask for references. You can ask the doctor who is caring for you during pregnancy. Ask family and friends. Ask people in your prenatal classes.

By choosing someone to care for your baby before it's born, you have a chance to take part in deciding who will have that important task. If you do not choose someone, the doctor who delivers your baby or hospital personnel will select someone. Another good reason for choosing someone ahead of time is if your baby has complications, your doctor will know whom to call.

After your baby is born, the pediatrician will visit him or her in the hospital. The pediatrician will do a physical exam on the baby within 24 hours after birth. Then he or she will visit you in the hospital and let you know how things are going for the baby.

Preregistering at the Hospital   During pregnancy, your doctor has recorded various things that have occurred during the past 37 weeks. A copy of this record is usually kept in the labor-and-delivery area.

It may be very helpful and save you time if you register at the hospital a few weeks before your due date. You will be able to do this with forms that you get at your doctor's office or by getting forms from the hospital. It's wise to do this before you go to the hospital in labor because you may be in a hurry or concerned with other things.

There are certain facts you should know that may or may not be included in your chart. It's helpful to know your blood type and Rh-factor. You should be able to tell them when your last period was and when your due date is. Be able to describe other pregnancies or complications with other pregnancies. Know your doctor's name and your pediatrician's name.

Will You Have an Enema?   Will you be required to have an enema when you arrive at labor and delivery? Most hospitals offer an enema at the beginning of labor, but it is not usually mandatory.

There are certain advantages to having an enema before labor. After your baby's delivery, you may not want to have a bowel movement because of discomfort with an episiotomy. Having an enema before labor can prevent this discomfort.

An enema before labor can also make the birth of your baby a more pleasant experience. When the baby's head comes out through the birth canal, anything in the rectum comes out, too.

Discuss it with your doctor. Find out his opinion and the policy at the hospital you're going to.

You Should also Know

What Is Back Labor?   Some women experience back labor. *Back labor* refers to a baby that is coming out through the birth canal looking straight up. With this type of labor, you will probably experience lower-back pain.

The mechanics of labor work better if the baby is looking down at the ground as it is coming out. It is able to extend its head as it comes out through the birth canal. If the baby is not coming out looking down at the ground, the baby is unable to extend its head. Its chin points toward its chest. This can cause more pain in your lower back during labor.

This type of labor may also take longer for delivery. It may require rotation of the baby's head by your doctor so it comes out looking down at the ground rather than looking up at the sky.

How Is Your Baby Presenting?   At what point in your pregnancy can your doctor tell how your baby is presenting—whether or not the baby's head is down or if you are carrying the baby breech? At what point will the baby stay in the position it is in?

Usually between 32 and 34 weeks of pregnancy, the baby's head can be felt in the lower abdomen below your umbilicus. In some women, it's possible to feel different parts of the baby earlier than this. But the baby's head may not be hard enough to feel to determine whether it's the head your doctor is feeling.

The head gradually becomes harder as calcium is deposited in the fetal skull. Your baby's head has a distinct feeling. It is different from the feeling your doctor gets with a breech. A breech position has a soft, round feeling.

✧

Beginning at 32 to 34 weeks, your doctor will probably feel your abdomen to determine how the baby is lying inside you. This position may change many times during pregnancy.

At 34 to 36 weeks of pregnancy, the baby usually gets into the position it's going to stay in. If you have a breech at 37 weeks, it's possible the baby can still turn and be head down. But this becomes less likely the closer you get to the end of your pregnancy.

It may be difficult at times to tell the exact location of different parts of the baby. You may have a good idea by where you feel kicks and punches. Ask your doctor to show you on your tummy how the baby is lying. Some doctors even take a pen and draw on your stomach to show you. You can leave it so you can show your partner how your baby was lying when you were seen in the office that day.

Will My Doctor Have to Use Forceps?   The use of *forceps*—metal instruments used in the delivery of babies—has decreased in recent years for a couple of reasons. One is the more-frequent use of Cesarean delivery to deliver a baby that might be very high up inside the pelvis. A C-section is much safer for the baby if it's not very close to delivering on its own.

Another reason for the decrease in the use of forceps is the use of a *vacuum extractor*. There are two types of vacuum extractors. One has a plastic cup that fits on the baby's head by suction. The doctor is able to pull on the vacuum cup as the baby's head is delivered. There is also a metal cup that can be placed on the baby's head. It also uses vacuum pressure to allow the doctor to pull on the baby for delivery. These vacuums easily release from the baby's head, so the baby can't be pulled as hard through the birth canal as with forceps.

The goal is to deliver the baby as safely as possible. If a large amount of traction with forceps to deliver the baby is needed, a Cesarean section would probably be better.

Your doctor won't be able to tell you how you're going to deliver until you're in labor. It's important to establish good communication with your doctor through regular visits so you can talk to each other and be able to communicate when you're in labor.

Week 38

Age of Fetus — 36 Weeks

How Big Is Your Baby?

At this time, your baby weighs about 6.8 pounds (3100g). Crown-to-rump length hasn't changed much; it's still about 14 inches (35cm). Total length is 21 inches (47cm).

How Big Are You?

You may still be getting bigger. However, many women don't grow larger during the last several weeks of pregnancy. But many feel very uncomfortable. Measuring your uterus from the pubic symphysis, it is 14.4 to 15.2 inches (36 to 38cm). From your bellybutton to the top of your uterus is about 6.4 to 7.2 inches (16 to 18cm).

How Your Baby Is Growing and Developing

Fetal Monitoring During Labor You may wonder how your doctor can tell your baby is all right, especially during labor. In many hospitals, the baby's heart rate is monitored throughout labor. An important goal during labor is the well-being of your baby. Being able to detect problems early is important so they can be resolved to avoid harming the baby.

Every time the uterus contracts during labor, there's a reduction in the flow of oxygenated blood from you to the baby. Most babies are able to handle this stress without any problem. However, if there are problems, this stress could be detrimental to your baby.

❖

Problems could include the cord being wrapped around the baby's neck or tied in a knot. It could be a problem with the placenta, such as placental abruption. A problem could be related to medications you have taken before labor or during labor.

There are two different ways to monitor the baby's heartbeat during labor. One can be used before your membranes rupture. It is called *external fetal monitoring.* A belt with a receiver is strapped to your abdomen. It uses a principle similar to ultrasound to detect the baby's heartbeat.

A more-precise method of monitoring the baby's heartbeat is with an *internal fetal monitor.* An electrode is placed on the fetal scalp. It is connected by wires to a machine that records the fetal heart rate. The use of an internal fetal monitor requires your membranes to be broken and for you to be dilated to at least 1cm.

An internal fetal monitor gives a more-exact reading of the fetal heart rate. This can be very helpful in determining the well-being of your baby.

The fetal heart rate is normally between 120 and 160 beats per minute. Fewer than 120 beats is slow and is called *bradycardia.* Faster than 160 is *tachycardia.*

Evaluating the Results of Fetal Monitoring In evaluating a fetal heart rate, it's important to look at a large portion of the fetal monitoring strip, not only a small section. Different things are noted besides the heart rate. If you are having contractions, it's important to know how the baby is affected. The pattern of most concern is a decreasing fetal heartbeat with a mother's contraction that takes a long time to recover.

Another test is called a *contraction stress test (CST).* Some believe this test is more accurate than the non-stress test, discussed on page 331, in evaluating the well-being of the baby. A monitor is placed on your abdomen to monitor the fetal heart rate and its reaction. An I.V. is started, and oxytocin is given in small amounts to make your uterus contract. This test gives an indication of how well the baby will tolerate contractions and labor. If the baby doesn't respond well to the contractions, it can be a sign of fetal distress.

If you've had problem pregnancies before, such as a stillbirth, or medical problems during pregnancy, such as diabetes, your doctor may have you tested often as you go through pregnancy. You may be tested weekly or biweekly to determine if the baby is doing well inside the uterus.

Fetal Blood Sampling   Another method of evaluating how well a baby is tolerating the stress of labor is the fetal blood pH. Membranes must be ruptured, and you must be dilated at least 2cm before this test can be done.

An instrument is applied to the scalp of the baby to make a small nick in the skin. The baby's blood is collected in a small tube or pipette, and its pH (acidity) is checked. If the baby is having trouble with labor and is under stress, the pH level can help determine this. This test may be useful in making a decision as to whether or not labor can continue or if a C-section needs to be done.

Changes in You

Depression During Pregnancy   Anti-depressant medication is not generally given during pregnancy because it is not considered safe. Prescribing anti-depressants during pregnancy involves the risk of fetal malformation or other harmful effects on a newborn.

If medication *is* necessary, most physicians prefer to use those that have been in use for a while, such as tricyclic anti-depressants (amitriptyline, desipramine, Sinequan®, Amoxopine®). Most evidence indicates there is no rate of increased malformations if these medications must be used during pregnancy. With some of the newer medications for depression, such as fluoxetine (Prozac®), there is little or no information about their use or safety in pregnancy. Without some type of evidence that they are safe, physicians hesitate to prescribe them.

All anti-depressant medications pass through the placenta to the fetus. There have been isolated case reports of teratogenic effects. See page 98. If these medications must be used during pregnancy, it's best to use the lowest dosage possible.

An infant born to a mother who takes anti-depressants during pregnancy may have withdrawal symptoms. These include tachycardia, decreased gastrointestinal motility, urinary retention, respiratory distress, difficulty feeding, diarrhea and other problems.

Treating depression during pregnancy can be a difficult problem. It must be done on an individualized basis. Your doctor and possibly a psychologist or psychiatrist may be involved in your treatment. Discuss medications you take for depression with your doctor.

What Are Postpartum Blues?   Depression after delivery is often called *postpartum blues* or *postpartum baby blues.* It may be a moderate form of depression that can become more severe. It can even become a psychosis.

Some estimates have indicated up to 70% of all women experience postpartum blues to some degree. This type of depression is often seen within the first week or 2 after delivery. It doesn't usually last more than a month to 6 weeks.

Emotions expressed with postpartum blues usually include:

✦ Anger at yourself or the newborn baby.
✦ Anger at other children.
✦ Feeling lonely.
✦ Sense of defeat.
✦ Headache.
✦ Confusion.
✦ Mood changes.
✦ Sleeplessness.
✦ Forgetfulness.

❖

Postpartum baby blues rarely require drug therapy. Usually support of family and friends helps you feel better.

Depression After Birth of a Baby Depression is the most frequently seen emotional problem during or immediately after pregnancy. Some studies indicate up to 10% of all women experience mild to moderate depression during pregnancy. About 15% of all women suffer from depression following delivery (beyond postpartum blues).

Women who seem most susceptible to depression related to pregnancy are those who have a personal or family history of depression. Women who have a highly stressful life at work or at home may also experience depression. Age seems to be important—the rate of depression increases as a woman gets older.

Depression can occur as long as a year after delivery. This type of depression often occurs because of lack of emotional support from the baby's father.

Warning signals for depression include:

+ Sleep disturbance.
+ A change in eating habits.
+ Weight loss.
+ Lack of bonding between mother and baby.
+ Prolonged or unusual fatigue.
+ Loss of interest in normal activities.
+ Mood swings.

True depression is a serious situation. A woman suffering from depression may be hostile to her baby. Or she may have thoughts of harming the baby or other children in the family. It can be a psychiatric problem.

This problem should be identified as soon as possible. Care may require hospitalization or the use of medication.

How Your Actions Affect Your Baby's Development

Breech Presentation As I've already discussed, it's common for your baby to be in the breech presentation early in pregnancy. However, at the time of labor, only 3 to 5% of all

✧

babies, not including twin or multiple pregnancies, present as a breech. Do your actions determine how your baby presents?

Certain factors make it more likely for a woman to have a breech presentation. One of the main causes is prematurity in the baby. Near the end of the second trimester, it's more common for the baby to be in a breech presentation. Taking care of yourself, as ordered by your doctor to avoid going into premature labor, can allow your baby the opportunity to change its position, if necessary.

Other factors include relaxation of the uterus because of previous pregnancies. Multiple fetuses, polyhydramnios, hydrocephalus and uterine abnormalities or tumors may increase the chance of a breech presentation.

There are different kinds of breech presentations. A *frank breech* occurs when the lower legs are flexed at the hips and extended at the knees. This is the most common type of breech found at term or the end of your pregnancy. The feet are up by the face or head.

With a *complete breech presentation,* one or both knees are flexed not extended. See the illustration on page 359. In an *incomplete breech presentation,* a foot or knee enters the birth canal ahead of the rest of the baby.

If a breech presentation is suspected, it's usually confirmed by ultrasound. This helps identify how the baby is lying inside you.

Delivering a Breech Baby　There is some controversy in obstetrics over the method of delivering a breech baby. For many years, breech deliveries were performed vaginally. Then it was believed the safest method was to deliver the breech by C-section, particularly if a woman was having her first baby.

Many doctors believe a Cesarean section is *still* the safest method of delivering a breech fetus. However, some doctors believe a woman can deliver a breech without difficulty if the situation is right. This usually includes a frank breech in

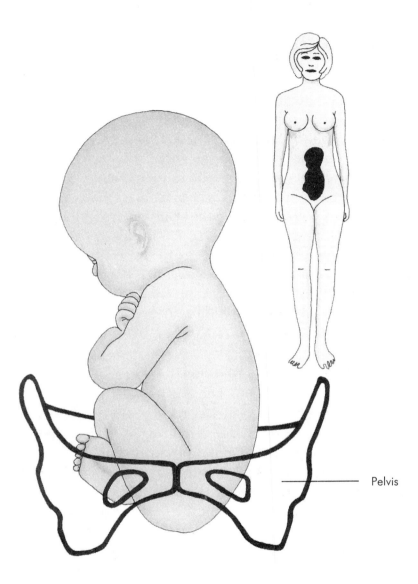

Pelvis

Baby aligned in the pelvis bottom-first, called a breech position.

✧

a mature fetus of a woman who has had previous normal deliveries. Most agree a footling breech presentation (one leg extended, one knee flexed) should be delivered by Cesarean section.

Most doctors believe a fetus in the breech position can probably be more safely delivered by a Cesarean section performed during early labor or before labor begins. Ask your doctor what he or she normally does in this situation.

Attempts may be made to turn the baby from a breech to a head-down (vertex) presentation. This is more difficult to do after your water breaks or if you are in labor.

If your baby is breech, it's important to discuss it with your doctor. When you get to the hospital, tell the nurses and hospital personnel you have a breech presentation. If you call with a question about labor and you have a breech presentation, mention this information to the person you talk with.

Other Types of Presentations   Another unusual presentation is a *face presentation*. The baby's head is hyperextended so the face comes into the birth canal first. This type of presentation is most often delivered by C-section if it does not convert to a regular presentation during labor.

Another unusual presentation is the *shoulder presentation*, also called the *transverse lie*. In this case, the baby is lying almost as if in a cradle in the pelvis. The head is on one side of your abdomen, and the bottom is on the other side. There is only one way to deliver this type of presentation, and that is by Cesarean section.

You Should also Know

What Is a Retained Placenta?   A complication following a normal delivery or C-section is an abnormally adherent placenta. In most cases, the placenta separates on its own from the implantation site on the uterus in the first few minutes after delivery. In some cases, a piece of placenta is retained

✧

inside the uterus. When this happens, the uterus cannot contract adequately, resulting in vaginal bleeding, which can be heavy.

In other cases, the placenta does not separate because it's attached to the wall of the uterus. This can be a very serious situation and may cause extreme blood loss. However, this unusual complication is not frequently encountered.

This condition assumes considerable importance because of the amount of bleeding that can occur. Below are descriptions of three types of retained placenta.

+ *Placenta accreta* adheres to the uterine wall. The placenta is directly attached to the muscle part of the uterus, the *myometrium.*
+ *Placenta increta* grows *into the muscle* of the uterus.
+ *Placenta percreta* grows *through the muscle* of the uterus.

Reasons for an abnormally adherent placenta are many. It is believed a placenta may attach over a previous Cesarean-section scar or other previous incisions on the uterus. The placenta may attach over an area that has been curetted, such as with a D&C, or over an area of the uterus that was infected.

Bleeding is usually severe after delivery. Problems occur when the placenta cannot be delivered. Surgery may be necessary to stop the bleeding. An attempt may be made to remove the placenta by D&C. However, if the placenta is attached *through* the wall of the uterus, it may be necessary to remove the uterus (hysterectomy).

Your doctor will pay attention to the delivery of your placenta while you are paying attention to your baby. It's an important part of the delivery experience and critical as far as blood loss is concerned. Some people ask to see the placenta after delivery; you may wish to have your doctor show it to you.

Week 39

Age of Fetus — 37 Weeks

How Big Is Your Baby?

Your baby weighs a little over 7 pounds (3250g). By this point in your pregnancy, crown-to-rump length is about 14.4 inches (36cm). Its total length is 21.5 inches (48cm).

How Big Are You?

Page 365 shows a side view of a woman with a very large uterus and her baby inside it. As you can see, she's about as big as she can get. You probably are, too!

If you measure from the pubic symphysis to the top of the uterus, it is 14.4 to 16 inches (36 to 40cm). Measuring from the umbilicus, the distance is 6.4 to 8 inches (16 to 20cm).

You're almost at the end of your pregnancy. However, your weight should not increase much from this point. It should remain between 25 and 35 pounds (11.4 and 15.9kg) until delivery.

How Your Baby Is Growing and Developing

The baby continues to gain weight, even up to the last week or two of pregnancy. It doesn't have much room to move inside your uterus.

At this point, all the organ systems are developed and in place. The last part of development is maturing of the lungs.

✧

Changes in You

It would be unusual for you not to be uncomfortable and feel huge at this time. Your uterus has filled up your pelvis and most of your abdomen. It has pushed everything else out of the way.

At this point in pregnancy, you may think you'll never want to be pregnant again because you're so uncomfortable. When this happens, some women consider permanent sterilization, such as tubal ligation.

Tubal Ligation After Delivery? Some women choose to have a tubal ligation done while they are in the hospital after having their baby. Now is *not* the time to make the decision about having a tubal ligation if you haven't considered it before now.

Being sterilized following delivery of a baby has some advantages. You're in the hospital and won't need another hospitalization.

But there are disadvantages to having a sterilization following delivery of a baby. The procedure should be considered permanent and not reversible. If you have your tubes tied within a few hours or a day after having your baby and then find out the baby has a serious problem, you may regret the tubal ligation.

If you have an epidural, it's possible to use the epidural for anesthesia for a tubal ligation. If you didn't have an epidural, it's necessary to put you to sleep. This is often done the morning after you've had your baby. This procedure does not usually lengthen the time you're in the hospital.

Different kinds of procedures are performed for permanent sterilization. Most common is a small incision underneath your bellybutton. Through this incision, the Fallopian tubes can be identified. A piece of tube can be removed, or a ring or clip can be placed on the tube to block it. This type of surgery usually requires about 30 to 45 minutes to perform.

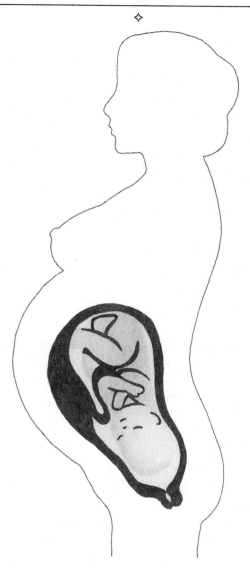

Comparative size of the uterus at 39 weeks of pregnancy (fetal age—37 weeks) with a baby that is close to full term.

No surgery is without possible complications. Problems associated with tubal sterilization are anesthetic complications and damage to the bladder or bowel. Failure rate after tubal ligation is up to 6 per 1000 sterilizations performed.

If you have second thoughts or are unsure about having it done, don't have the surgery performed. Consider this procedure as permanent. Tubal ligations can be reversed, but it's very expensive and requires a longer hospital stay—3 to 4 days. The success rate following sterilization reversal depends on several factors. These include the experience of the surgeon, the type of tubal ligation originally performed and any complications at that time. Reversal may be about 50% effective, but pregnancy cannot be guaranteed.

How Your Actions Affect Your Baby's Development

This discussion of how your actions affect your baby's growth and development actually concerns your actions *after* your baby is born! I'm talking about your decision as to whether or not you will breast-feed your baby.

Is Breast-Feeding Right for You and Your Baby? Your decision about whether or not to breast-feed is a personal one. Today, more than half of all babies born are breast-fed. One of the more compelling reasons to breast-feed is the bonding that occurs between you and your baby. This close relationship can begin as soon as your baby is born—some women breast-feed on the delivery table. It helps stimulate uterine contractions, which can prevent hemorrhage.

Breast-feeding encourages the natural intimacy of a newborn baby with its mother and the mother with her baby. The opportunity to breast-feed may be a relaxing time for you. It may give you a chance to relax and spend some wonderful time with your new baby.

If you're considering breast-feeding your baby, give it a try. There's no harm in trying to breast-feed. It may be something you enjoy. It will bring you close to your baby. But if it doesn't work out, don't feel like you're a failure. It's all right to stop and switch to formula.

Benefits of Breast-Feeding   There are benefits for you and your baby if you breast-feed. Mother's milk is good for your baby because it contains all the nutrients it will need during its first months of life. Commercial formulas have good mixtures of vitamins, protein, sugar, fat and minerals, but none can match the formula of your breast milk.

Another advantage of breast-feeding is you pass protection against infection (via antibodies) to your baby in your breast milk. Many people feel a breast-fed baby is less likely to get colds and infections than a bottle-fed baby.

Breast-feeding is also good for the baby because the baby will probably have to nurse more vigorously than is necessary with some bottle nipples. This encourages good tooth and jaw development.

Advantages for you include decreased cost as compared to buying formula. It's convenient to breast-feed; you don't have to carry bottles and formula with you for the baby.

Some women find breast-feeding makes it easier for them to regain their figure. Some say it helps them trim down more quickly.

You may have noticed during your pregnancy that your breasts got larger. They were probably tender at times. This occurs because increased hormonal activity makes the alveoli in the breasts get larger. Milk in the breast is stored in small sacs of these alveoli.

Late in pregnancy, your breasts begin to secrete colostrum. It is rich in antibodies that provide the baby with protection against various infections.

The first milk that comes from the breasts usually arrives 2 or 3 days after delivery. Its arrival involves stimulation by having the baby suckle at your breast. This sends a message to your brain where prolactin is made. This hormone stimulates milk production in the alveoli. Women who choose not to breastfeed are no longer given medication to block prolactin so they don't produce milk.

Talk with your doctor during pregnancy about breast-feeding. Ask friends about their experiences and how much they enjoyed it. You may also want to contact your local La Leche League. This organization encourages and promotes breast-feeding. It offers support and help for women who may be having trouble getting started with breast-feeding. Give them a call if you need information and/or support.

Some women have trouble breast-feeding because of inverted nipples. This can happen when the nipple retracts inward instead of pointing outward. If you have inverted nipples, it is possible to breast-feed. Plastic breast shields are available to wear under clothing to help bring out an inverted nipple. Some doctors also recommend pulling on the nipple and rolling it between the thumb and index finger.

A woman who has a Cesarean delivery may breast-feed. Twins can also be nursed simultaneously. There will be a greater demand for milk, but it can be done.

Some women find wearing a support bra is very helpful in the last few weeks of pregnancy. A nursing bra is useful while nursing. Many doctors suggest wearing a nursing bra all the time, even when you sleep. You may be more comfortable.

There may be times when you are away from the baby but you want to continue to nurse. If this is your desire, there are ways to pump your breasts with small battery-operated or suction-type pumps. Electrical pumps may be available to help you remove your breast milk and save it for the baby. Your local La Leche League may have some pumps to loan to members.

Learning to Breast-Feed   Learning how to breast-feed may be a goal while you're in the hospital. Ask the nurses to show you some of the tricks they've learned to help your baby catch on to breast-feeding. Ask them any questions you have. It may make the difference in whether or not you are able to keep your baby happy with breast-feeding.

Many women like to nurse their baby immediately after birth. If the baby is stable and can be kept warm, this can be an enjoyable experience for both of you.

When you breast-feed, find a place that is comfortable. Brush your breast against the baby's cheek; usually the baby will begin to suck instinctively. You may want to express a small amount of milk into the baby's mouth. Once the baby begins sucking, place the breast inside the baby's mouth. After you have fed on one side, it's usually helpful to burp the baby before moving to the other breast.

Breast-feeding requires a healthy nutrition plan, just as you consumed during pregnancy. You'll need at least 500 extra calories each day. Some doctors recommend you continue taking vitamin/mineral supplements after pregnancy while you are nursing.

Be careful about what you eat and drink. Certain foods may not "sit" well with you or your baby. Spicy foods you eat may result in an upset stomach in your baby! Caffeine can also pass to your baby. Any alcohol you drink passes to your baby through your breast milk, so be careful about your consumption of alcoholic beverages. The longer you breast-feed, the more you'll realize what you can and cannot eat and drink.

Breast-Feeding Problems   A common problem you may experience if you breast-feed is breast engorgement. *Engorgement* means the breast becomes very swollen and tender and filled with breast milk. The best cure is to drain the breast, if possible. Some women take a hot shower and empty their breast in the warm water. Ice packs may also help.

Mild pain medicines, such as acetaminophen (Tylenol®), are often useful in relieving the pain of engorgement. Acetaminophen (Tylenol) is recommended by the American Academy of Pediatrics as safe to use while you're breast-feeding. It might be necessary to use stronger medications, such as Tylenol with codeine, a prescription medication. Call your doctor if engorgement is especially painful. He or she will decide on treatment.

One way to prevent breast engorgement is to feed from *both* breasts each time you feed. Don't feed on only one side. When you're away from your baby, try to express some breast milk to keep your milk flowing and breast ducts open. You'll feel more comfortable.

Most nursing mothers have sore nipples at some time, particularly in the beginning. Try to keep your breasts dry and clean. It may be helpful to use a lanolin lotion on the breasts to keep the nipples from getting too dry. In a short period of time—a few days to a few weeks— your breasts will become accustomed to breast-feeding, and you won't have problems.

It is possible to get an infection in your breast while breast-feeding. If you think you have an infection, it's important to call your doctor. An infection may cause pain in the breast, and the breast may turn red and become more swollen. You may have streaks of red discoloration on the breast. You may also feel like you have the flu.

If you're concerned about the baby getting enough nutrition, talk to your baby's doctor.

You Should also Know

Pain Relief During Labor   For some women, labor can be a very painful experience. The ability to relieve pain during labor can be a difficult problem and is approached in many ways. In trying to relieve pain, you must remember there are two patients to consider—you and your unborn baby.

We haven't found one completely safe, satisfactory method of pain relief during delivery. It is best to know about all the possible choices for pain control during labor— what's available—then see how labor goes for you. Different types of pain relief may even be regional. One type of pain control may be used more in one area of the country. Much

❖

depends on what's available and what is commonly used in the area where you live and at the hospital where you deliver your baby.

A valuable part of your experience in labor and delivery is your preparation for it. This includes being aware of things that are happening to you and not being frightened by the pain you feel. You should have confidence in those taking care of you, including the staff at the hospital and your doctor.

When labor begins, meaning contractions are regular and the cervix is beginning to dilate, uterine contractions may be very uncomfortable for you. For pain in this early stage of labor, many hospitals use a narcotic analgesic drug, such as meperidine (Demerol®) and a tranquilizer, such as promethazine (Phenergen®). This decreases pain and causes some sleepiness or sedation. Medication may be given through an I.V. or by injection into a muscle.

A drawback to using narcotic analgesics is the medication passes to your baby through the placenta. This can cause a decrease in the respiratory function in the newborn infant. It can also affect your baby's Apgar Scores. These medications should *not* be given close to the time of delivery.

Very occasionally it is necessary to use general anesthesia for delivery of a baby. This is usually done for an emergency Cesarean section when there's no time to use an epidural or spinal anesthesia. A pediatrician is in attendance at the birth because of the possibility of the baby being asleep following delivery.

In many locations, anesthesia for delivery is given by a local injection of a particular medication. This is called a *block*, such as a pudendal block, an epidural block or a cervical block. Medication is similar to the type used to block pain when you have a tooth filled. The agents are xylocaine or xylocaine-like medications.

What Is an Epidural Block?   A local or regional block that is used very frequently in many areas is the *epidural block*. It provides relief from the pain of uterine contractions and

✧

delivery. A local anesthetic is injected into the space around the spinal cord (the epidural space). It should be done *only* by someone trained and experienced in this type of anesthesia. Some obstetricians have this experience, however, in most areas an anesthesiologist is required to administer this type of anesthesia.

A continuous epidural block can be started when you are sitting up or lying on your side. An area of skin over your lower back in the middle of your spinal cord is numbed. A needle is introduced through the numbed area of the skin; anesthetic is placed around the spinal cord but not into the spinal canal. A plastic catheter is left in place.

Pain medication may be given during labor either continuously with a pump that injects a small amount of medication on a regular basis or by the anesthesiologist at regular intervals or as needed. An epidural provides excellent relief from labor pain.

A problem with an epidural block is the possibility of a decrease in your blood pressure, which may affect blood flow to the baby. This problem can be avoided through the use of I.V. fluids to help reduce the risk of hypotension (low blood pressure). Another problem is you may have problems pushing during delivery.

Other Pain Blocks   Other types of blocks include a *pudendal block;* it is given through the vaginal canal with a long needle. It decreases pain in the birth canal itself. You still feel the contraction and tightening with pain in the uterus.

A *paracervical block* is used in some hospitals. It provides pain relief for the dilating cervix. It doesn't relieve the pain of contractions. Concern has been expressed about this block because of possible fetal bradycardia—slowing of the baby's heartbeat. Usually this complication can be avoided through the use of I.V. fluids in the mother to avoid hypotension or other problems following a paracervical block.

Spinal anesthesia may be used for a Cesarean section. With this anesthesia, pain relief lasts long enough for the

✧

Cesarean section to be performed. However, epidural anesthesia is used more often than spinal anesthesia for labor. Medication can be continuously or repeatedly given through the epidural catheter, which is left in the space around the spinal cord. With a spinal block, enough medication must be given in one dose to control pain.

No method is perfect for relief of pain during labor and delivery. Discuss it with your doctor, and mention your concerns. Find out what types of anesthesia are available and the risks and benefits of each.

Anesthesia Complications   In addition to some of the complications I've already mentioned, there are other complications from use of anesthesia. These include increased sedation of the baby with use of narcotics, such as Demerol®. The newborn may have lower Apgar Scores and depressed breathing. It may require resuscitation or administration of a reversal agent, such as naloxone (Narcan®).

Increased sedation, slower respiration and a slower heartbeat may also be observed in a baby whose mother is given general anesthesia. This type of anesthesia is rarely used today, except in emergency C-sections or when epidural or spinal blocks don't work. The mother is usually "out" for over an hour and is unable to see her newborn infant until later.

It may be impossible to determine *before* you go into labor which anesthesia will be best for you. But it's helpful to know what's available and what types of pain relief you might be able to count on during your labor and delivery.

Contraction of the Uterus After Delivery   After you deliver your baby, the uterus shrinks from about the size of a watermelon to the size of a volleyball. When this happens, the placenta detaches from the uterine wall. At this time, there may be a gush of blood from inside of the uterus signaling delivery the placenta.

After the placenta is delivered, you may be given oxytocin (Pitocin®). This helps the uterus contract and clamp

❖

down so it won't bleed. Heavy bleeding after delivery is called *postpartum hemorrhage*, which is bleeding more than 17 ounces (500ml) in a vaginal delivery. It can often be prevented by massaging the uterus and using medications to help the uterus contract.

The main reason a woman experiences heavy bleeding after delivering a baby is her uterus does not contract. This is called an *atonic uterus*. Your doctor or the nurse attending you may massage your uterus after delivery. They may tell you how to do it so your uterus will stay firm and contracted. This is important so you won't lose more blood and become anemic.

Week 40

Age of Fetus — 38 Weeks

How Big Is Your Baby?

Your baby weighs about 7.5 pounds (3400g). Its crown-to-rump length is about 14.8 to 15.2 inches (37 to 38cm). Total length is 21.5 inches (48cm).

Your baby is about as big as it's going to get! It fills your uterus and has very little room to move. See the illustration on page 377.

How Big Are You?

You're not going to get much bigger. From the pubic symphysis to the top of the uterus, you probably measure 14.4 to 16 inches (36 to 40cm). From your bellybutton to the top of your uterus is 6.4 to 8 inches (16 to 20cm).

By this time, you probably don't care an awful lot about how much you measure. You feel you're as big as you could ever be, and you're ready to have your baby. You may continue to grow and even get a little bit bigger until you have your baby. But don't be discouraged—you'll have your baby soon.

How Your Baby Is Growing and Developing

Before your baby is born, bilirubin is transferred easily across the placenta from the fetus to the maternal circulation. *Bilirubin* is a breakdown product from red blood cells. Through this process, your body is able to get rid of the bilirubin from the baby.

❖

Once your baby is delivered and the umbilical cord is clamped, the baby is on its own to handle the bilirubin produced in its own body.

Jaundice in a Newborn   After birth your baby may have problems dealing with bilirubin. High levels may develop. The occurrence of jaundice is not uncommon. With *jaundice,* your baby develops yellow coloring of the skin and the sclera of the eyes. Bilirubin levels increase for 3 or 4 days after delivery then decrease.

The infant's color is observed by your pediatrician and the nurses in the nursery. The bilirubin level may be measured while the baby is in the nursery or at the pediatrician's office after the baby goes home.

Treatment for jaundice is *phototherapy.* The baby is placed under special lights; the light penetrates the skin and destroys the bilirubin. By some unknown mechanism, the bilirubin is excreted from the baby's body. Exchange blood transfusion is used for very high levels of bilirubin.

Kernicterus in a Newborn   A serious concern with extremely high levels of bilirubin, called *hyperbilirubinemia,* in a newborn infant is the development of *kernicterus.* Kernicterus is seen more frequently in premature infants than in babies delivered at full term. Very high levels of bilirubin are required for kernicterus to develop.

If the baby survives the kernicterus, it may have neurologic problems: spasticity, lack of muscle coordination and varying degrees of mental retardation. However, kernicterus in a newborn is an infrequent occurrence.

Changes in You

What Happens When You're Overdue?   By now you're anticipating the delivery of your baby. You're probably counting the days to your due date. As I've already mentioned, not every woman delivers by her due date. A pregnancy is

✧

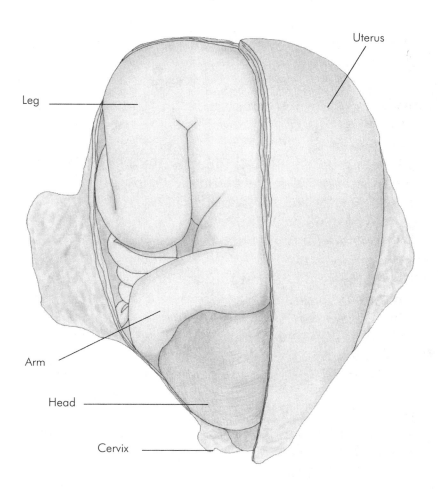

Uterus

Leg

Arm

Head

Cervix

A full-term baby in the uterus has little room to move. This is one reason fetal movements may slow down in the last few weeks of pregnancy.

considered to be *post-date* when it exceeds 42 weeks or 294 days from the first day of the last menstrual period.

While the fetus is growing and developing inside your uterus, it depends on two important functions performed by the placenta. These are respiration and nutrition. The baby relies on these functions for continued growth and development inside the uterus.

When a pregnancy is post-date, the placenta can fail to provide the respiratory function and essential nutrients the

❖

baby needs to grow and survive. An infant may begin to suffer nutritional deprivation; the baby is called *dysmature* or *post-mature*.

At birth, a post-mature baby has dry, cracked, peeling, wrinkled skin, long fingernails and abundant hair. It also has less vernix covering its body. The baby appears almost malnourished, with decreased amounts of subcutaneous fat.

Because the post-date infant is in danger of losing nutritional support from the placenta, it's important to know the true dating of your pregnancy. This is one reason it's important to go to all of your prenatal visits.

Most doctors agree that once a woman reaches 42 weeks of pregnancy, the baby should be delivered if the cervix is beginning to dilate and thin and the baby is in the proper presentation, with the head down. Placental function may also be assessed.

A decision must be made whether to continue watching and evaluating the baby or to elect to induce labor or do a C-section. Your doctor will discuss the situation with you.

Inducing Labor   If your doctor must induce labor, you receive oxytocin (Pitocin®) intravenously. Medication is given in a gradual, increasing manner until contractions begin. The amount of oxytocin you receive is controlled by a pump. It allows only a certain amount of the medication to be given so you can't receive too much of it.

When you receive oxytocin, you are monitored to watch for the baby's reaction to your labor.

How Your Actions Affect Your Baby's Development

The delivery of your baby is the event you've been planning for! If this is your first baby, you may be very excited and a little frightened. Delivery of your baby is something you'll remember for a very long time.

You need to decide who you want with you during delivery. In some cases, family members assume they're

❖

invited to the delivery of the baby. This might include your mother or mother-in-law or a sister. There's nothing wrong with having other people in attendance at your delivery. But make sure it's something you discuss with your partner and you both agree on.

Some couples choose to bring young children into the delivery room to see the birth of a new brother or sister. Discuss this with your doctor ahead of time and get his or her opinion. The delivery of the baby might be very exciting and special to you and your partner, but it may be frightening to a young child to see you in pain and bleeding as the baby delivers.

Many other places offer special classes for brothers- and sisters-to-be to help prepare them for their new brother or sister. This is probably a better way to make them part of the birth experience.

You Should also Know

What Happens When You Arrive at the Hospital?   Don't be embarrassed if you have to go to the hospital to be checked for labor. This isn't a nuisance to hospital personnel or your doctor. That's why they're there! If you're concerned you might be in labor and you aren't sure, talk with your doctor or the nurses at labor and delivery. They'll tell you if you should come in to be evaluated.

When you go to the hospital, many things will be done to evaluate you. A record from your doctor's office is kept in the labor and delivery area. Those seeing you in the hospital should know about any problems or complications that have occurred during your pregnancy and any other information that is important.

You will probably be asked many questions when you arrive to check in. Some of these include:

✦ Have your membranes ruptured? At what time?
✦ Are you bleeding?

✧

✦ Are you having contractions? How often do they occur?
  How long do they last?
✦ You may be asked about the last thing you had to eat and
  at what time.

Other important information for you to share with the
people in labor and delivery include medical problems you
have and any medications you take or have taken during
pregnancy. If you've had complications, such as placenta
previa, it's important information. Tell them when you first
come into labor and delivery.

If you think you're in labor, don't eat. This avoids having a stomach full of pizza or spaghetti that can make you
sick and cause you to vomit. Even something light in your
stomach can cause nausea. You may have to ask for an
antacid for relief of stomach upset.

After you check in, you will be put in a labor room or an
evaluation room to determine if you're actually in labor. It's
important to evaluate whether you're having contractions,
how often they occur and how strong they are. This is normally done with an external fetal monitor, discussed on
pages 353-354. The monitor is placed on your abdomen; it
shows the frequency and duration of your contractions. The
nurse or doctor also feels your abdomen and checks the frequency and duration of contractions.

It's very important to know whether or not your membranes have ruptured (your water has broken). Ruptured
membranes can be confirmed in any of several ways.

✦ By your description of what happened, such as a large
  gush of fluid.

✦ With nitrazine paper. Fluid is placed on the paper; if
  membranes have ruptured, the paper changes color.

✦ With a ferning test. Fluid is placed on a glass slide and
  allowed to dry. It is then examined under a microscope.
  Amniotic fluid has a characteristic "fern" appearance
  when dry.

❖

Another important part of your evaluation at the hospital is checking to see if you are dilated. It's helpful to know if you were dilated (and how much) when last checked by your doctor. This exam may be done by a nurse, resident, intern or doctor.

In addition to your doctor's prenatal chart kept in labor and delivery, you will also be asked to give a brief history of your pregnancy. Mention any other medical problems you have. If you've had any complications during pregnancy, such as bleeding, or if you know your baby is breech, tell your nurse or doctor. Don't assume everyone already knows. Vital signs, including your blood pressure, pulse and temperature, are also noted.

Evaluation and determination of whether or not you're in labor is usually not a 5-minute experience. It takes time to check it all out.

If you are in labor and remain at the hospital, other things will occur. It may be necessary for your partner to admit you to the hospital if you haven't already filled out preadmittance papers. You may be asked to sign a release form or a permission slip from the hospital, your doctor or the anesthesiologist. This is done to ensure that you are informed and aware of the procedures that will be done for you and the risks that are involved.

After you have been admitted, you may receive an enema or an I.V. may be started. Your doctor may want to discuss an epidural, or you may have an epidural put in place.

Blood will probably be drawn. It is tested for hematocrit and complete blood count (CBC). Blood may be drawn and stored in case you need a blood transfusion, although this is unlikely in routine labor and delivery.

Other things that are done at the hospital vary depending on the hospital you go to, the preferences of your doctor and arrangements you have made ahead of time.

Your Labor Coach In most instances your labor coach will be your partner. However, this isn't an absolute requirement. A close friend or relative, such as your mother or a

✧

sister, can also serve as your labor coach. Ask someone ahead of time; don't wait until the last minute. Give the person time to prepare for the experience and to make sure he or she will be able to be there with you.

Not everyone feels comfortable watching the entire labor and delivery. This may include your partner. Don't force your partner or labor coach to watch the delivery if he or she doesn't want to. It can be hard for those who love and care about you to see you in pain. It is not unusual for a labor coach to get lightheaded, dizzy or pass out during labor and delivery. On more than one occasion, I've had a coach or partner faint or become extremely lightheaded when we just *talked about* plans for labor and delivery or a C-section!

Preparation ahead of time, such as prenatal classes, helps avoid some problems. In the past, you would have been alone with the nurses and doctor while your partner paced in the waiting room. Things have changed!

The most important thing about the labor coach is the support he or she gives you during pregnancy, labor, delivery and recovery following the birth of the baby. Choose this person carefully.

What Can a Partner or Labor Coach Do?   Your partner is one of the most valuable assets you may have with you during labor and delivery. He can help you prepare for labor and delivery in many ways. He can be there to support you as you go through the experience of labor together. He can share with you the joy of the delivery of your baby.

In most cases, your partner will be your labor coach. As I've already mentioned, in some situations your partner may not be able to be with you. You may choose to have someone else—a sister, a friend, your mother—as your labor coach. Whomever you choose, keep in mind that he or she should be someone you *want* to be with you at this time.

An important role of the labor coach is to make sure you get to the hospital! Before going to the hospital, your labor

❖

coach can time your contractions so you are aware of the progress of your labor. Work out a plan during the last 4 to 6 weeks of pregnancy so you know how to reach your coach. It's helpful to have an alternate driver, such as a neighbor or friend, who is available in case you are unable to reach your labor coach immediately and need to be taken to the hospital.

Once you arrive at the hospital, both you and your labor coach are going to be nervous. Your coach can do things to help you both *relax*. Some of these include:

+ Talking to you while you're in labor. This can distract you and help you relax.
+ Encouraging and reassuring you during labor. Even though you've gone through prenatal classes and have read about labor and delivery, there's still a lot that leaves room for fear and uncertainty. Encouragement is also helpful when it comes time for you to push. Many coaches have said they're exhausted after the baby is delivered and felt like they were pushing, too. Prenatal classes often teach breathing techniques to use during labor. You and your coach can learn and practice the techniques together; they may be helpful for both of you during labor. One of the best techniques is for the coach to breathe with you.
+ Helping create a mood in the labor room. This can include music and lighting. Discuss it ahead of time; bring things with you that you would like to have available during labor. It always amazes me when people choose to have a baby with the television on! There's nothing wrong with watching TV during labor, but when the baby is ready to deliver, turn off the TV and enjoy what is occurring.
+ Keeping a watch on the door and your privacy. As the nurses, doctor and other support people come and go during labor, you may want to have the door kept shut. Your coach can take this responsibility and make sure the door is closed.
+ Traffic control is also important. By traffic control, I mean the visits of family members or friends while you're in

labor and during delivery. Some friends and relatives assume they can come and go as they please during *your* labor and delivery. The birth of your baby is a very personal event. You may be in pain. You may not want to see others while you're in labor. Or you may not want them to be present at the delivery. Discuss this ahead of time. This is *your* special experience, and it doesn't need to be shared with anyone unless you choose to share it.

+ Reporting symptoms or pain to the nurse and/or doctor.
+ Coaches stay around during labor. If your coach is going to get something to eat, he or she shouldn't leave the hospital. Make sure the nurse knows where your coach is.
+ Humor may relieve tension during labor. But this isn't the time for a party or a wild celebration.
+ It's OK to touch each other, to hug and to kiss. But you may not want to be touched during labor. If this is how you feel, tell your coach. Many women concentrate on labor and block out other things. A labor coach shouldn't be offended by this.
+ It's all right for your labor coach to rest and take a break during labor. This is especially true if labor lasts a long time. It's better if your coach eats in the lounge or hospital cafeteria.
+ Your labor coach can reassure you it's permissible for you to deal vocally with your pain. You don't need to apologize for loud or strong expressions, such as obscenities, in response to the pain of labor.
+ Many people do different things to distract themselves and to help time pass during labor. These include picking names for the baby, playing games, watching TV or listening to music.
+ A labor coach shouldn't bring work to the labor room. Talking on the phone to clients or doing work is inappropriate and shows little support of the laboring woman.
+ Your coach can do many things to help with physical discomfort and show emotional support. This includes wiping your face or your mouth with a washcloth,

✧

rubbing your abdomen or your back, supporting your
back while pushing.

✦ Talk to your doctor about your coach's participation in the
events of delivery, such as cutting the umbilical cord or
bathing the baby after birth. Things that can be done vary
from one place to another. But you must understand the
responsibility of your doctor is the well-being of you and
your baby—don't impose requests or demands that are
foolish and could cause complications for you or your
baby.

✦ After delivery of the baby, enjoy the moment together.
There is no other moment like hearing the first cry of your
newborn baby. Don't immediately pick up the phone and
call friends or family. Talk about who needs to be called
ahead of time. Bring a list of names and phone numbers
with you.
There are some people you may want to call yourself.
In most places, a telephone is available in labor and
delivery rooms.

✦ Talk to your labor coach about showing the baby to those
who are waiting. If you want to be with your partner
when friends or relatives first see the baby, make it clear.
Don't allow your baby to be taken out of the room unless
that's what you want. In most instances, you need some
cleaning up. Take 10 or 15 minutes for yourselves, then
you can show the baby to friends and relatives and share
the joy with them.

✦ A labor coach can be responsible for taking pictures.
Pictures should be in good taste. Many people have made
videotapes of labor and delivery. These may show some
inappropriate views of you and expose parts of your body
you'd rather keep private. Videotapes also record sound;
you may not enjoy the sounds of your pain during labor
and delivery. Many couples find still pictures taken of the
baby after the delivery help them best remember these
wonderful moments of joy.

✧

What Happens to You After Birth? What happens to you after the birth of your baby depends on the facilities of the hospital or birthing center where you have your baby. Hospitals vary in the arrangements and accommodations they have available.

A relatively new concept is an LDRP—this stands for labor, delivery, recovery and postpartum. With this concept, the room you are admitted to at the beginning of your labor is the room you labor in, deliver in, recover in and remain in for your entire hospital stay. This facility isn't available everywhere; it's available on a limited basis. However, more LDRP facilities are being built to meet the increasing demand for them.

The concept of LDRP has evolved because many women don't want to be moved from the labor area to another part of the hospital after delivery. The nursery is usually close to labor and delivery and the recovery area. This allows you to see your baby as often as you like and to have your baby in your room often.

In many places, you will labor in a room in the labor and delivery suite and then be moved to a delivery room at the time of delivery. Following this, you may go to a postpartum floor, which is an area in the hospital where you will spend the remainder of your hospital stay.

Most hospitals allow you to have your baby in your room as much as you want. However, this also varies from one hospital to another. It is called *rooming in* or *boarding in*. Some hospitals also have a cot, couch or chair that makes into a bed in your room so your partner can stay with you after delivery. Check the availability of various facilities in the hospitals in your area.

Another concept is the birthing room. This generally refers to having your baby in the same room you labor in. You don't have to be moved from the room you're laboring in to another place to have the baby. Even if you use a birthing room, it may be necessary for you to move to another area of the hospital for recovery.

Whatever you choose, the most important thing is the health of your baby and the welfare of you both. When you examine where you will have your baby, there are several questions you should have answered.

+ Ask them about the facilities and staff they have available.
+ Ask about the availability of anesthesia. Is an anesthesiologist available 24 hours a day?
+ How long does it take them to respond to and to perform a Cesarean delivery, if necessary? This time period should be 30 minutes or less.
+ Is a pediatrician available 24 hours a day for an emergency or problems?
+ Is the nursery staffed all the time?
+ In the event of an emergency or a premature baby that needs to be transported to a high-risk nursery, how is it done? Is it by ambulance? How far away is the nearest high-risk nursery if it is not at your hospital? Is the baby transported by helicopter?

These may seem like a lot of questions to ask, but the answers can help put your mind at rest. Most women won't have to worry about many of these concerns, but the birth of a baby carries with it the risk of complications. And when it's *your* baby and *your* health on the line, it's nice to know emergency measures can be employed in an efficient and timely manner when necessary.

What Happens to Your Baby After It's Born? When your baby is delivered, the doctor clamps and cuts the umbilical cord. The baby's mouth and throat are suctioned out. The baby may be placed on your abdomen in clean blankets. Or the baby may be passed to a nurse or pediatrician for initial evaluation and attention. The Apgar Scores, see page 340, are recorded at this time, at 1- and 5-minute intervals. An identification band is placed on the baby's wrist so there's no mix-up in the nursery!

It's important to keep the baby warm immediately after birth. To do this, the nurse will dry the baby and wrap it in warm blankets. This will be done whether the baby is on your chest or attended to by a nurse or doctor.

If your labor is complicated with fetal distress or other complications, the baby may need to be evaluated more thoroughly in the nursery. The baby's well-being and health are of primary concern. You'll be able to hold and nurse the baby, but if your child is having trouble breathing or needs special attention, such as monitors, immediate evaluation is the most appropriate procedure at this time.

Your baby will be taken to the nursery by a nurse and your partner or labor coach. In the nursery, the baby is weighed, measured and footprinted (in some places). Drops to prevent infection are placed in the baby's eyes. A vitamin-K shot is also given to help with the baby's blood-clotting factors. Then the baby is put in a heated bassinet for 30 minutes to 2 hours. This time period varies, depending on how stable the baby is.

Your pediatrician is notified immediately if there are problems or concerns. Otherwise, he or she will be notified soon after birth, and a physical exam will be performed within 24 hours.

Keep Your Options Open During Labor and Delivery   An important consideration in planning for your delivery and labor is the method(s) you may use to get through labor and delivery. Will you have an epidural anesthesia? Are you going to attempt a drug-free delivery? Will it be necessary for you to have an episiotomy?

Every woman is different, and every labor is different. It's difficult to anticipate what will happen for you and what you will need during labor and delivery for pain relief. It's impossible to know how long labor will last—3 hours or 20 hours. It's best to adopt a flexible plan for your labor and delivery. Understand what's available and what options you can choose during labor.

During the last 2 months of your pregnancy, discuss these concerns with your doctor and become familiar with his or her philosophy about labor. Know what can be provided for you at the hospital you're going to. Availability of some medications is limited in some areas.

What Is Natural Childbirth?   Some women decide before the birth of their baby that they are going to labor and deliver with "natural childbirth." What does this mean? The description or definition of natural childbirth varies from one couple to another.

Many people equate natural childbirth with "drug-free" labor and delivery. Others equate natural childbirth with the use of mild pain medications or local pain medications, such as numbing medications in the area of the vagina, for delivery or episiotomy and repair of episiotomy. Most agree that natural childbirth is birth with as few artificial procedures as possible. Instruction is usually necessary to prepare a woman to labor and deliver with natural childbirth.

Natural childbirth isn't for every woman. If you arrive at the hospital dilated 1cm, with terrible contractions and in great pain, you have a long way to go. Natural childbirth may be very hard for you. In this situation, an epidural might be very appropriate.

On the other hand, if you arrive at the hospital dilated 4 or 5cm and contractions are OK, natural childbirth might be a reasonable choice. It's difficult or impossible to know what will happen ahead of time. But it helps to be aware of, and ready for, everything.

A very popular, widely available method of childbirth education is the *Lamaze method*. It provides both education and practice or training before labor. Intensive teaching and practice involves the expectant mother and partner or labor coach. The labor coach is an important part of the training. Psychological preparation for labor and delivery helps you achieve a "mind over matter" approach.

The concentration and preparation gained through Lamaze training is more successful when the labor coach participates in the breathing exercises practiced before labor and used during labor. The woman is also instructed to concentrate on objects to block out pain, or other methods of concentration are used to help reduce labor pain.

The Lamaze approach works very well for many women in labor. But this approach to childbirth requires a *very serious commitment* from you and your partner or labor coach.

It's important to keep an open mind and to be open to possible complications that can occur during the unpredictable process of labor and delivery. Don't feel guilty or let down if you can't do all the things you planned before labor. You may *need* an epidural. Or the birth may not be accomplished *without* an episiotomy. Don't let anyone make you feel guilty or make you feel like you've accomplished less if you end up needing a C-section, an epidural or an episiotomy.

Beware of instruction that tells you labor is free of pain or no one really needs a C-section, I.V.s are unnecessary or an episiotomy is foolish. This can create unrealistic expectations for you. If you do need any of the above procedures, you may feel like you failed during your labor.

The goal in labor and delivery is a healthy baby. If this means you end up with a C-section, you haven't failed. Be grateful a Cesarean delivery can be performed safely. Babies that would not have survived birth in the past can be delivered safely. This *isn't* a failure! It's a wonderful accomplishment!

Every pregnant woman should be aware of the possibility of alternatives to natural childbirth. Don't be afraid of the consequences. They may save your baby's life or at the very least give him or her a healthier start.

Glossary

Abortion—Termination or end of pregnancy. Giving birth to an embryo or fetus before it can live outside the womb, usually defined as before 20 weeks of gestation. Abortion may be spontaneous, often called a *miscarriage*, or induced as in a medical or therapeutic abortion performed to terminate a pregnancy.

Abruptio placenta—See *Placental abruption*.

Acquired-Immune-Deficiency Syndrome (AIDS)—Debilitating and frequently fatal illness that affects the body's ability to respond to infection. Caused by the human immune deficiency virus (HIV).

Aerobic exercise—Exercise that increases your heart rate and causes you to consume oxygen.

Afterbirth—See *Placenta*.

Albuminuria—See *Proteinuria*.

Alphafetoprotein (AFP)—Substance produced by the unborn baby as it grows inside the uterus. Large amounts of AFP are found in the amniotic fluid. Larger-than-normal amounts are found in the maternal bloodstream if neural-tube defects are present in the fetus.

Alveoli—Ends of the ducts of the lung.

Amino acids—Substances that act as building blocks in the developing embryo and fetus.

Amniocentesis—Removal of amniotic fluid from the amniotic sac. Fluid is tested for some genetic defects.

Amnion—Membrane around the fetus. It surrounds the amniotic cavity.

Amniotic fluid—Liquid surrounding the baby inside the amniotic sac.

Amniotic sac—Sac that surrounds baby inside the uterus. It contains the baby, the placenta and the amniotic fluid.

Ampulla—Dilated opening of a tube or duct.

Anemia—Any condition in which the number of red blood cells is less than normal. Term usually applies to the concentration of the oxygen-transporting material in the blood, which is the red blood cell.

Anencephaly—Defective development of the brain combined with the absence of the bones normally surrounding the brain.

Angioma—Tumor, usually benign, or swelling composed of lymph and blood vessels.

Anovulatory—Lack of or cessation of ovulation.

Anti-inflammatory medications—Drugs to relieve pain or inflammation.

Areola—Pigmented or colored ring surrounding the nipple of the breast.

Arrhythmia—Irregular or missed heartbeat.

Aspiration—Swallowing or sucking a foreign body or fluid, such as vomit, into an airway.

Asthma—Disease marked by recurrent attacks of shortness of breath and difficulty breathing. Often caused by an allergic reaction.

Atonic uterus—Flaccid; relaxed; lack of tone.

Autoantibodies—Antibodies that attack parts of your body or your own tissues.

❖

Back labor—Pain of labor felt in lower back.

Beta-adrenergics—Substances that interfere with transmission of stimuli. They affect the autonomic nervous system.

Bilirubin—Breakdown product of pigment formed in the liver from hemoglobin during the destruction of red blood cells.

Biophysical profile—Method of evaluating a fetus before birth.

Biopsy—Removal of a small piece of tissue for microscopic study.

Birthing center—Facility in which a woman labors, delivers and recovers in the same room. It may be part of a hospital or a freestanding unit.

Blastomere—One of the cells egg divides into after it has been fertilized.

Bloody show—Small amount of vaginal bleeding late in pregnancy; often precedes labor.

Board certification—Doctor has had additional training and testing in a particular specialty. In the area of obstetrics, the American College of Obstetricians and Gynecologists offers this training. Certification requires expertise in care of a pregnant woman.

Braxton-Hicks contractions—Irregular, painless tightening of uterus during pregnancy.

Breech presentation—Abnormal position of the fetus. Buttocks or legs come into the birth canal ahead of the head.

Carcinogen—Any cancer-producing substance.

Carcinoma-in-situ—Cancer that has not spread to surrounding tissues. It is usually the most-curable type of cancer.

Cataract, congenital—Cloudiness of the eye lens present at birth.

Cell antibodies—See *Autoantibodies*.

Cesarean section (delivery)—Delivery of a baby through an abdominal incision rather than through the vagina.

Chadwick's sign—Dark-blue or purple discoloration of the mucosa of the vagina and cervix during pregnancy.

Chemotherapy—Treatment of disease by chemical substances or drugs.

Chlamydia—Sexually transmitted venereal infection.

Chloasma—Extensive brown patches of irregular shape and size on the face or other parts of the body.

Choriocarcinoma—Highly malignant cancer that grows in the uterus during pregnancy or at the site of an ectopic pregnancy.

Chorion—Outermost fetal membrane found around the amnion.

Chorionic villus sampling—Diagnostic test done early in pregnancy. A biopsy of tissue is taken from inside the uterus through the cervical opening to determine abnormalities of pregnancy.

Cleft palate—Defect in the palate, the part of the upper jaw or mouth.

Colostrum—Thin, yellow fluid, which is the first milk to come from the breast. Most often seen toward the end of pregnancy. It is different in content from milk produced later during nursing.

Condyloma acuminatum—Skin tags or warts that are sexually transmitted. Also called *venereal warts*.

Congenital problem—Problem present at birth.

Conization of the cervix—Surgical procedure performed on premalignant and malignant conditions of the cervix. A large biopsy of the cervix is taken in the shape of a cone.

✧

Conjoined twins—Twins connected at the body; they may share vital organs. Also called *Siamese twins.*

Constipation—Bowel movements are infrequent or incomplete.

Contraction stress test—Response of fetus to uterine contractions to evaluate fetal well-being.

Corpus luteum—Area in the ovary where the egg is released at ovulation. A cyst may form in this area after ovulation. Called a *corpus luteum cyst.*

Crown-to-rump length—Measurement from the top of the baby's head (crown) to the buttocks of the baby (rump).

Cystitis—Inflammation of the bladder.

Cytomegalovirus (CMV) infection—Group of viruses from the herpes virus family.

D&C (dilatation and curettage)—Surgical procedure in which the cervix is dilated and the lining of the uterus is scraped.

Developmental delay—Condition in which the development of the baby or child is slower than normal.

Diastasis recti—Separation of abdominal muscles.

Diethylstilbestrol (DES)—Non-steroidal synthetic estrogen. Used in the past to try to prevent miscarriage.

Dizygotic twins—Twins derived from two different eggs. Often called *fraternal twins.*

Dysplasia—Abnormal, precancerous changes in the cells of the cervix.

Dysuria—Difficulty or pain urinating.

EDC (estimated date of confinement)—Anticipated due date for delivery of the baby. Calculated from the first day of the last period counting forward 280 days.

Eclampsia—Convulsions and coma in a woman with pre-eclampsia. Not related to epilepsy.

Ectodermal germ layer—Layer in the developing embryo that gives rise to developing structures in the fetus. These include skin, teeth and glands of the mouth, the nervous system and the pituitary gland.

Ectopic pregnancy—Pregnancy that occurs outside the uterine cavity.

Effacement—Thinning of cervix.

Electroencephalogram—Recording of the electrical activity of the brain.

Embryo—Organism in the early stages of development.

Embryonic period—First 10 weeks of gestation.

Endodermal germ layer—Area of tissue in early development of the embryo that gives rise to other structures. These include the digestive tract, respiratory organs, vagina, bladder and urethra. Also called *endoderm* or *entoderm.*

Endometrial cycle—Regular development of the mucous membrane lining the inside of the uterus. It begins with the preparation for acceptance of a pregnancy and ends with the shedding of the lining during a menstrual period.

Endometrium—Mucous membrane that lines inside of the uterine wall.

Enema—Fluid injected into the rectum for the purpose of clearing out the bowel.

Engorgement—Congested; filled with fluid.

Enzyme—Protein made by cells. It acts as a catalyst to improve or cause chemical changes in other substances.

Epidural block—Type of anesthesia. Medication is injected around the spinal cord during labor or other types of surgery.

Episiotomy—Surgical incision of the vulva (area behind the vagina, above the rectum). Used during delivery to avoid tearing or laceration of the vaginal opening and rectum.

Estimated date of confinement—See *EDC.*

Exotoxin—Poison or toxin from a source outside the body.

Face presentation—Baby comes into the birth canal face first.

Fallopian tube—Tube that leads from the cavity of the uterus to the area of the ovary. Also called *uterine tube.*

False labor—Tightening of uterus without dilatation of the cervix.

Fasting blood sugar—Blood test to evaluate the amount of sugar in the blood following a time period of fasting.

Ferrous gluconate—Iron supplement.

Ferrous sulfate—Iron supplement.

Fertilization—Joining of the sperm and egg.

Fertilization age—Dating a pregnancy from the time of fertilization. 2 weeks earlier than the gestational age.

Fetal anomaly—Fetal malformation or abnormal development.

Fetal arrhythmia—See *Arrhythmia.*

Fetal goiter—Enlargement of the thyroid in the fetus.

Fetal-growth retardation (IUGR)—Inadequate growth of the fetus during the last stages of pregnancy.

Fetal monitor—Device used before or during labor to listen to and record the fetal heartbeat. Can be *external* monitoring (through maternal abdomen) or *internal* monitoring (through maternal vagina) of the baby inside the uterus.

Fetal period—Time period following the embryonic period (first 10 weeks of gestation) until birth.

Fetus—Refers to the unborn baby after 10 weeks of gestation until birth.

Fibrin—Elastic protein important in the coagulation of blood.

Forceps—Instrument used to help remove baby from the birth canal during delivery.

Frank breech—Baby presenting buttocks first. Legs are flexed and knees extended.

Fraternal twins—See *Dizygotic twins.*

Genetic counseling—Consultation between a couple and a specialist about genetic defects and the possibility of genetic problems in a pregnancy.

Genital herpes simplex—Herpes simplex infection involving the genital area. It can be significant during pregnancy because of the danger to a newborn fetus infected with herpes simplex.

Genitourinary problems—Defects or problems involving genital organs and the bladder or kidneys.

Germ layers—Layers or areas of tissue important in the development of the baby.

Gestational age—Dating a pregnancy from the first day of the last menstrual period; 2 weeks longer than fertilization age. See *Fertilization age.*

Gestational diabetes—Occurrence or worsening of diabetes during pregnancy (gestation).

Gestational trophoblastic disease (GTN)—Abnormal pregnancy with cystic growth of the placenta. Characterized by bleeding during early and middle pregnancy.

Globulin—Family of proteins from plasma or serum of the blood.

Glucose-tolerance test—Blood test done to evaluate the body's response to sugar. Blood is drawn at intervals following ingestion of a sugary substance.

Glucosuria—Glucose in the urine.

Gonorrhea—Contagious venereal infection, transmitted primarily by intercourse. Caused by the bacteria *Neisseria gonorrhea.*

Grand mal seizure—Loss of control of body functions. Seizure activity of a major form.

❖

Group-B streptococcal infection—Serious infection occurring in the mother's vagina and throat.

Gyri—Prominent, rounded elevation found on the surface of the brain tissue.

Habitual abortion—Occurrence of three or more spontaneous miscarriages.

Heartburn—Discomfort or pain that occurs in the chest. Often occurs after eating.

Hematocrit—Determines the proportion of blood cells to plasma. Important in diagnosing anemia.

Hemoglobin—Pigment in red blood cell that carries oxygen to body tissues.

Hemolytic disease—Destruction of red blood cells. See *Anemia.*

Hemorrhoids—Dilated blood vessels in the rectum or rectal canal.

Heparin—Medication used to thin the blood.

Homans' sign—Pain caused by flexing the toes when a person has a blood clot in the lower leg.

Human chorionic gonadatropin—Hormone produced in early pregnancy. Measured in a pregnancy test.

Human placental lactogen—Hormone of pregnancy produced by the placenta. Found in the bloodstream.

Hyaline membrane disease—Respiratory disease of the newborn.

Hydatidiform mole—See *Gestational trophoblastic disease.*

Hydramnios—Increased amniotic fluid.

Hydrocephalus—Excessive accumulation of fluid around the brain of the baby. Sometimes called *water on the brain.*

Hyperbilirubinemia—Extremely high level of bilirubin in the blood.

Hyperemesis gravidarum—Severe nausea, dehydration and vomiting during pregnancy. Occurs most frequently during the first trimester.

Hyperglycemia—Increased blood sugar.

Hypermastia—More than two breasts present in a woman. Also called *polymastia.*

Hypertension, pregnancy-induced—High blood pressure that occurs during pregnancy. Defined by an increase in the diastolic and/or systolic blood pressure.

Hyperthyroidism—Elevation of the thyroid hormone in the bloodstream.

Hypoplasia—Defective or incomplete development or formation of tissue.

Hypotension—Low blood pressure.

Hypothyroidism—Low or inadequate levels of thyroid hormone in the bloodstream.

Identical twins—See *Monozygotic twins.*

Immune globulin preparation—Substance used to protect against infection with certain diseases, such as hepatitis or measles.

In utero—Within the uterus.

Incompetent cervix—Cervix that dilates painlessly, without contractions.

Incomplete abortion—Miscarriage in which part, but not all, of the uterine contents are expelled.

Inevitable abortion—Pregnancy complicated with bleeding and cramping. Usually results in miscarriage.

Insulin—Peptide hormone made by the pancreas. It promotes the use of glucose.

Intrauterine-growth retardation (IUGR)—See *Fetal-growth retardation.*

Invasive squamous-cell carcinoma—Cancer of the cervix that extends beyond the cervix into surrounding tissues or deeper layers.

Iodides—Medications made up of negative ion of iodine.

Iron-deficiency anemia—Anemia produced by lack of iron in the diet. Often seen in pregnancy. See *Anemia.*

Isoimmunization—Development of specific antibody directed at the red blood cells of another individual, such as a baby in utero. Often occurs when an Rh-negative woman carries an Rh-positive baby or is given Rh-positive blood.

❖

Jaundice—Yellow staining of the skin, sclera (eyes) and deeper tissues of the body. Caused by excessive amounts of bilirubin. Treated with phototherapy.

Ketones—Breakdown product of metabolism found in the blood, particularly in starvation or uncontrolled diabetes.

Kidney stones—Small mass or lesion found in the kidney or urinary tract. Can block the flow of urine.

Labor—Process of expelling a fetus from the uterus.

Laparoscopy—Minor surgical procedure performed for tubal ligation, diagnosis of pelvic pain or diagnosis of ectopic pregnancy.

Leukorrhea—Vaginal discharge characterized by a white or yellowish color. Primarily composed of mucus.

Lightening—Change in the shape of the pregnant uterus a few weeks before labor. Often described as the baby "dropping."

Linea nigra—Line of increased pigmentation running down the abdomen from the bellybutton to the pubic area during pregnancy.

Malignant GTN—Cancerous change of gestational trophoblastic disease. See *Gestational trophoblastic disease*.

Mammogram—X-ray study of the breasts to identify normal and abnormal breast tissue.

Mask of pregnancy—Increased pigmentation over the area of the face under each eye. Commonly has the appearance of a butterfly.

McDonald cerclage—Surgical procedure performed on an incompetent cervix. A drawstring-type suture holds the cervical opening closed during pregnancy. See *Incompetent cervix*.

Meconium—First intestinal discharge of the newborn; green or yellow in color. It consists of epithelial or surface cells, mucus and bile. Discharge may occur before or during labor or soon after birth.

Melanoma—Pigmented mole or tumor. It may or may not be cancerous.

Meningomyelocele—Congenital defect of the central nervous system of the baby. Membranes and the spinal cord protrude through an opening or defect in the vertebral column.

Menstrual age—See *Gestational age*.

Menstruation—Regular or periodic discharge of a bloody fluid from the uterus.

Mesodermal germ layer—Tissue of the embryo that forms connective tissue, muscles, kidneys, ureters and other organs.

Metaplasia—Change in the structure of a tissue into another type that is not normal for that tissue.

Microcephaly—Abnormally small development of the head in the developing fetus.

Microphthalmia—Abnormally small eyeballs.

Miscarriage—See *Abortion*.

Missed abortion—Failed pregnancy without bleeding or cramping. Often diagnosed by ultrasound weeks or months after a pregnancy fails.

Mittelschmerz—Pain that coincides with release of an egg from the ovary.

Molar pregnancy—See *Gestational trophoblastic disease*.

Monilial vulvovaginitis—Infection caused by yeast or monilia. Usually affects the vagina and vulva.

Monozygotic twins—Twins conceived from one egg. Often called *identical twins*.

Morning sickness—Nausea and vomiting, with ill health, found primarily during the first trimester of pregnancy. See *Hyperemesis gravidarum*.

Morula—Cells resulting from the early division of the fertilized egg at the beginning of pregnancy.

Mucus plug—Secretions in cervix; often released just before labor.

Mutations—Change in the character of a gene. Passed from one cell division to another.

Neural-tube defects—Abnormalities in the development of the spinal cord and brain in a fetus. See *Anencephaly; Hydrocephalus; Spina bifida.*

Nurse-midwife—Nurse who has received extra training in the care of pregnant patients and the delivery of babies.

Obstetrician—Physician who specializes in the care of pregnant women and the delivery of babies.

Oligohydramnios—Lack or deficiency of amniotic fluid.

Omphalocele—Presence of congenital outpouching of the umbilicus containing internal organs in the fetus or newborn infant.

Opioids—Synthetic compounds with effects similar to those of opium.

Organogenesis—Development of the organ systems in the embryo.

Ossification—Bone formation.

Ovarian cycle—Regular production of hormones from the ovary in response to hormonal messages from the brain. The ovarian cycle governs the endometrial cycle.

Ovulation—Cyclic production of an egg from the ovary.

Ovulatory age—See *Fertilization age.*

Oxytocin—Medication that causes uterine contractions.

Palmar erythema—Redness of palms of the hands.

Pap smear—Routine screening test that evaluates presence of premalignant or cancerous conditions of the cervix.

Paracervical block—Local anesthetic for cervical dilatation.

Pediatrician—Physician who specializes in the care of babies and children.

Pelvimetry—Evaluation of the size of the birth canal or pelvis. Performed by X-ray.

Perinatologist—Physician who specializes in the care of high-risk pregnancies.

Petit mal seizure—Attack of a brief nature with possible short impairment of consciousness. Often associated with blinking or flickering of the eyelids and a mild twitching of the mouth.

Phosphatidyl glycerol—Lipoprotein present when fetal lungs are mature.

Phospholipids—Fat-containing phosphorous. The most important are lecithins and sphingomyelin, which are important in the maturation of fetal lungs before birth.

Phototherapy—Treatment for jaundice in a newborn infant. See *Jaundice.*

Physiologic anemia of pregnancy—Anemia during pregnancy caused by an increase in the amount of plasma (fluid) in the blood compared to the number of cells in the blood. See *Anemia.*

Placenta—Organ inside the uterus that is attached to the baby by the umbilical cord. Essential during pregnancy for growth and development of the embryo and fetus. Also called *afterbirth.*

Placenta accreta—Placenta that attaches to muscle of uterus.

Placenta increta—Placenta that grows into muscle of uterus.

Placenta percreta—Placenta that penetrates muscle of uterus.

Placenta previa—Low attachment of the placenta, covering or very close to the cervix.

Placental abruption—Premature separation of the placenta from the uterus.

Placentamegaly—Abnormally large growth of the placenta during pregnancy.

Pneumonitis—Inflammation of the lungs.

Polyhydramnios—See *Hydramnios.*

Post-mature baby—Pregnancy of 42+ weeks gestation.

Postpartum blues—Mild depression after delivery.

Postpartum depression—Depression after delivery.

Postpartum hemorrhage—Bleeding greater than 15 ounces (450ml) at time of delivery.

Pre-eclampsia—Combination of symptoms significant to pregnancy, including high blood pressure, edema, swelling and changes in reflexes.

Pregnancy diabetes—See *Gestational diabetes.*

Premature delivery—Delivery before 38 weeks gestation.

Presentation—Describes which part of the baby comes into the birth canal first.

Propylthiouracil—Medication used to treat thyroid disease.

Proteinuria—Protein in urine.

Pruritis gravidarum—Itching during pregnancy.

Pubic symphysis—Bony prominence in the pelvic bone found in the midline. Landmark from which the doctor often measures during pregnancy to follow growth of the uterus.

Pudendal block—Local anesthesia during labor.

Pulmonary embolism—Blood clot from another part of the body that travels to the lungs. Can cause closed passages in the lungs and decrease oxygen exchange.

Pyelonephritis—Serious kidney infection.

Quickening—Feeling the baby move inside the uterus.

Radiation therapy—Method of treatment for various cancers.

Radioactive scan—Diagnostic test in which radioactive material is injected into the body and scanned to find a problem within a particular part of the body.

Rh-negative—Absence of rhesus antibody in the blood.

RhoGAM™—Medication given during pregnancy and following delivery to prevent isoimmunization. See *Isoimmunization.*

Rh-sensitivity—See *Isoimmunization.*

Round-ligament pain—Pain caused by stretching ligament on the sides of the uterus during pregnancy.

Rupture of membranes—Loss of fluid from the amniotic sac. Also called *breaking of waters.*

Seizure—Sudden onset of a convulsion.

Sexually transmitted disease (STD)—Infection transmitted through sexual intercourse.

Sickle-cell anemia—Anemia caused by abnormal red blood cells shaped like a sickle or a cylinder.

Sickle-cell trait—Presence of the trait for sickle-cell anemia. Not sickle-cell disease itself.

Sickle crisis—Painful episode caused by sickle-cell disease.

Skin tag—Flap or extra buildup of skin.

Sodium—Element found in many foods, particularly salt. Ingestion of too much sodium may cause fluid retention.

Spina bifida—Congenital abnormality characterized by a defect in the vertebral column. Membranes of the spinal cord and the spinal cord protrude outside the protective bony canal of the spine.

Spinal anesthesia—Anesthesia given in the spinal canal.

Spontaneous abortion—Loss of pregnancy during the first 20 weeks of gestation. See *Abortion.*

Stasis—Decreased flow.

Station—Estimation of the descent of the baby.

Steroids—Group of medications of hormone origin. Often used to treat various diseases. Includes estrogen, testosterone, progesterone, prednisone.

Stigma—Area on the ovary where the egg has been released at the time of ovulation.

Stretch marks—Areas of the skin that are torn or stretched. Often found on the abdomen, breasts, buttocks and legs.

Striae distensa—See *Stretch marks*.

Sulci—Groove or furrow on the surface of the brain.

Surfactant—Phospholipid present in the lungs. Controls surface tension of lungs. Premature babies often lack sufficient amounts of surfactant to breathe without assistance.

Syphilis—Sexually transmitted venereal infection caused by treponema pallidum.

Systemic lupus erythermatosus (SLE)—Connective-tissue disorder common in women in the reproductive ages. Antibodies made by the person act against his or her own tissues.

Tay-Sachs disease—Inherited disease characterized by mental and physcial retardation, convulsions, enlargement of the head and eventually death. Trait is usually carried by Ashkenazi Jews.

Telangiectasias—Dilatation or swelling of a small blood vessel. Sometimes called an *angioma*. During pregnancy, another common name is a *spider angioma*.

Teratogenic—Causes abnormal development.

Teratology—Branch of science that deals with teratogens.

Thalassemia—Group of inherited disorders of hemoglobin metabolism, which results in a decrease in the amount of hemoglobin formed. Found most commonly in people of Mediterranean descent.

Threatened abortion—Bleeding during the first trimester of pregnancy without cramping or contractions.

Thrombosis—Formation of a blood clot (thrombus).

Thrush—Monilial or yeast infection occurring in the mouth or mucous membranes of a newborn infant.

Thyroid disease—Abnormality of the thyroid gland and its production of thyroid hormone. See *Hyperthyroidism; Hypothyroidism*.

Thyroid hormone—Chemical made in the thyroid that affects the entire body.

Thyroid panel—Series of blood tests done to evaluate the function of the thyroid gland.

Thyroid stimulating hormone (TSH)—Hormone made in the brain that stimulates the thyroid to produce thyroid hormone.

Tocolysis—Stopping contractions during premature labor.

Tocolytic agents—Medications to stop labor. See *Beta-adrenergics*.

Toxemia—See *Pre-eclampsia*.

Toxoid—Poison.

Toxoplasmosis—Infection caused by toxoplasma gondii.

Transverse lie—Fetus is turned sideways in uterus.

Trichomonal vaginitis—Venereal infection caused by trichomonas.

Trimester—Method of dividing pregnancy into three equal time periods of about 13 weeks each.

Trophoblast—Cell layer important in early development of the embryo and fetus. It provides nourishment from the mother to the fetus and participates in the formation of the placenta.

Umbilical cord—Cord that connects the placenta to the developing baby. It removes waste products and carbon dioxide from the baby and brings oxygenated blood and nutrients from the mother through the placenta to the baby.

Umbilicus—Bellybutton.

Ureters—Tubes from the kidneys to the bladder that drain urine.

Urinary calculi—See *Kidney stones*.

Uterine atony—Lack of tone of uterus.

Uterus—Organ an embryo/fetus grows in. Also called a *womb*.

Vaccine—Mild infection given to cause production of antibodies to protect against subsequent infections.

Vacuum extractor—Device used to provide traction on fetal head during delivery.

Varicose veins—Blood vessels (veins) that are dilated or enlarged.

Vascular spiders—See *Telangiectasias*.

Vena cava—Major vein in the body that empties into the right atrium of the heart. It returns unoxygenated blood to the heart for transport to the lungs.

Venereal warts—See *Condyloma acuminatum*.

Vernix—Fatty substance made up of epithelial cells that covers fetal skin inside the uterus.

Vertex—Head first.

Villi—Projection from a mucous membrane. Most important within the placenta in the exchange of nutrients from maternal blood to the placenta and fetus.

Womb—See *Uterus*.

Yeast infection—See *Monilial vulvovaginitis; Thrush*.

Zygote—Cell that results from the union of a sperm and egg at fertilization.

Bibliography

American College of Obstetricians and Gynecologists, *Guide to Planning for Pregnancy, Birth and Beyond*. Penguin Books, 1992.

American College of Obstetricians and Gynecologists, Technical Bulletins 59, 62, 64, 74, 79, 81, 84, 86, 87, 89, 90, 91, 92, 94, 95, 96, 97, 99, 104, 105, 106, 107, 108, 110, 112, 113, 114, 115, 116, 117, 119, 122, 123, 127, 130.

Briggs, G.G., Freeman, R.K., Yaffe, S.J. *Drugs in Pregnancy and Lactation*. Second Edition. Williams and Wilkins, 1986.

Clark. S.L. "Bleeding During Early Pregnancy." *The Female Patient*. Vol. 14, Feb. 1989.

Cunningham, Gary, *Williams Obstetrics*. 19th Edition. Appleton & Lange, 1993.

Cunningham, F.G., MacDonald. P.C., Gant, N.F. *Williams Obstetrics*. Eighteenth Edition. Appleton & Lange, 1989.

Disaia, P.J., Creasman, W.T. *Clinical Gynecologic Oncology*. Third Edition. C.V. Mosby Company, 1989.

Dorfman, S.F. "Aids and Pregnancy." *The Female Patient*. Vol. 14, Feb. 1989.

England, M.A. *Color Atlas of Life Before Birth, Normal Fetal Development*. Year Book Medical Publishers, Inc., 1983.

Freeman, R.F., "Problems of Postdate Pregnancy." *Contemporary OB/GYN*. Oct. 1986.

Friedman, E.A., Acker, D.A., Sachs, B.P. *Obstetrical Decision Making*. Second Edition. B.C. Decker, Inc., 1987.

Gershon, A.G. "Chickenpox: How Dangerous Is It?" *Contemporary OB/GYN*. March, 1988.

Hansmann, M., Hackloer, B.J., Staudach, A. *Ultrasound Diagnosis in Obstetrics and Gynecology*. Springer-Verlag, 1985.

Hollingsworth, Dorothy, M.D. *Medical Counselling Before Pregnancy*. Churchill Livingstone, 1988.

Kibayashi, M. *Illustrated Manual of Ultrasonography in Obstetrics and Gynecology*. Second Edition. Igaku-Shoin, 1980.

Mattingly, R.F. *TeLinde's Operative Gynecology*. Fifth Edition. J.B. Lippincott Company, 1977.

Netter, F.H. *The CIBA Collection of Medical Illustrations. Volume 2, Reproductive System*. CIBA Pharmaceutical Company, 1965.

Niswander, K.A. *Manual of Obstetrics, Diagnosis and Therapy*. Little, Brown and Company, 1987.

O'Brien, G.D. "Screening for Anomalies." *Contemporary OB/GYN*. July,1989.

Phelan. J.P. "Postdatism." *Clinical Obstetrics and Gynecology*. Lippincott. Vol. 32, No. 2, June, 1989.

Platt, L.D. "Obstetric Ultrasound." *Clinical Obstetrics and Gynecology.* Harper and Row, Vol. 27, No. 2, June, 1984.

Platt, L.D. "Predicting Fetal Health with the Biophysical Profile." *Contemporary OB/GYN.* Feb. 1989.

Precis III, An Update in Obstetrics and Gynecology. The American College of Obstetricians and Gynecologists, 1986.

Pritchard, J.A., MacDonald, P.C., Gant, N.F. *Williams Obstetrics.* Seventeenth Edition. Appleton-Century-Crofts, 1985.

Sadler, T.W. *Langman's Medical Embryology.* Fifth Edition. Williams and Wilkins, 1985.

Scialli, A.R., Lione, A. "Environmental Toxicants and Adverse Pregnancy Outcome." *Contemporary OB/GYN.* August, 1989.

Stedman's Medical Dictionary. Twenty-second Edition. Williams and Wilkins, 1972.

Sussman, John R., M.D. *Before You Conceive.* Bantam Books, 1989.

Theeson, K., Alderson, M., Hill, W. "Caring for the Depressed Obstetric Patient." *Contemporary OB/GYN.* Feb. 1989.

Index

❖

✧

✧

✧

✧

✧

✧

✧

❖

✧

❖

✧